… Collins

NEW GCSE MATHS
Functional Skills

Andrew Bennington • Andrew Manning • Dr Naomi Norman

William Collins' dream of knowledge for all began with the publication of his first book in 1819. A self-educated mill worker, he not only enriched millions of lives, but also founded a flourishing publishing house. Today, staying true to this spirit, Collins books are packed with inspiration, innovation and practical expertise. They place you at the centre of a world of possibility and give you exactly what you need to explore it.

Collins. Do more.

Published by Collins
An imprint of HarperCollins*Publishers*
77 – 85 Fulham Palace Road
Hammersmith
London
W6 8JB

Browse the complete Collins catalogue at
www.collinseducation.com

© HarperCollins*Publishers* Limited 2010

10 9 8 7 6 5 4 3 2 1

ISBN-13 978 0 00 741007 1

Andrew Bennington, Andrew Manning and Dr Naomi Norman assert their moral rights to be identified as the authors of this work

All rights reserved. No part of this publication may be reproduced, stored in a retrieval system, or transmitted in any form or by any means, electronic, mechanical, photocopying, recording or otherwise, without the prior written permission of the Publisher or a licence permitting restricted copying in the United Kingdom issued by the Copyright Licensing Agency Ltd., 90 Tottenham Court Road, London W1T 4LP.

British Library Cataloguing in Publication Data.
A Catalogue record for this publication is available from the British Library

Commissioned by Katie Sergeant
Project managed by Aimee Walker and Sue Chapple
Edited and proofread by Joan Miller, Christine Vaughan and Rosie Parrish
Cover design by Julie Martin
Cover photography by Caroline Green
Illustrations by Ann Paganuzzi
Design concept by Linda Miles, Lodestone Publishing
Production by Kerry Howie

Printed and bound by Hobbs the Printer, Totton

With thanks to Dr Naomi Norman, Howard Marsh and Jonathan Miller for their support and contribution of ideas.

Contents

* Beginner

Birds	6–10
Getting ahead in the job market	11–15
Blood donors	16–20
Tuning in	21–24
Making your own fuel	25–28
Thumbelina	29–34
Off your trolley	35–39
The honey bee	40–45
Money – making the world go round?	46–50
Flags	51–57
Commuting	58–62
Website design	63–66

** Improver

Eat well, live longer?	67–70
Coastguard search	71–77
Photography: past, present and future	78–81
Teabag design and production	82–85
Small-scale farming	86–88
Coastguard rescue	89–94
Tomorrow's world	95–99
Time management	100–103
GM foods	104–108
Flying the world	109–113
Your plaice or mine?	114–117
Sleep	118–124
Selling online	125–128
Jewellery design	129–133
Buying your first car	134–139
Fish and chips	140–143

*** Advanced

The Milky Way	144–148
On your bike	149–152
Water usage	153–155
Crash investigation	156–159
Glastonbury Festival	160–164
Leaving smaller footprints	165–169
Can we hold back the sea?	170–176
Facebook	177–181
Population and pensions	182–187
London black cabs	188–191
Extreme sports	192–196
Maths – music to your ears?	197–203

Matching charts

Foundation matching chart	204–205
Higher matching chart	206–207

Data sheets can be found on the CD-Rom

Introduction

Welcome to *Collins New GCSE Maths Functional Skills*. The 2010 GCSE Mathematics curriculum made functional skills central to GCSE assessment. 30-40% of foundation tier questions and 20-30% of higher tier questions have a functional mathematics element. This Teacher's Pack, which accompanies the Student Book, provides you with the lesson plans you need to make functional skills an integral part of your GCSE Mathematics course.

What is functional mathematics?

Some people may think that functional mathematics is using mathematics in a real-life context. More broadly it means giving students the knowledge and skills they need to use mathematics confidently and effectively in life and work. What does that mean in practice for you? We want students to recognise when they could use mathematics in a particular situation; to choose a way to tackle a problem; to be confident about applying their knowledge; to use mathematics to provide answers; to interpret and check their results; and to judge how successful they have been.

Planning for progression

The point to remember is that students can be taught to be confident and reflective users of mathematics and over time we can help them move towards that goal. So what does 'progression' look like when we are talking about functional mathematics? It helps to look at these four factors:

- The **complexity** of the application. Is it a routine or a non-routine problem? Does it require a number of steps to reach a solution? Does it involve extended enquiry?
- The **familiarity** of the context. Is the scenario drawn from other subjects or from other aspects of students' lives?
- The **technical demand** of the mathematics required. How advanced are the concepts and procedures needed?
- The degree of **independence** and autonomy of the student. Can the students make decisions and choices for themselves?

About this book

Levels

The book has been written at three levels: Beginner[*], Improver[**] and Advanced[***].

- Beginner topics cover Level 1 functional skills and GCSE grades G, F and E.
- Improver topics cover Level 1/2 functional skills and GCSE grades E, D and C.
- Advanced topics cover Level 2 functional skills and GCSE grades B, A and A*.

Learning objectives

The objectives are written in a student-friendly way and show how the content of each topic relates to 'Representing', 'Analysing' and 'Interpreting' Functional Skills Standards.

Assessing Pupils' Progress (APP)

The work students produce when carrying out these Functional Maths activities can support APP, especially for 'Using and applying mathematics'.

Personal, Learning and Thinking Skills (PLTS)

PLTS is a core requirement of the National Curriculum and we think these are closely related to functional mathematics. For example, deciding on the appropriate mathematical tools to use requires creative thinking; evaluating the success of a particular approach requires reflective learning; and so on. Because of this we have included references to PLTS for each activity.

Every child matters outcomes
'Every Child Matters' references identify how the topics build on student awareness of these important aims.

Self-assessment
At the end of each topic in the Student Book we've included questions which will encourage students to evaluate the different elements of the lesson.

Matching charts
The lessons in this book are designed to be a flexible resource that can be used as part of your Scheme of Work for teaching mathematics in KS4. Your decision on when to use the activities will depend upon the ability of your students and their stage of development. We have provided two matching charts at the back of this Teacher's Pack which map the topics to the *Collins New GCSE Maths* Foundation and Higher courses for AQA Modular, Edexcel Linear and Edexcel Modular. These should help you to decide where to integrate the topics into your Scheme of Work.

Underpinning maths
Each topic tests a variety of underpinning mathematics. On occasions students are stretched beyond the maths covered in the GCSE curriculum. We've done this to demonstrate how mathematical skills are required in more demanding aspects of other subjects and to stimulate students with new challenges.

Practical questions

How do I know that the lessons will be successful?
Be brave; try it out and see what happens! Teachers who try this sort of activity for the first time are often surprised by how well they turn out. Your students will appreciate the opportunity to work on these activities. Why not get some feedback from them afterwards?

When is the best time to do them?
This is an interesting question. For example, if a task involves students applying their knowledge of symmetry should they do it just after they have been taught a unit on symmetry? It may be better to do it a month or two later, to see if they can recall what they did when the topic is no longer fresh in their minds. Then the task of 'choosing the appropriate mathematical tools' becomes a more realistic task and closer to the situation students are likely to experience in life outside school.

What if the students do not do what I expect them to do?
It can be hard to 'let go' and not tell students what to do, particularly if you think that a student is using an inefficient or inappropriate technique. However if students are going to learn to be effective and confident users of mathematics, being able to make mistakes and learn from them is an important part of the process.

My Scheme of Work is already full. How can I fit this in as well?
Do you think that they have too much to teach and too little time in which to teach it? Try to think 'instead of' rather than 'as well as'. Lessons that focus on developing the ability of students to use and apply their mathematics are often the best way to foster real understanding. See if you can find some lessons in your Scheme of Work that could be replaced by an activity in this book. You might even find that as the students undertake some of these tasks, their reasoning and thinking skills improve so that they grasp future mathematical topics more quickly, actually saving time.

How long will should each activity take?
Try not to rush through the tasks and resist the temptation to hurry things along if progress seems slow. The time students need to complete these activities will vary according to their level of expertise: try to give them the time they need. We provided an approximate guide for each topic.

*Beginner **

Birds

Learning objectives
- **Representing Level 1**: understand problems in unfamiliar situations or represented in unfamiliar ways
- **Analysing Level 1**: analyse mathematical results to make simple comparisons
- **Interpreting Level 1**: interpret and communicate solutions to practical problems, drawing simple conclusions and giving explanations

APP
Evidence for Using and applying mathematics Level 5, Numbers and the number system Level 4, Handling data Level 5

PLTS
Develops Independent enquirers, Team workers, Creative thinkers

Every child matters outcomes
Make a positive contribution, Enjoy and achieve

Cross-curricular links
Science, English

Underpinning maths
- Surveys
- Averages
- Rounding decimals to the nearest whole number
- Statistical representation

Resources
- *Student book*, pages 6–9
- Data sheet: Birds
- Calculator
- Internet access (optional)
- Bird fact book (optional)

Useful websites
- www.rspb.org.uk/wildlife/birdguide/name

Context
Although students will recognise many birds, they may not know many individual bird species.

In this activity, students will reflect on the ways in which data can be collected and presented.

Lesson plan
This activity takes two lessons. You may do it in one lesson, just using Tasks 1, 2 and 5. Task 4 would make a good homework and Task 6 would make an excellent whole-class project.

Beginner *

Starter

- Ask students which kinds of bird they can recognise. You could show the RSPB bird list, available from their website, or use a book about birds. Choose a particular bird to look at with the class.
- Discuss the information about the bird you have chosen and ask students how this information may have been collected.
- Focus on where the bird is found and when to see it. Explain that this information has been collected by **surveys** and **observation**.
- Look at population numbers, also collected by surveys and using **sampling**. Ask students what it means to sample. (Answer: Select a smaller set because it is not possible to examine the whole population.) Discuss with students why bird population numbers cannot be collected by observation. (Answer: They are too large and widespread.)

Main activity

- Explain that, every year, groups of people carry out all kinds of bird surveys, all over the world. Ask students to discuss, in pairs, the kinds of survey that may be conducted to learn more about birds or particular bird species. Encourage students to share ideas with the rest of the class.
- **Let students do Task 1**. Remind them to think about whether it is possible to observe or whether sampling may be necessary.
- Tell students that sometimes it is useful to compare survey data. For example:
  - We may wish to compare observations of different birds species. Ask students why this comparison may be useful. (Answer: So that we know which birds are most and least common.)
  - We may wish to compare observations of the same kind of bird over several years. Ask students why this comparison may be useful. (Answer: So that we know which birds have a growing or shrinking population.)
- Look at Task 2 with students. Ask them to look at the table and discuss what it shows. Ask students to imagine that hundreds of people had done this survey. It would be very difficult to read all the data in the table.
- Explain that an **average** enables us to describe a whole set of data by providing a typical value. There are several ways of expressing an average but the most common are the **mode**, **median** and **mean**.
- Remind students that the mode is the value that occurs most frequently in a set of data. Ask students to look at the data and find the **modal number** of robins. (Answer: Two) Now ask them to find the modal number of wood pigeons. (Answer: Three)
- Ask students what they can now say about the number of wood pigeons compared to robins in this survey. (Answer: When looking at the modal average, this survey suggests there are more wood pigeons than there are robins.)
- Remind students that the median is the middle value when all values in a set of data are arranged in order of size, from lowest to highest. Ask students to look at the data and work with the person next to them to find the **median number** of blue tits. (Answer: Two)
- Discuss with students the fact that, because there are eight children in the survey shown in the table, they need to look at the fourth and fifth values to find the median. Ask students what the median would be if Toby had not taken part in the survey. (Answer: Two) Ask students what the median would be if Toby, Ross and Miguel had not taken part in the survey. (Answer: One)
- Remind students that the mean is the sum of all values in a set of data, divided by the number of values. Ask students to look at the data and find the sum of all sightings of blue tits. (Answer:

Beginner *

    18) Then ask students to use their calculators to divide that sum by the number of values, which is 8. (Answer: 2.25)

- Comment that it is not possible to have 0.25 of a bird! Ask students to round to the nearest whole number. (You could use a number line showing tenths between two and three, with 2.25 marked on it, to illustrate why 2.25 rounds to two.)
- Ask students what they notice about the median number and mean number of blue tits. (Answer: Both averages are the same.)
- **Let students do Task 2**. Suggest they write down the definition of each type of average (mode, median and mean) to help them complete this task.
- **For Task 3 (extension)**, students require reasonable literacy skills. If literacy is a challenge for some students, whom you believe to be otherwise capable of this extension, you could use the task as basis for a discussion rather than as a written exercise.
- To prepare for Task 4, ask students to look at the data sheet. Explain that the diagrams were drawn by the children who completed the survey in Task 2. Ask students to identify the types of diagram. (Answer: Bar charts, pie charts and pictograms) Look together at the first bar chart. Ask students how many house sparrows this child has spotted. (Answer: Two). Now ask students to look at the table in Task 2 to find which of the children spotted two house sparrows, and therefore to identify which child produced the chart. (Answer: Isy)
- Ask students to imagine that there were two children who had spotted two house sparrows. What could they have done then? Suggest looking at which birds had not been spotted at all according to this bar chart. (Answer: Great tit, goldfinch, collared dove and chaffinch) Ask students to look at Table 2 and confirm that this data does indeed relate to Isy.
- **Let students do Task 4**. This would work well as a paired exercise.
- Ask students if they know what a **bird of prey** is. (Answer: A bird that eats other birds or small animals.) You could return to the RSPB webpage or the bird reference book, to look at a bird of prey.
- Look together at how children conducted their survey on birds of prey, in Task 5. Ask students whether the children were using observation or sampling. (Answer: Sampling)
- Ask students to comment on the method of sampling. Why didn't the children just choose places where they knew they would see birds of prey? (Answer: This would bias their results.)
- Ask students to point to each square the children are covering and then to compare this to the corresponding diagram of results with the coloured dots. Ask students what they notice about squares 2 and 24. (Answer: These squares were covered by children but no birds of prey were seen.)
- Ask students which bird of prey was spotted in square 19, and by which child. (Answer: Kestrel, by Louise)
- **Let students do Task 5**. It may help them to begin by drawing one 5 × 5 grid that includes all the data. In each of the cells 21, 2, 10, 19, 24, 11, 13 and 3, they write the number, with the corresponding child's name, and draw any coloured dots to represent that child's bird sightings.
- Ask students to work in small groups as they begin to plan their own bird survey. You could start them off by suggesting that they first discuss exactly what it is they wish to survey. Does it require observation or sampling? If observation, where and when will they observe? If sampling, how will they sample?
- Ask students for some of their ideas, and conduct a vote among the class to decide which bird survey(s) they will do.
- **Let students do Task 6**.

Beginner ＊

Plenary
- Ask students to list all the mathematics they used to help them understand the bird survey data.
- Ask them whether they think the same kind of mathematics would be relevant to other surveys. For example, would it be relevant to a survey of the hedgehog population? What about a survey of traffic at a busy roundabout?

Outcomes
o Students will have used mathematics to gain insights into survey data.
o Students will have read and interpreted mathematical information from a variety of diagrams.

Answers

Task 1

| 1 | Observation | 2 | Observation | 3 | Sampling | 4 | Observation |
| 5 | Observation | 6 | Observation | 7 | Observation | 8 | Sampling |

Task 2

1 a 5 b 2 or 0
2 a 2 b 0
3 a 3 b 2 c 2.25 (rounds to 2) d 0.75 (rounds to 1)
4 a 4 b 2

Task 3 (extension)

1 Mean, because the numbers include decimal fractions, rounded to two decimal places.
2 The charity's survey shows a slightly higher average for starlings than that of the children's survey.
  The charity's survey shows a lower average for robins than that of the children's survey.
3 When the charity's survey results for starlings and robins are rounded, the number of starlings seen is three and of robins is two. This is the same as the children's survey.
4 The charity's survey is likely to be more accurate because it involved 729 people. The children's survey involved only eight people.

Task 4

A: Isy; B: Edward; C: Sophie; D: Toby; E: Ross; F: Jamie; G: Miguel; H: Louise

Task 5

1 a Kestrel b Red kite
2 a Edward; Ross
   b Jamie; Isy; Sophie
   c Louise; Toby
   d Miguel
3 10 ÷ 8 = 1.25
4 1.25 × 25 = 31.25
5 31

© HarperCollins*Publishers* 2010

Beginner *

Task 6

Students should use Tasks 1–5 for ideas of how to plan, record and analyse their bird survey findings. For example:

- **for planning**, they may use Task 1 to help them decide if they wish to observe or sample; and Tasks 1 and 2 to decide if they wish to observe birds in their gardens for an hour on a particular day
- **for recording**, they may use Tasks 2 and 3 to decide if they wish to record their findings in a table, and Task 4 to decide if they wish to display them as bar charts, pie charts or pictograms
- **for analysing**, they may use Task 2 to decide if they wish to find averages and Task 5 to decide if they wish to make an estimate of bird population in a wider area (assuming they have used sampling).

Beginner *

Getting ahead in the job market

Learning objectives
- **Representing Level 1**: find required information from graphs, diagrams and direct questioning
- **Analysing Level 1**: calculate wages including percentages and check calculations make sense
- **Interpreting Level 1**: use results to explain findings and draw conclusions

APP
Evidence for Handling data Level 3, Using and applying mathematics Level 3, Numbers and the number system Level 4, Calculating Level 5

PLTS
Develops Independent enquirers, Creative thinkers, Reflective learners, Self-managers, Effective participators

Every child matters outcomes
Make a positive contribution, Achieve economic well-being, Enjoy and achieve

Cross-curricular links
PSHE, Geography, English

Underpinning maths
- Extracting information from graphs
- Interpreting diagrams
- Collecting information
- Calculating percentages
- Producing graphs

Resources
- *Student book* pages 10–13
- Data sheet: Getting ahead in the job market
- Calculators, graph paper, ruler
- Internet access

Useful websites
- www.statistics.gov.uk/cci/nugget.asp?id=19
- lwww.hmrc.gov.uk/paye/payroll/day-to-day/nmw.htm

Context
All students should be familiar with the term 'unemployment' and the types of job available in their local area. Students should have heard the terms 'national minimum wage' and 'inflation rate' (the increase each year in living costs, such as food, fuel and goods). In this activity students think about the patterns of unemployment in the UK, analyse living costs and payment methods.

Lesson plan
This activity takes one or two lessons. It could be completed in one lesson, using Task 4 as homework.

Beginner *

Starter
- Ask students if they know what the national minimum wage is and if they know the current figure set by the Government. Either supply the information from your own research or refer to Task 2 in the *Student book* for examples.
- Explain to students what the **inflation rate** is. (Answer: The increase in the cost of living, for example, the percentage increase in a price of a loaf of bread, clothes, fuel bills.) Ask how many students want to go on to further education after school (A-levels or a college course).
- Tell students that the UK economy is influenced by world trade. When the UK went into a recession, in 2009, so did many other countries, with Greece being one of the hardest hit.

Main activity
- Discuss with students the sorts of job available in their local area. Refer to newspapers or the internet, having searched beforehand so that examples are current. Explain to students the difference between **hourly pay** and **salary**. If a job is described as hourly paid, you only get paid for the time you are at work. If you are permanently employed you will get holiday pay and sick pay. Salary means that you get the same amount of money each month and usually have fixed hours of employment.
- Read Task 1 with students. Remind students that they should try to be as accurate as possible when transferring information from the bar chart, recording the numbers in a table and using a suitable scale.
- **Let students do Task 1**. Encourage them to use a ruler to read information from the bar graph and to draw up a small table to record their findings. Distribute graph paper. Check that students have the correct values before they start to draw their line graphs and encourage them to start the scale on the vertical axis at zero. They could use graph-drawing computer software for this part of the task. Make sure that students' comments on unemployment include mathematical evidence.
- Explain that people with good qualifications can generally earn more money than those without, and that people with A-levels have a greater chance of getting a job because they have more to offer an employer. Suggest that, in the current job market, it is helpful to have as many relevant qualifications as possible.
- Read Task 2 with students. Explain that the increases in the minimum wage for people as they get older might not look a lot but it makes a significant difference to the yearly figure. Explain the differences in gross and net pay and write them on the board. Make it clear that gross pay is the amount earned, without any stoppages. Explain that tax, national insurance and possibly pension contributions are deducted from gross pay. Then net pay is the amount paid into your bank after stoppages or deductions. Explain the principle of tax allowances as the amount that HMRC allow you to earn before they start charging tax. Remind students how to find a percentage. Work through an example on the board. (For example: 8% of £120 = 120 × 8 ÷ 100 = 9.6 = £9.60.) Explain the term 'annual' (Answer: Relating to a period of one year.) Remind students there are 52 weeks in a year, not four weeks per month × 12 months, as this is only 48 weeks.
- **Let students do Task 2**. Move around the classroom as students work and make sure they are taking the tax allowance of £6475 off the annual wages before finding 20% and 6%. Check students' answers and give praise and feedback on their progress. Students could work in pairs if less able students are struggling with the ideas of gross and net pay.
- Ask students where they would they want to live, if they had a job. Would they stay with their family or aim to have their own flat? Ask them to suggest the essential things they would spend their money on. What things would they need to pay, wherever they lived? (Answer: For example, rent, council tax, phone bill, broadband, food, insurance, gas/electric, TV licence.)

Beginner

- List their answers randomly on the board. Tell students that when they have their own homes everything, including shower gel and toilet rolls, comes out of their wage. Ask if they have planned for a holiday, at home or abroad.
- Read Task 3 with students. Tell students to allow plenty of room for their lists and to use the whole of the sheet of paper, drawing a line down the centre of their page and then writing the title 'Essential' on the left and 'Luxury' on the right. Let students work in appropriate pairs but make sure they write their lists themselves.
- **Let students do Task 3**. Suggest any expenses students may have missed but do not tell them which category they fall into. Set a time limit for students to complete their lists and remind them as time runs out. When their lists are complete, ask pairs of students to move into groups of four. Move among groups and encourage discussions. Ask each group to elect a spokesperson to offer feedback to the class, writing key items on the board. Direct students to the internet to find the prices of items on their lists.
- Read Task 4 (extension) with students. Distribute the data sheet and look at the payment methods listed in the table. Ask students to explain how each method works. If necessary, explain by means of these examples.
    - Cash is the usual way to pay for inexpensive items. Cheques are a means of paying for goods through a bank, with the money being taken out of the customer's account in three to five working days. A cheque can only be cashed by the person whose name is on the cheque.
    - Postal orders are similar to cheques but go though the post office, which takes the money in return for a postal order, made out to a specific person (like the cheque).
    - Debit card payments are taken straight out of the bank account; the customer must have enough money in their account.
    - Credit card payments allow a customer to buy now and pay at the end of the month in full, or over several months (plus interest on the amount still owed). Explain that goods bought on credit card, over a certain value, are covered by insurance if they are lost or damaged.
    - Standing orders authorise the bank to pay a fixed amount of money out of a customer's account each month, for example, to pay off a loan for a car.
    - Direct debits authorise someone else to take a variable amount of money, within limits, out of a customer's account each month, for example, under a mobile-phone contract.
    - Telephone or internet banking offer on-demand ways to pay bills or transfer money.
    - E-money accounts, such as Paypal, are supposed to be reliable and secure and are becoming more popular.
- Warn students of the hazards of paying for goods on the internet. Remind students that online fraud is on the increase.
- **Let students do Task 4 (extension)**. They can use the data sheet, or draw their own tables. If they choose to do this, remind them to make sure the boxes are big enough for them to write in. Remind students of the difference between a standing order and a direct debit. If internet access is available let students find definitions for each method of payment and the pros and cons of using each method.
- Distribute graph paper and guide students as needed to the types of graphs they can draw from their results.

Beginner *

Plenary
- Ask students how many of them now want to go into further education or training after they leave school.
- Ask students to describe unemployment patterns in the UK and in their area.
- Ask what the difference is in net and gross pay.
- Ask a student to explain what essential items are and how much money per week or year they need to support their lifestyle.

Outcomes
o Students will have used maths to identify the information they needed to solve the problem.
o Students will have carried out appropriate research and calculations to find solutions to the problem.
o Students will have interpreted their results and drawn mathematical justification.

Answers

Task 1

1 The vertical axis doesn't start at zero so the figure for 2001, for example, looks to be much lower than it really is.

2

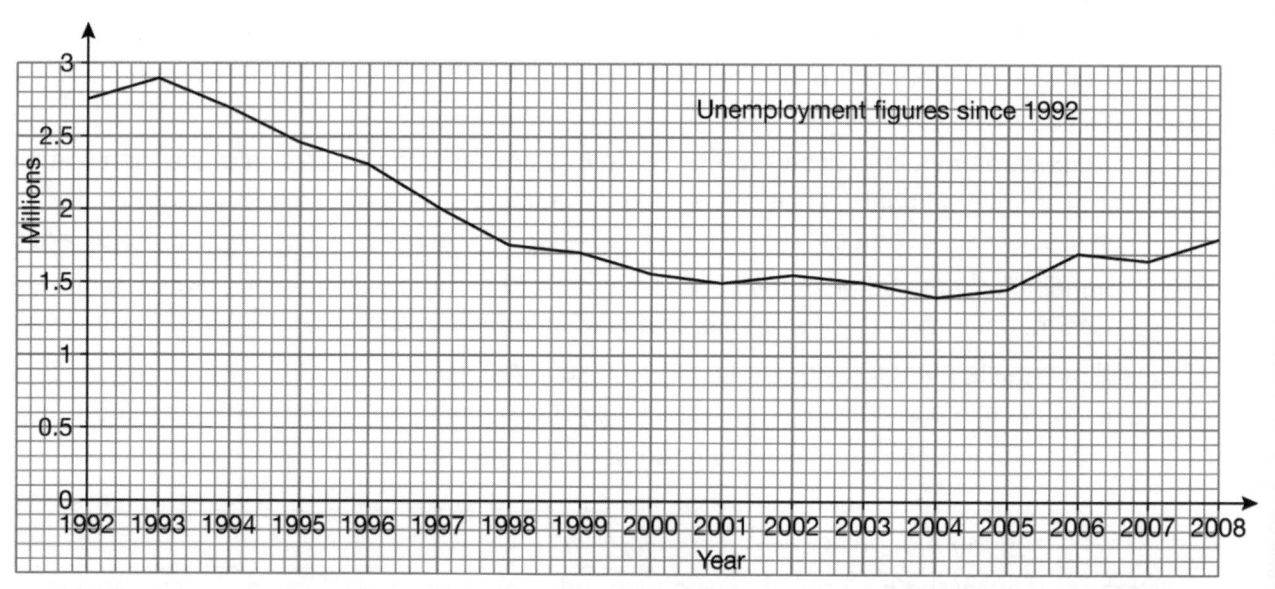

3 The choice of graph depends on whether the aim is to give the impression that unemployment is high or low. The block graph reduces the visual impact by starting from a base of 1 million. The line graph starts at zero so gives a truer impression; it also smoothes out the changes more than a block graph would.

4 The general pattern is that a higher percentage of people are now unemployed across the UK. The largest change is in the south of England.

Task 2

1 a 16-year-old: £3.57 x 35 =£124.95 x 52 = £6497.40

19-year-old: £4.83 x 35 = £169.05 x 52 = £8790.60

25-year-old: £5.80 x 35 = £203 x 52 = £10 556

b 16-year-old: £6497.40 – £6475 = £22.40

20% of £22.40 = £4.48; 6% of £22.40 = £1.34

Take-home pay = £6497.40 – £4.48 – £1.34 = £6491.18

19-year-old: £8790.60 – £6475 = £2315.60

20% of £2315.60 = £463.12; 6% of £8790.60 = £527.44

Take-home pay = £8790.60 – £463.12 – £527.44 = £7800.04

25-year-old: £10 556 – £6475 = £4081.00

20% of £4081.00 = £816.20; 6% of £4081.00 = £244.86

Take-home pay = £10 556 – £816.20– £244.86 = £9494.94

Task 3

1 a Students should list items such as, essential: rent, council tax, insurance, gas/electric, food, water rates, clothes allowance, travel costs (mobile phone – basic use), luxuries, takeaways, mobile phone, socialising, designer clothes, game stations and associated games.

b Students should use the internet and get individual prices.

2 a Students should calculate their salary after deductions.

b Students should calculate the amount of money they would have left over.

c Students should adjust their list of luxuries and recalculate, if necessary.

d Students should calculate the cost of the items after the cost of living increase, and state whether or not they can still afford all the things on their lists.

e Students should use local papers or the internet to investigate the job market. They should use the information they find to complete the answers to this question.

Task 4 (extension)

1 Students should complete each row of the table.

2 Students should complete suitable tables for collecting data, to include each method of payment and 'like' and 'dislike' columns or 'would use' and 'would not use'.

3 Students could use spreadsheet software to produce, for example, pie charts and comparative bar charts. They should comment on their results and compare them to their own opinions of methods of payment.

4 Students should make appropriate comments, based on the information they have found.

Beginner *

Blood donors

Learning objectives
- **Representing Level 1**: understand problems in unfamiliar situations and identify necessary mathematical information to find solutions
- **Analysing Level 1**: apply mathematics in an organised way to find solutions to practical problems
- **Interpreting Level 1**: interpret and communicate solutions to practical problems, drawing simple conclusions and giving explanations

APP
Evidence for Using and applying mathematics Level 4, Numbers and the number system Level 5, Handling data Level 5

PLTS
Develops Effective participators, Creative thinkers

Every child matters outcome
Make a positive contribution, Be healthy

Cross-curricular links
Science, English

Underpinning maths
- Systems of measurement
- Frequency tables
- Calculating probabilities
- Equivalent fractions and percentages
- Interpreting and organising data

Resources
- *Student book*, page 14–17
- Data sheet: Blood donors
- Calculator
- Internet access

Useful websites
- www.blood.co.uk/video-audio-leaflets/tv-radio-ads for the advertisements
- www.blood.co.uk/video-audio-leaflets/publications for leaflets and *Donor* magazine

Context
- Students may not be totally familiar with this context, although they will have some knowledge of blood from their work in science.
- Bear in mind that some students may have religious beliefs, such as those of Jehovah's Witnesses, that would reject blood transfusions. In addition, some sensitivity may be required in case any students, or their relatives, have needed an emergency blood transfusion.

Beginner *

Lesson plan

This activity takes two lessons. You may do it in one lesson by using Task 1 and Task 6 for mathematical investigation (using just the tables from Tasks 2 and 4). Task 7 could be used for homework.

Starter

- Play a TV or radio advertisement for the National Blood Service, downloaded from their website. If there is no internet access in the classroom, show students a leaflet about blood donation or a copy of *The Donor* magazine (published by the National Blood Service); these are also available from the website.
- Explain that people who give blood are called **blood donors**. Discuss why people may need to receive blood, for example, because they are injured and have lost blood, or because they are ill and their own blood does not work properly.
- Tell students that the UK's National Blood Service states that:
- **96% of us rely on the other 4% to give blood**.
- Ask students, if that statistic were applied to their class, how many of them would be blood donors. (Answer: 0.04 × number of students in class)
- Tell students that, in fact, only people who are at least 17 years old and weigh more than 7 stone 12 lb may donate blood, so none of them would currently be allowed to give blood.

Main activity

- Ask students what units can be used for weight. Make a list. Students should at least mention stones, pounds, kilograms and grams.
- Ask students how many pounds there are in a stone (Answer: 14) and how many grams in a kilogram (Answer: 1000). Suggest students make a note of these conversions.
- Remind students that pounds and stones are traditional, older units of weight and belong to the **imperial** system of measure, while grams and kilograms are newer units and belong to the **metric** system of measure.
- Tell students that it is possible to convert between imperial and metric weights:
- 1 pound ≈ 450 grams or 2.2 pounds ≈ 1 kilogram
- Suggest students make a note of this conversion. Ask them what the symbol ≈ means, in the conversion statements. (Answer: They are approximate, not exact.) Tell students that, for this activity, they should use the conversion 1 pound ≈ 450 grams.
- Let students do Task 1.
- Discuss with students whether they found it easy to read the Year 12 students' weights from the table. Ask if they can think of any other ways the data could be represented. For example, it could have been shown in a frequency table, like the one shown on the data sheet.
- Remind students that '< weight' means 'weight greater than' and 'weight ≤' means 'weight less than or equal to'.
- Ask students to copy and complete the table. (Answer: See the table below.)

Weights	Tally	Frequency
44.5 kg < weight ≤ 49.5 kg	//	2
49.5 kg < weight ≤ 54.5 kg	//// //// //	12
54.5 kg < weight ≤ 59.5 kg	//	2
More than 59.5 kg	//	2

© HarperCollins*Publishers* 2010

Beginner *

- Discuss with students how this frequency table would have been useful for Task 1 (Answer: It shows how many students weigh exactly 49.5 kg or less, so cannot give blood. **Note**: they should have worked out in Task 1, question 4 that 7 st 12 lb is equivalent to 49.5 kg.)
- Discuss how this frequency table would **not** have been useful for Task 1. (Answer: It does not show ages; it does not show the names of the students who do not weigh enough to give blood.)
- Remind students how to find the probability of an **outcome** of an event.
- $$P(\text{outcome}) = \frac{\text{number of ways the outcome can happen}}{\text{total number of possible outcomes}}$$
- Ask students to discuss, in pairs, how they would use the frequency table and this formula to work out this problem.
- If a student is picked at random from the Year 12 class, what is the probability of that student weighing exactly 49.5 kg or less? (Answer: Number of students weighing exactly or less than 49.5 kg = 2; total number of students = 18; so probability = $\frac{2}{18}$.)
- Ask students if it is possible to cancel this fraction. If necessary, remind them that this involves checking the numerator and the denominator for common factors. (Answer: In this case, 2 is a factor of both numerator and denominator, so $\frac{2}{18} = \frac{1}{9}$.)
- **Let students do Task 2**. You could construct the appropriate frequency table together, before asking students to complete the tallies and frequencies and work out probabilities independently.
- Look at Task 3 with students. Ask them how they are going to make comparisons. Expect them to recognise that they need to convert the fractions to percentages, or percentages to fractions. Suggest they work with percentages as fractions may have different denominators, which will make comparisons difficult. Remind students that to convert a fraction to a percentage you multiply by 100. **Let students do Task 3 (extension)**.
- Look at Task 4 with students. Ask them to look at the table and say which blood groups can donate blood to group O. (Answer: O) Now ask them which blood groups can receive blood from group O. (Answer: All)
- **Let students do Task 4**. When they answer question 2, remind students to complete the blanks to create their four questions, and then swap with the person next to them to answer.
- **For Task 5 (extension)**, encourage students to list all the students who can donate to the boy, and all the students who can donate to the girl, to help them find the probabilities. Remind them that to compare the fractions, they need the same denominator; this requires finding equivalent fractions.
- Look at Task 6 with students. Discuss how they might represent the different matches. For example, they may choose to copy both lists and draw arrows from donors to recipients, or copy only the list of donors and then, beside each one, add the names of students to whom they can donate. **Let students do task 6**.
- Look at Task 7 with students. Discuss what information they have learnt that would it be useful to include in a leaflet encouraging people to give blood. **Let students do task 7**.

Plenary

- Ask students what mathematics they used in these tasks to learn more about blood donors.
- Ask students what other mathematical information might be useful to understand blood donation further. Students may suggest:
  - the number of people in the UK who are able to give blood, i.e. who are 17 or over, who weigh more than 7 stone 12 lbs and who are healthy

Beginner *

- o the number of people who require blood each year
- o the amount of blood someone can donate and how often.
- You could ask students to find this information for their homework.

Outcomes

- o Students will have used mathematics to gain insight into a real-life problem.
- o Students will have interpreted data to enable them to do calculations from which they can draw conclusions.

Answers

Task 1

1 98 lb **2** 110 lb **3** 49 500 g **4** 49.5 kg

5 Phoebe and Roman are too young (age 16); Abbie and Charlie weigh too little (under 49.5 kg).

Task 2

1

Blood group	Tally	Frequency
A	## /	6
B	//	2
AB	/	1
O	## ////	9

2 O

3 AB

4 18

5 a AB = $\frac{1}{18}$ **b** A = $\frac{1}{3}$ **c** O = $\frac{1}{2}$ **d** B = $\frac{1}{9}$

Task 3 (extension)

Students should make their comparison by converting their fractional answers to question 5 to percentages.

Blood group	UK population (percentage)	Year 12 class (percentage)
O	44	50
A	42	33.3
B	10	11.1
AB	4	5.6

They should note that the proportions of the different blood groups among the Year 12 class are roughly similar to those for the UK population. However, there are higher percentages of blood groups O, B and AB among the Year 12 class compared to the UK population, and there are lower percentages of blood group A.

Task 4

1 a Coral, Richard, Emily, Jordan, Georgia, James, Carla, Caroline

 b Fred, Lucy, Abbie, Ginny, Phil, Heidi, Greg

© HarperCollins*Publishers* 2010

*Beginner **

2

Question	Answer
How many of the Year 12 students can donate blood to group A?	11
How many of the Year 12 students can donate blood to group B?	8
How many of the Year 12 students can donate blood to group AB?	14
How many of the Year 12 students can donate blood to group O?	6
How many of the Year 12 students can receive blood from group A?	7
How many of the Year 12 students can receive blood from group B?	11
How many of the Year 12 students can receive blood from group AB?	1
How many of the Year 12 students can receive blood from group O?	18

Task 5 (extension)

The boy (group O) can only receive blood-type O. Six students can donate to O. P(boy finding a donor) = $\frac{6}{18} = \frac{1}{3}$. The girl (group AB) can receive blood from A, B, AB and O. 14 students can donate to AB. So P(girl finding a donor) = $\frac{14}{18} = \frac{7}{9}$. The girl has a better chance, at $\frac{7}{9}$ compared to $\frac{1}{3} = \frac{3}{9}$.

Task 6

Name	Blood group	Can donate to:	Name	Blood group	Can receive from:
Greg	A	Abbie, Heidi, Lucy, Phil	Abbie	A	Greg, Ginny, Caroline, Jordan, Coral, Emily, Richard, Fred
Carla	B	Phil, Georgia	Heidi	A	Greg, Ginny, Caroline, Jordan, Coral, Emily, Richard, Fred
Ginny	A	Abbie, Heidi, Lucy, Phil	Roman	O	Caroline, Jordan, Coral, Emily, Richard
Caroline	O	All	James	O	Caroline, Jordan, Coral, Emily, Richard
Jordan	O	All	Charlie	O	Caroline, Jordan, Coral, Emily, Richard
Coral	O	All	Lucy	A	Greg, Ginny, Caroline, Jordan, Coral, Emily, Richard, Fred
Emily	O	All	Phil	AB	All
Richard	O	All	Phoebe	O	Caroline, Jordan, Coral, Emily, Richard
Fred	A	Abbie, Heidi, Lucy, Phil	Georgia	B	Caroline, Jordan, Coral, Emily, Richard, Carla

1 Yes, Caroline, Jordan, Coral, Emily, Richard and James
2 No
3 Phil cannot donate to anyone. This means there will be one recipient who has not got a donor.

Task 7

To persuade people to give blood, students should include:

- some mathematical background information, e.g. age, weight, percentages of those in different blood groups.
- the implications of the lack of a match in Task 6, question 3.

Beginner *

Tuning in

Learning objectives
- **Representing Level 1**: understand practical problems and use scales
- **Analysing Level 1**: perform calculations with large numbers; calculate percentages
- **Interpreting Level 1**: draw and interpret graphs

APP
Evidence for Using and applying maths Level 4, Calculating Level 5, Shape, space and measure Level 4, Handling data Level 5

PLTS
Develops Independent enquirers, Team workers, Effective participators

Every child matters outcomes
Enjoy and achieve, Make a positive contribution, Achieve economic well-being

Cross-curricular links
Music, Science, Media studies

Underpinning maths
- Using scales and marking a range of values
- Interpreting graphs
- Calculating with large numbers
- Calculating with money
- Calculating percentages
- Devising and conducting a survey

Resources
- *Student book*, pages 18–21
- Calculators
- Internet access

Useful websites
- www.listenlive.eu/uk
- www.rajar.co.uk

Context
Students will be aware of the availability of radio from a variety of sources, but they may be unaware of the full range. This includes normal radio broadcasts, both analogue and digital, radio over the internet or mobile phone, and radio channels broadcast on digital TV frequencies.

They may not be aware of how radio stations are financed, or that, for commercial stations, audience size and reach are very important, as they determine revenue.

Lesson plan
This activity will take one or two lessons. The extensions to Tasks 1 and 2 can be set for homework. Task 6 could be done as a class project.

Beginner *

Starter
- Ask students, in pairs, to discuss their musical tastes.
- Hold a brief class discussion about what types of music they like, which bands or singers they like and how they hear about new performers.

Main activity
- Discuss whether students listen to the radio, and list their reasons. Examples might include listening:
    - to music channels that play their favourite type of music
    - in the car
    - to commentaries on sport when it is not televised
    - to sports commentaries on local radio
    - to local radio for information of school closures during bad weather
    - through their mobile phones.
- Ask how they find a particular station. Do they know the frequencies of any stations they tune in to?
- Many radios have the facility for stations to be preset; some tune into them automatically. Digital radios find all available radio broadcasts.
- **Let students do Task 1**. If students need help in finding information about other stations, they could use an internet search. **Extend the task** for more able students by asking: Why do the stations have a range of frequencies rather than a single one?
- Look at Task 2 with students. Discuss regional and national radio. Ask: What is the difference? (Answer: Regional or local stations only cover a small part of the country, whereas national stations cover the entire country.) Ask students to name any regional stations. (Answer: These vary from area to area.)
- **Let students do Task 2**. **Extend the task** for more able students by asking them to try to find out the audience share for their local station(s). They could use an internet search.
- Discuss how you can listen to the radio without a radio. (Answer: Via the internet, digital TV or mobile phone.) Ask: What are the advantages of these? (Answer: They receive digital signals that provide access to many more stations. Mobile phones are portable, so can be listened to wherever there is a signal. The internet allows access to radio programmes that we may have missed, and the internet also allows us to hear local stations when we're away from the area.)
- Explain that because radio has become more available, the sizes of radio audiences have increased. Say that students will see later why audience size and reach are important.
- **Let students do Task 3**, in which they will see how internet listening is growing. Questions 2 and 3 require students to select the correct information from the text above, and to calculate a percentage. If necessary, remind students how to do this before they attempt the task. Question 4 requires students to use the information in their graphs and compare it to their calculations.
- Discuss with students where radio stations get their money from. (Answer: The TV license fee funds BBC national and local radio stations. Independent commercial stations charge a fee for advertising to cover funding.)
- **Let students do Task 4**, which requires them to work out how much money per year (and then per week) it costs to run a radio network. As an alternative method, students could arrive at the answer to question 2 by finding what percentage of each licence fee goes towards the cost of radio (Answer: 1.8%) and then finding that percentage of the £3.45 billion total. (Answer: £63.5 million)

- The graph in Task 2 shows that Radio B is the most popular station in the UK, with approximately 14.6 million listeners.
- Discuss whether these people are listening all day. When are the most people likely to listen? (Answer: In the mornings, before and on the way to work, evenings after work and at weekends.) When will they have the smallest audience? (Answer: Probably between 1am and 5am.) The average number of listeners to Radio B during the day will almost certainly be well under half of the 14.5 million.
- Explain that audience figures are very important – particularly to commercial stations – because their advertising revenue depends on the number of listeners.
- Look at Task 5, which focuses on a local station. It might have an audience of up to 50 000 but because of fluctuation of listeners during the day and overnight, the average might be as low as 20 000. Using the information given, students can calculate the weekly revenue of the station.
- Compare the costs of the national radio and the local station. Why is there such a huge difference? (Answer: A national network has higher costs because it runs a number of national stations as well as many local stations. It also transmits to the analogue and digital networks and provides the repeat radio coverage facility.)
- The figures for the local station are based on average listening figures, but most businesses will want to advertise – at higher cost – when the audience is at its highest. So the station will actually receive greater income by broadcasting more adverts during peak listening times, and fewer during the 'quiet' listening times. **Let students do Task 5.**
- **Task 6 (extension)** can be tackled as a class project. Students need to design a data collection sheet to allow them to ascertain favourite stations and average daily listening times.

Plenary

- Discuss TV and radio advertising, as follows:
    - As more and more commercial TV and radio stations are launched, do you think there is a danger that there will not be enough advertising revenue to finance them all?
    - Name (or ask students to name) some local radio stations and what these stations advertise. Then discuss target audiences (who the station is aimed at) and the link with the advertised products.

Outcomes

- Students will have drawn and interpreted scales and graphs.
- Students will have extrapolated from a graph.
- Students will have calculated percentages.
- Students will have estimated the running cost of BBC radio.

Answers

Task 1

1 Students may recognise the frequencies of some of these national radio stations.

Frequency (FM)	86	88	90	92	94	96	98	100	102	104	106
Station				B	C	D		A	E		D

2 Students should add their local stations.

Beginner *

Extension

A transmitter has a limited range. If adjacent transmitters used the same frequency, the signals would interfere, so they use slightly different frequencies. Most car radios will automatically retune to a stronger signal during a journey.

Task 2

1 Radio B is the most popular.
2 14.6 million people listen to Radio B every week.
3 Although the Hampshire radio station has a larger audience share than Radio A, it has a much smaller potential audience, so its overall listening figures are much lower.

Task 3

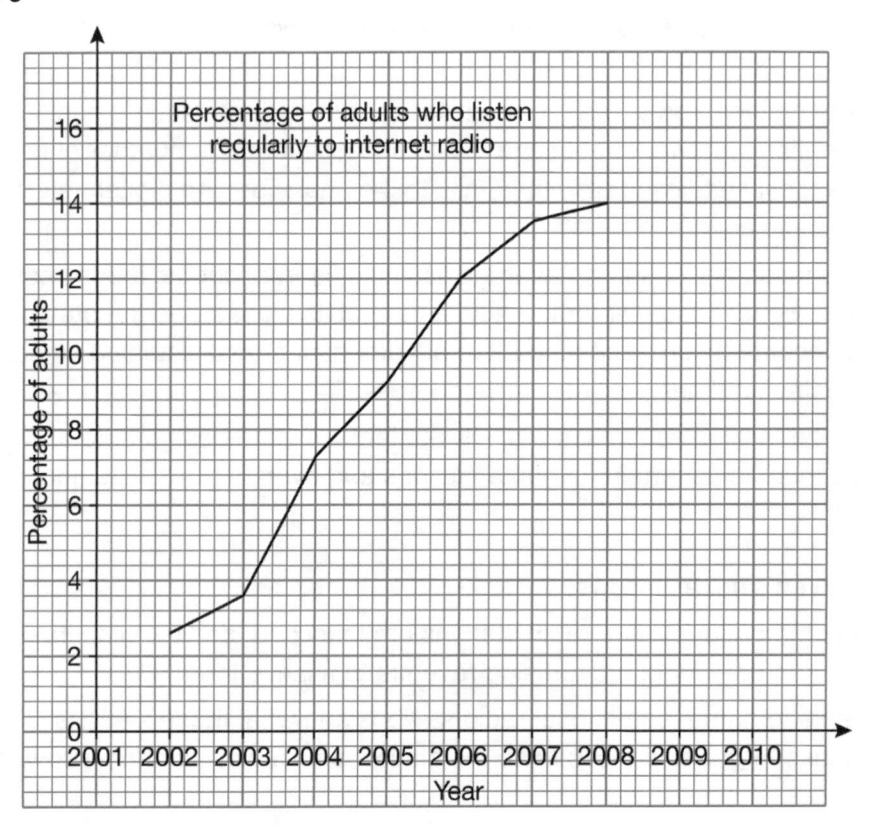

1 [Graph: Percentage of adults who listen regularly to internet radio, plotted from 2001 to 2010, rising from about 3% to about 14%]
2 According to the research, 11.6 million people listened to internet radio every week.
3 According to the research, 23.2% regularly listened to internet radio.
4 It seems unlikely that the figure would rise to 23.2%, but the increase in repeat radio facilities, as well as the growing number of broadband connections, means it is not impossible.

Task 4

1 About 23.7 million licences were bought last year.
2 Of the licensing fee, £63.5 million was spent on radio.
3 This is £1.22 million per week.

Task 5

1 A 30-second advertisement would cost £40.
2 They will receive £53 760 per week.

Task 6 (extension)

Students should conduct a survey among their age group to see which radio stations they listen to. They should have created questionnaires structured to provide the appropriate answers.

Beginner *

Making your own fuel

Learning objectives
- **Representing Level 1**: find information needed from the internet and select mathematics in an organised way to find the solution
- **Analysing Level 1**: apply mathematics in an organised way to calculate the costs of producing biodiesel
- **Interpreting Level 1**: interpret results and draw simple conclusions and explanations

APP
Evidence for Using and applying mathematics Level 3, Numbers and the number system Level 2, Calculating Level 2, Algebra Level 4, Handling data Level 3

PLTS
Develops Independent enquirers, Creative thinkers, Team workers

Every child matters outcomes
Achieve economic well-being, Make a positive contribution, Enjoy and achieve

Cross-curricular links
Science, ICT, PSHE

Underpinning maths
- Carry out research
- Calculating ratios and percentages
- Using formula
- Converting volume to litres
- Reading instruments
- Solving problems with money
- Working with network diagrams
- Producing charts

Resources
- *Student book*, page 22–25
- Data sheet: Making your own fuel
- Calculators
- Internet access

Context
All students are likely to be familiar with increasing fuel prices and the need to reduce the use of fossil fuels. Many will be keen to conserve fossil fuel resources and reduce the amount of carbon dioxide being released into the atmosphere. In this topic, they consider the costs associated with producing biodiesel and make comparisons between running a car on biodiesel and conventional diesel.

Lesson plan
This activity takes one or two lessons. Task 6 (extension) is suitable as a homework assignment.

Beginner *

Starter
- Ask students if they know the cost of a litre of petrol and a litre of diesel and how the prices have changed over the past decade. (Answer: Lowest at 79p per litre, highest at about £1.28, depending where in the country you are.) Ask if they know what **biodiesel** is and talk about the yellow fields that are full of rapeseed oil plants. Most of these are used for vegetable oil but, increasingly, are being used to produce biodiesel industrially.
- Explain that biodiesel is not new and has been around for a century. Rudolf Diesel was the inventor of the diesel engine, which bears his name. It was designed to run on vegetable oil as an incentive to farmers to buy it.

Main activity
- Discuss the process of producing biodiesel. Vegetable oil, either new or filtered waste, is collected in a large conical-shaped container. If necessary, explain the term **conical** and draw the shape on the board. The shape of the container enables the finished product to be drawn off.
- The oil is heated, then chemicals are added. The oil is washed and dried before it can be used. Explain that the process costs used in the task are simplified but are still realistic.
- Read Task 1 with students. Distribute the data sheet. Suggest that the prices given on the sheet are typical but the equipment could probably be sourced more cheaply via the internet.
- **Let students do Task 1**. Make sure they add all the start-up costs together, including the £50 for the equipment.
- Explain to the class that energy is measured in **kilowatt hours** (**kWh**). This is how much it takes, for example, to run a 1 kW heater for 1 hour and is the basis for electricity charges, with 1 kWh being referred to and costed as 1 **unit**. Show on the board the example of a 60 watt light bulb left on for four hours with the unit cost per kWh of 14p, costing $\frac{60}{1000} \times 4 \times 14p = 3.36p$. A 3kW heater left on for 2.5 hours will cost $3 \times 2.5 \times 14p = 105p$ or £1.05.
- **Let students do Task 2**. Remind them to deduct the smaller reading on the meter from the larger one. Tell them to find the volume of 1 cubic metre (m^3) in cubic centimetres (cm^3) and check that they have the correct answer of 1 000 000 cm^3 before they find the cost of water per litre. Make sure students work through the questions logically and underline their answers as they will be used later.
- Read Task 3 with students. Explain that they need to devise a route that goes to every village once every two weeks but are only visiting villages A, B and F on alternate weeks. Tell students to assume there are four weeks in a month; remind them, though, that if they were working out the answer for a year they would have to consider 52 weeks in a year, not $4 \times 12 = 48$ weeks.
- **Let students do Task 3**. Remind them to total the mileage for their two trips to A, B and F per month. Stress that 1 gallon is equivalent to 4.55 litres and remind them to multiply the total number of litres by the cost of fuel per litre.
- **Let students do Task 4** in suitable pairs, if necessary. Check that students have added the costs of electricity, water, methyl alcohol and fuel used for the journeys to collect the waste oil. Remind them they have made 50 litres of biofuel so they need to divide their total costs by 50 to find the price per litre. Explain that the actual process makes a little less than 50 litres as,

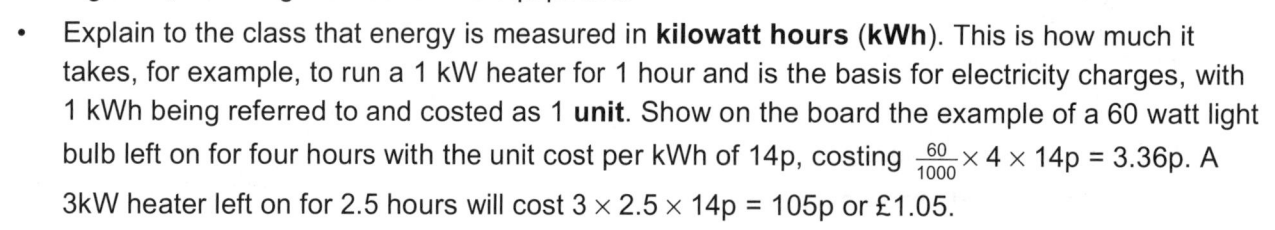

Beginner *

once the waste oil has been cleaned, some unwanted solid matter will have been removed during washing.

- Read Task 5 with students. Say that they need to divide 14 000 miles by the number of miles per gallon achieved by their car, and convert that to litres, before multiplying by the cost of a litre of fuel. Alternatively, they could find the number of gallons needed for 14 000 miles and divide by the cost of a gallon of fuel.
- **Let students do Task 5**. Make sure they are using one of the methods they have been shown. Help students check their answers, using either a reverse calculation or estimation. Remind them that, for question **2a**, they need to add 38p to the cost of their biodiesel per litre and redo the calculation from question **1b**.
- **Let students do Task 6 (extension)**. Put them into pairs to research the amount of biofuel used around the world now. Students could use a suitable spreadsheet package to produce their diagrams, which should be bar charts or pie charts.
- An increasing number of fuel companies and supermarkets now stock biofuels or biofuel blends. Students could find the prices and use a spreadsheet to calculate the savings from different suppliers.

Plenary

- Ask students about the process of producing biofuel. How long do they think it could take to make 50 litres of fuel at home? Do they think it is cost effective for the saving they would make? Is it something they would do?
- Ask students to refer to their calculations to say how much the savings would be per year, for a total of 14 000 miles. Ask if they think there are enough sources of waste oil near where they live. Remind students that the waste has to be based on vegetable oil, as animal fats are solid at room temperature.
- Tell students that people who produce their own biofuel put an additive into it or mix it with regular diesel in winter. Why would they need to do this? Ask what happens when you put vegetable oil in a fridge. (Answer: it goes very thick.)

Outcomes

o Students will have used maths to identify a situation and identified the methods needed to find solutions.
o Students will have used appropriate checking procedures.
o Students will have interpreted the solutions to their calculations and drawn conclusions.

Answers

Task 1

1 Total cost, e.g. £99 + £(20 × 2) + £30 + £20 + £80 + £50 = £319
2 500 − 319 = £181 ≈ 36% saving

Task 2

1 **a** Stages 2, 6 and 8: electricity costs and cost of water (assume water meter)
   b 6551 (end reading) − 6548 (start reading) = 3 kWh
   c Running 2 × 3kW heaters for 1 hour uses 6 kWh, so heaters only on for 0.5 hours.
   d $\frac{180}{60} \times 3 \times 2 = 18$ kWh (units)
   e (3 + 18) × 14p = £2.94

*Beginner ***

2 a 25 : 100 = 1 : 4 (not 4 : 1)

b 1 000 000 ÷ 1000 = 1000 litres per cubic metre (m^3),
113 ÷ 1000 = 0.113p per litre (do not round)

c 200 × 0.113p = 22.6p

Task 3

1 a i A suitable route that covers all villages, must start and end at G.

e.g. G → D → C → D → E → F → A → B → G
= 13.5 + 16.5 + 16.5 + 15.5 + 12 + 15 + 13 + 11 = 113 miles

ii A suitable route for villages C, D and E, must start and end at G.

e.g. G → E → D → C → D → G = 12 + 15.5 + 16.5 + 16.5 + 13.5 = 74 miles

b Check if all students have found the shortest route, accept any route that starts and ends at village G.

2 Students should realise that all villages are visited the first week then only C, D and E are visited the second week, e.g. (74 + 113) × 2 = 374 miles per month

374 ÷ 55 = 6.8 gallons

3 6.8 × 4.55 × 1.17 = £36.20

Task 4

1 (10 × 3) × 2 + (5 × 3) × 4 = 120 litres per month

2 £2.94 (heat) + £8.66 (methyl alcohol) + £0.23 (water) + £36.20 ÷ 120 × 50 (fuel used in collections) = £26.91

3 26.91 ÷ 50 = 53.8p per litre overall

Task 5

1 a 14 000 ÷ 55 = 254.5454 gallons, 254.5454 × 4.55 = 1158.1818 litres, 1158.1818 × £1.17 = £1355.07

Students could check: 14 000 ÷ 50 × 4.5 × 1.2 = £1512 or reverse check,
1355.07 ÷ 1.17 ÷ 4.55 × 55 = 13 999.97 OK

b 14 000 ÷ 55 × 4.55 × £0.538 = £623.10

c Annual savings are £1355.07 − £623.10 = £731.97

2 a Cost per litre = 53.8p + 38p = 91.8p or £0.92

b 14 000 ÷ 55 × 4.55 × 0.92 = £1065.53

New saving = £1355.07 − £1065.53 = £289.54

c The saving is marginal considering set-up costs and time spent producing the fuel.

Task 6 (extension)

1 Students should find figures for current biodiesel usage. Less able students should use ICT or draw a bar chart by hand. More able students should produce a pie chart. They should make reasoned comments analysing their own charts and any changes since 2007.

2 Students should research high street prices for biodiesel and should be aware of the fact that a 5% mix of biodiesel with standard diesel is becoming common. If savings are indicated, then they should recalculate the cost of driving 14 000 miles per year and compare this to their previous answers.

Beginner *

Thumbelina

Learning objectives
- **Representing Level 1**: undertake problem-solving in an unfamiliar context and recognise where mathematical skills are required
- **Analysing Level 1**: analyse information, using appropriate mathematical approaches and understand their impact on creative design
- **Interpreting Level 1**: interpret and communicate solutions to practical problems and draw simple conclusions

APP
Evidence for Using and applying mathematics Level 5, Calculating Level 6, Shape, space and measure Levels 6/7

PLTS
Develops Independent enquirers, Creative thinkers

Every child matters outcomes
Enjoy and achieve, Make a positive contribution

Cross-curricular links
Design and technology, English, Drama

Underpinning maths
- Ratios
- Scale drawings
- Isometric grids
- Plans and elevations
- Pythagoras' theorem

Resources
- *Student book*, pages 26–2
- Data sheet 1: Thumbelina characters
- Data sheet 2: Thumbelina sets
- Ruler, tape measure, thimble (optional)
- 1 cm × 1 cm × 1 cm cubes (optional)
- Calculator
- Internet access (optional)

Useful websites
- www.ncetm.org.uk/resources/9680 (video clip, National Centre for Excellence in the Teaching of Mathematics)

Context
All students should be familiar with fairy tales, even if they do not know the story of *Thumbelina*. They should also be familiar with plays and the theatre, even if they have no knowledge of theatre production. This activity uses the mathematics involved in creative design for a theatre production.

Beginner *

Lesson plan
This activity takes two lessons. You may do it in one lesson by doing Tasks 1, 2 and 4 only (no extensions). Task 6 and one of the extensions may then be used for homework.

Starter
- Ask students if they have been to the theatre. Discuss the sorts of tasks that need to be done to prepare for putting on a play at the theatre. Ask whether any of these tasks may involve mathematics.
- If the internet is available, you could show the video clip from the National Centre for Excellence in the Teaching of Mathematics (see list of websites, above).

Main activity
- Ask students to estimate the length of their little fingers. Ask one volunteer student to stand up and, as a class, estimate how many times the length of that student's little finger will divide into their height.
- Ask students how they would write this estimate as a ratio. (Answer: Little finger : height = 1 : n)
- Now provide a ruler and a tape measure; ask a pair of volunteers to measure the little finger and the height of the volunteer student accurately and give their answers correct to the nearest centimetre. Encourage students to write these measurements as the ratio, little finger : height.
- Ask students how they could judge their estimate. Discuss with them the problem that it is difficult to make a comparison between the ratios, because their estimate is in the form 1 : n, but their measured ratio is not.
- Discuss how they could write their measured ratio in the form 1 : n. (Answer: Divide the second number by the first, then write as the ratio '1 : second number divided by the first'.) Encourage students to comment on the accuracy of their estimate.
- Introduce the students to the story of *Thumbelina*, as outlined in the introduction to the activity.
- You could draw a face on the little finger of the volunteer student and put a thimble on it. Alternatively, show students a sketch of this. Tell students this is Thimbelina!
- Now tell students to imagine that Thimbelina grows to the height of the student and the thimble grows proportionately to become her hat. Ask students how they could use their measured ratio to work out how much bigger the thimble would become. (Answer: Measure the height or width of the thimble and multiply by n, as calculated for their ratio.)
- Read Task 1 with students and distribute data sheet 1. **Let students do Task 1**. Remind them to think about how they found ratios in the form 1 : n and how they used that ratio to make the thimble proportionately large.
- Read Task 2 with students and distribute data sheet 2. Ask students to look at this sheet, which shows the notes for the sets for the play, *Thumbelina*. Ask what dimensions students will use for the old woman's home, when they draw it on the isometric paper, if the scale is 1 cm to represent 1 m. (Answer: 4 cm × 2 cm × 3 cm)
- Ask students to write the scale '1 cm represents 1 m' as a ratio. Discuss with them the use of different dimensions in the scale, which means it is not a ratio 1 : 1 but, instead, 1 : 100.
- Explain that the **plan** view is the view from above. Ask students the shape and dimensions of their plan view for the set for scene 1. (Answer: A rectangle, 4 cm × 2 cm)
- Tell students that the front and side elevations are the views from the side and the front.
- Ask students the shapes and dimensions of their side and front elevations for the set for scene 1. (Answer: Side – rectangle, 2 cm × 3 cm; front – rectangle, 4 cm × 3 cm)

Beginner *

- **Let students do Task 2**. It may help them to have small cubes, each 1 cm × 1 cm × 1 cm, to aid visualisation for elevations and also to work out the number of blocks.
- Discuss considerations For Task 3 (extension) with students before they begin to design their set for Scene 4. For example, they could think about using increasingly smaller blocks on top of each other to resemble a hill, but using fewer than 30 blocks. **Let students do Task 3 (extension)**.
- Look at the introduction to Task 4 with the students. Make sure that students know that the **throw distance** is the distance between the light and the point where the beam hits the stage. Ask students what they notice about the shape made by the distance to the stage, the height and the throw distance. (Answer: It is a right-angled triangle.)
- Ask students how, if they know the distance from the stage and the height of a light, they can be sure whether it will light a scene. (Answer: Work out the throw distance, using Pythagoras' theorem: $c^2 = a^2 + b^2$, where c is the hypotenuse.)
- Ask students how they could work out the height of a light if they know the throw distance and the distance from the stage. (Answer: Use Pythagoras' theorem: $b^2 = c^2 - a^2$, where c is the hypotenuse.)
- **Let students do Task 4**. You may need to remind them how to find a square and a square root on their calculators.
- For Task 5 (extension), encourage students to use the whole triangle to find the height of light G, and then ratios to find the heights of lights E and F. **Let students do Task 5**.
- In preparation for Task 6, ask students to revisit Tasks 1, 2 and 4 and think back over the mathematics they used to find their answers. Encourage them to jot down all the mathematical skills they have used. This would work well as a paired exercise.
- **Let students do Task 6**. They can use their reflections to help them.

Plenary
- Ask students if they are surprised by the variety of mathematical skills required to put on a play.
- Ask students what other tasks for putting on a play may require mathematical skills; for example, the box office manager will need to manage money and sales, the choreographer will need to understand space and time.

Outcomes
- Students will have used a range of mathematical skills as they are applied in a real-life scenario.
- Students will have used a range of problem-solving techniques to reach their answers. Ratio will have been required throughout.

Answers

Task 1
1.   a   1 : 2   b   1 : 1   c   1 : 0.5
   d   1 : 1.2   e   1 : 30
2. Toad: 300 cm; fish: 150 cm; butterfly: 75 cm; field mouse: 180 cm
3. Woman: fish; stilt-walking man: toad; man: field mouse; child: butterfly

Beginner *

Task 2

1 Students should produce diagrams of 3D shapes, based on data sheet 2, but drawn on an isometric grid, with 1 cm representing 1 m.

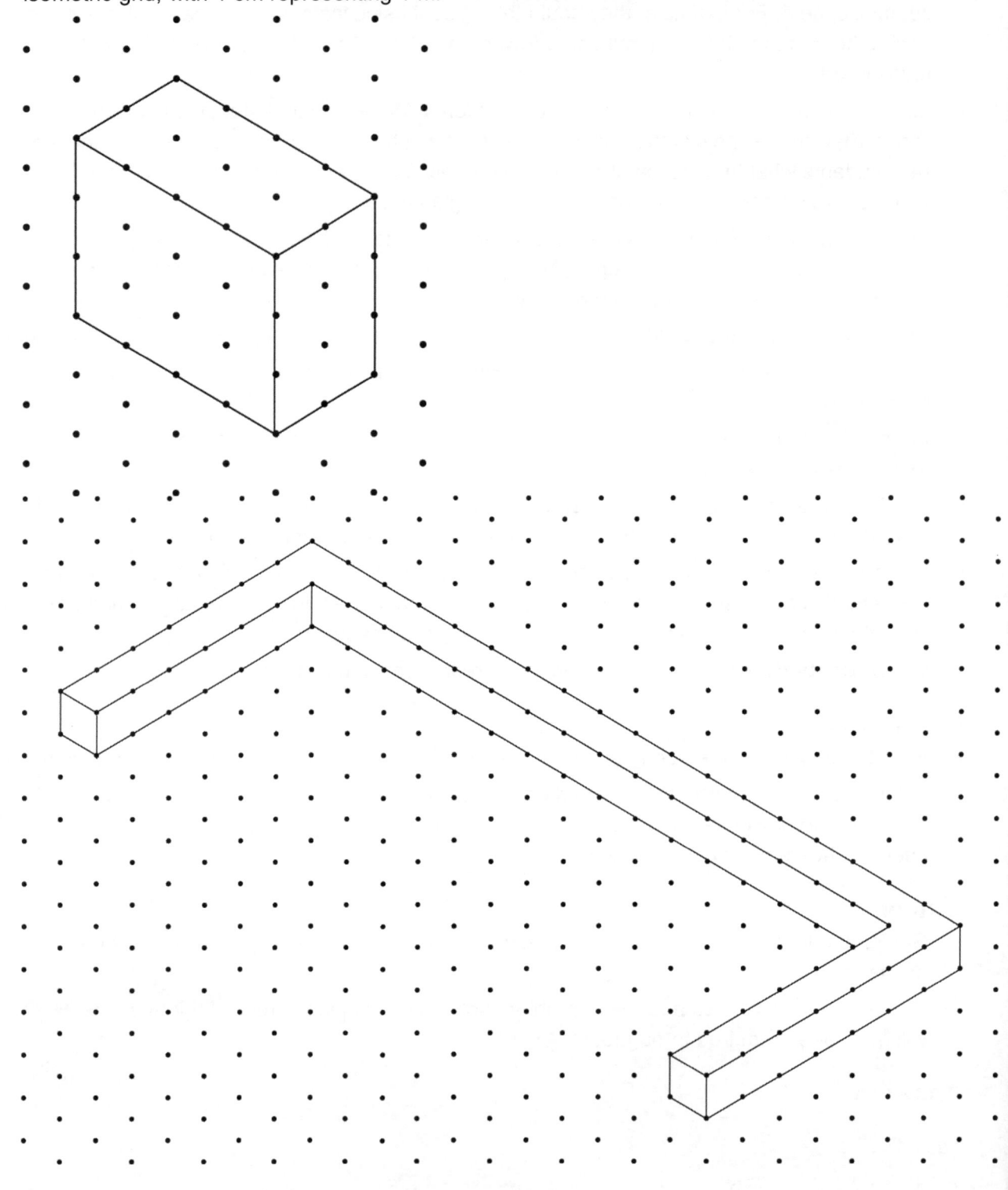

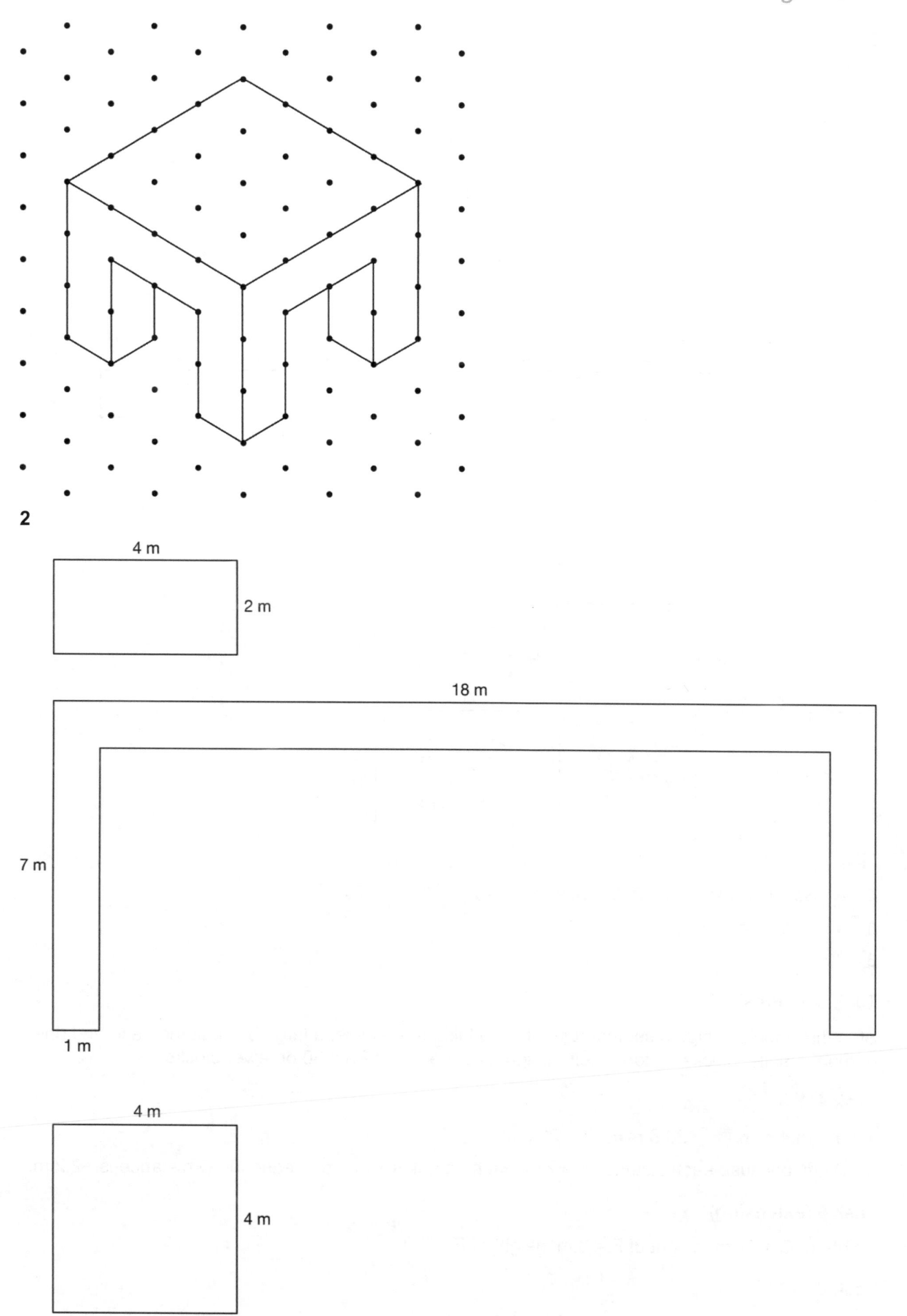

*Beginner ***

2

4 m
2 m

18 m
7 m
1 m

4 m
4 m

*Beginner ***

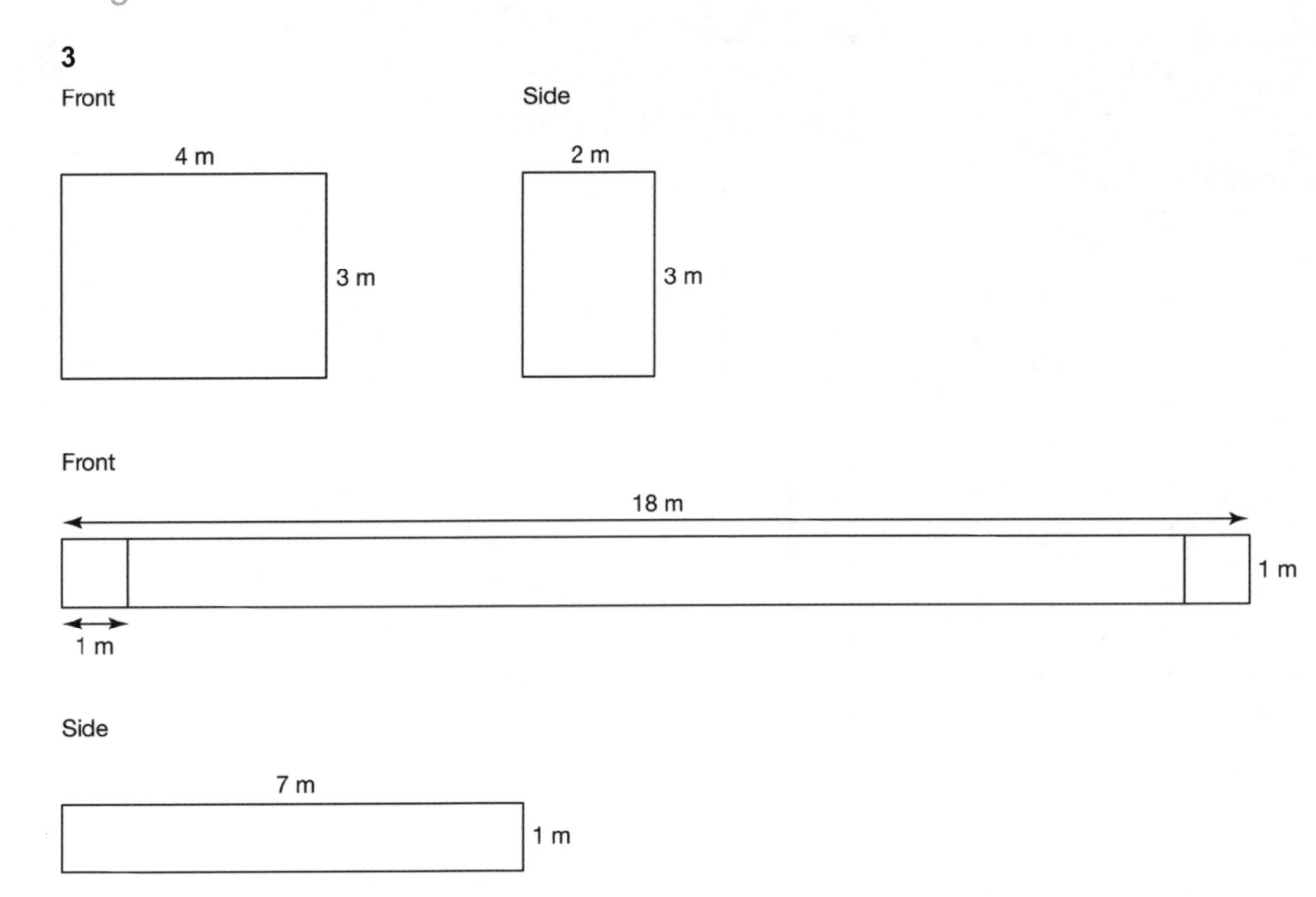

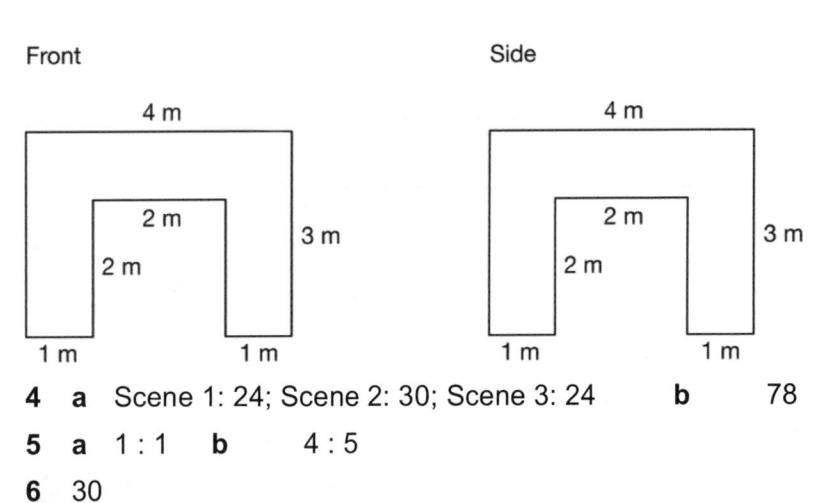

3

Front

4 m

3 m

Side

2 m

3 m

Front

18 m

1 m

1 m

Side

7 m

1 m

Front

4 m

2 m

2 m

3 m

1 m   1 m

Side

4 m

2 m

2 m

3 m

1 m   1 m

4 a Scene 1: 24; Scene 2: 30; Scene 3: 24   **b**   78

5 a 1 : 1   **b**   4 : 5

6 30

Task 3 (extension)

Students should design a set that resembles a hill, for example, a large block at the base and one or more smaller blocks on top. Their design must be made from 30 or fewer blocks.

Task 4

1 a 18.4 m **b**   20.6 m **c**   22.8 m

2 25 m, because each distance is +2 m, each height is +1 m, and each throw distance is +2.2 m.

Task 5 (extension)

Height of G = 12 m, height of F = 8 m, height of E = 4 m

Task 6

Students should include at least the following mathematical skills, as used in Tasks 1, 2 and 4:

costume designer: ratios; set designer: scale drawing; lighting designer: Pythagoras' theorem.

Off your trolley

Learning objectives
- **Representing Level 1**: identify and obtain necessary information to tackle the problem
- **Analysing Level 1**: solve problems requiring calculation with common measures, including money
- **Interpreting Level 1**: interpret and communicate solutions to practical problems, drawing simple conclusions and giving explanations

APP
Evidence of Using and applying mathematics Level 3, Numbers and the number system Level 3, Calculating Level 4

PLTS
Develops Creative thinkers, Reflective learners

Every child matters outcomes
Be healthy, Achieve economic well-being

Cross-curricular links
Food technology, Science, Economics

Underpinning maths
- Calculating with measures including money
- Best value
- Simple proportion

Resources
- *Student book*, pages 30–33
- Data sheet: Shopping list
- Calculators

Context
Students will be familiar with supermarket shopping. This activity enables them to investigate carbon footprints, compare prices between supermarkets and find best-value products. Discussion will encourage them to look beyond just calculation.

Lesson plan
These tasks will take one to two lessons. Task 5 (extension) could be done as homework.

Starter
- Discuss video games. Where do students buy them? Where is the cheapest place to buy them? (Answer: Very often, supermarkets are the cheapest; they regularly beat internet prices.)
- How can supermarkets sell the games so cheaply? (Answer: They buy them in very large quantities to distribute to all their stores. This is true for everything they sell.)

Beginner *

Main activity

- Ask students what they understand by the term **carbon footprint**. Many will associate it with cars, aeroplanes and other forms of transport. Explain that it is the total amount of carbon dioxide (CO_2) released into the atmosphere by the actions of an organisation, event, product or person. Sometimes the definition is expanded to include any **greenhouse gas** emissions. Make sure students know that greenhouse gases (and these include carbon dioxide) are gases that help to trap solar radiation in the Earth's atmosphere. Explain that many greenhouse gases are given off during the creation of power, such as electricity, by motor vehicles and by home heating using gas or oil. Students may have other examples.

- Look at Task 1 with students. In this, they will consider the carbon footprint of some everyday foods. It might be worth saying that, because of the way we farm animals, meat has the highest carbon footprint of any food. Fertilisers and pesticides are used in the production of grain to feed animals. These animals are routinely sprayed with pesticides and treated with antibiotics. All of this adds to their carbon footprint. Sheep and cows give off a lot of methane – a greenhouse gas – as well as carbon dioxide in their breath.

- **Let students do Task 1**. Discuss the results. What else adds to an individual's carbon footprint? (Answer: As well as those factors mentioned already, transporting, refrigerating and cooking food; travel by car, bus, train and aeroplane produces greenhouse gases. Heating our houses and using any electrical gadgets, from TVs to chargers for mobile phones, has an effect. Many cosmetics, hairsprays and deodorants will have yielded greenhouse gases in their manufacture, although propellants in most aerosols have been changed, to reduce the effect.)

- Discuss how you could reduce the carbon footprint of food you buy. (Answer: By not travelling so far to buy, or visiting local farm shops or farmers' markets for locally produced food.)

- Discuss the fact that supermarkets advertise that they are cheaper than their competitors. However, in many cases, the prices are identical. Discuss **loss leaders**, explaining that supermarkets sell some items at a loss to entice customers, assuming that, once inside, they will do all their shopping there. Distribute the data sheet.

- **Let students do Task 2**. If necessary, point out that Georgie can buy the potatoes from A at two packs for £2, in which case the cost is only £1 for the shopping list. Georgie has to pay £2, but will have an extra £1 worth of potatoes.

- Discuss the savings made by shopping around: is it worth spending the time to work out which is cheaper? What other factors might influence buying decisions? (Answer: Ease of parking or parking charges; whether you prefer one supermarket's own-brand products to another's.)

- Discuss 'bulk' offers. Which is potentially the least useful? (Answer: The potatoes, as they might sprout before you eat them all. All the others can be frozen.)

- Discuss value for money and the economy of buying larger sizes. Are larger sizes always best buys? What are the disadvantages? (Answer: Sometimes smaller packs on offer can work out cheaper; you may not finish the large pack before the use-before date; larger packs may be more difficult to store.)

- **Let students do Task 3**. Students often have difficulty in deciding which way to divide. Discuss or explain that the price of 333 grams of chicken for £3 can be calculated as 333 g ÷ £3 = 111 grams per pound (g/£1), or £3 ÷ 333 g = 0.009 pounds per gram (£/g). Best value is the most g/£ or the least £/g. (The answer section uses a mixture of methods, avoiding answers of less than one where possible.)

Beginner *

- Read Task 4 with students. Explain that when you plan a meal, you usually find that you already have some ingredients. In this task, they are going to have to buy them all, irrespective of what they may already have in their homes. They will work out the cost of all the ingredients, and then work out the cost of the quantities they have used. This is an ideal task for solution by spreadsheet, although many students will need support in setting up the appropriate columns. **Let students do Task 4**. **Extend the task**, asking students to choose their own favourite recipe, then work out the costs of the ingredients and calculate the cost per person.
- Read Task 5 (extension) with students. This highlights how much cheaper it can be to prepare your own food. **Let students do Task 5**.

Plenary

- At some stage in their lives, students will have to feed themselves. Will they rely on ready meals or cook their own?
- What are the advantages and disadvantages of preparing your own food? (Answer: You can change the recipe to suit yourself; it is usually cheaper, and probably healthier as it is less likely to be loaded with salt and preservatives. However, it takes time.)

Outcomes

- Students will have calculated with money and other measures.
- Students will have calculated with proportion.
- Students will have made fair comparisons to calculate best value.

Answers

Task 1

1 240 lb
2 1170 lb
3 Transporting, refrigerating and cooking all produce greenhouse gases.

Task 2

1 £45.22, reduced to £43.05 by buying the offers.
2 £41.39, reduced to £40.42 by buying the offers.
3 £40.71, reduced to £39.89 by buying the offers.
4 Supermarket A: with transport costs, £47.02, or £44.85 with offers

   Supermarket B: with transport costs, £45.59, or £44.62 with offers

   Best of both: with transport costs, £45.21, £44.39 with offers.

   It's slightly cheaper to go to Supermarket B, unless Georgie goes to both and takes advantage of the offers.

Beginner *

Task 3

1

Chicken breasts	333 g for £3	111g/£	613 g for £6.74	90.9 g/£	950 g for £10.43	91.1 g/£
Carrots	500 g for 71p	7.0 g/p	600 g for 90p	6.7 g/p	750 g for 92p	8.2 g/p
Baked beans	220 g for 30p	7.3 g/p	420 g for 44p	9.5g/p	4 × 420 g for £1.48	11.4 g/p
Orange squash	64p for 1 litre	64p/litre	£1 for 1.5 litres	66.7p/litre	£1.35 for 2 litres	67.5 p/litre
Shower gel	150 ml for £1	150 ml/£	250 ml for £2.32	107.8 ml/£	400 ml for £2.75	145.5 ml/£
Cheddar cheese	400 g for £3.98	100.5 g/£	600 g for £4	150 g/£	2 × 400 g for £5	160 g/£

Cheapest item tinted darker grey.

2 The chicken breasts can be frozen; the baked beans, orange squash and shower gel have a long life. The cheese and carrots would be the first to go to waste.

Task 4

Item	Needed		Buy		Cost	Part cost
Bacon	6	rashers	10	rashers	£1.64	£0.98
Butter	20	g	250	g	£0.98	£0.08
Olive oil	15	ml	500	ml	£1.84	£0.06
Boneless chicken breasts	6	breasts	2 packs	pack of 4	£7.80	£5.85
Onion	1	onion	1 pack	pack of 3	£0.50	£0.17
Garlic	3	cloves	1	1 bulb (12 cloves)	£0.24	£0.06
Grated cheddar cheese	50	g	250	g	£1.50	£0.30
Total cost					£14.50	£7.50
Cost per person					£2.42	£1.25

1 Cost of ingredients bought = £14.50
2 Cost per person (including ingredients left over) = £2.42
3 Cost of ingredients used = £7.50, Cost per person = £1.25

Extension

Students' recipes and prices will vary.

Task 5 (extension)

Students need to take care that they are comparing like with like.

For example, a beef lasagne recipe for 8 might look like this.

Beef lasagne for 8

Meat sauce	Unit price	Unit quantity	Part price
1 tablespoon (20 ml) oil	£1.84	500 ml	£0.07
1 large (about 200 g) onion, peeled and finely chopped	£0.50	3 onions	£0.17
100 g shortcut bacon, finely chopped	£1.64	250 g	£0.66
750 g lean beef mince	£1.61	500 g	£2.42
2 medium garlic cloves, peeled and crushed	£0.24	1 bulb	£0.04
100 g (4 tablespoons) tomato puree	£0.40	200 g	£0.20
800 g chopped tomatoes	£0.33	400 g	£0.66
0.5 g dried oregano leaves	£0.95	9 g	£0.05
0.25 g dried basil leaves	£0.90	7 g	£0.03
1 bay leaf (approximately 2 g)	£0.46	80 g	£0.01
Cheese sauce			
90 g butter	£0.98	250 g	£0.35
75 g plain flour	£0.42	1500 g	£0.02
800 ml milk	£1.25	2272 ml	£0.44
1 g ground nutmeg	£0.92	44 g	£0.02
65 g grated Parmesan cheese	£2.23	180 g	£0.81
Pasta			
250 g packet dry instant lasagne sheets	£0.30	250 g	£0.30
Cheese topping			
60 g grated Mozzarella cheese	£0.47	125 g	£0.23
60 g grated tasty Cheddar cheese	£1.50	250 g	£0.36
Total			**£6.84**

Shop-bought beef lasagne for two: £2.97

Home-made lasagne for eight costs £0.86 per person.

Shop-bought ready-made lasagne for eight costs £1.49 per person

Beginner *

The honey bee

Learning objectives
- **Representing Level 1**: find information, from the internet and tables, required to tackle a problem
- **Analysing Level 1**: apply mathematics in an organised way when working with straightforward problems
- **Interpreting Level 1**: interpret results and draw simple conclusions for the problem that is set

APP
Evidence for Using and applying mathematics Level 3, Numbers and the number system Level 3, Calculating Level 4, Shape, space and measure Level 3, Handling data Level 3

PLTS
Develops Independent enquirers, Creative thinkers, Team workers, Effective participators

Every child matters outcomes
Make a positive contribution, Enjoy and achieve

Cross-curricular links
Science, Geography, ICT, English, PSHE

Underpinning maths
- Extracting information for and from tables
- Converting between different units of measure
- Using significant figures
- Calculating averages
- Working with scales
- Displaying data graphically

Resources
- *Student book*, pages 34–37
- Data sheet: Honey bee map
- Maps of the UK
- Scientific calculators, graph paper, plain paper, tracing paper
- Internet access

Context
All students are likely to be familiar with the sight of bees collecting nectar and pollen, and know that bees produce honey. Most will be familiar with the fact the bees are kept by beekeepers and live in hives. In this activity, which is about the honey bee and its population in the UK, students will look at the life span of the bee and its work to produce honey.

Lesson plan
This activity takes one or two lessons. It could be limited to one lesson, with Task 5 (extension) being set for homework. Task 4 could be adapted for less able students, by reducing the number of areas to be visited.

*Beginner ***

Starter

- Ask students what they know about the honey bee. Ask them to suggest how long a bee might live (Answer: one to four months, depending on the type of bee) and how far it might fly in its lifetime. (Answer: A worker bee might fly up to 500 miles in its lifetime) Ask if they know how many bees there are in the average hive. (Answer: Up to 50 000)

- Tell students that, over the past few years, the bee population, worldwide, has been in decline. This is thought to be due mainly to extensive farming, which reduces the number of hedgerows and wild flowers, and a disease that is killing tens of thousands of bees every year. Remind students that bees are important as they pollinate plants and crops in the fields. One-third of the food we eat comes from plants pollinated by insects.

Main activity

- Explain that the loss of bees each year is measured as a percentage, which is an estimation based on figures from beekeepers. Tell students that most honey bees in the UK are **domesticated**: they live in hives and are looked after by beekeepers.

- Read Task 1 with students. Remind them that, although there is no such thing as 0.7 of a hive, the figures have been worked out from the average number of hives per beekeeper.

- **Let students do Task 1**. Distribute graph paper and discuss with students how to predict numbers over the next two two-year periods. Some may suggest drawing a graph; ask what sort of graph would allow them to make predictions.

- Guide students to include in their tables the **years** as headings, to calculate the **number of bees** that each beekeeper has per year **multiplied by** the **number of recorded beekeepers**.

- Remind students that when they are asked to **compare**, this generally means they will need to calculate an average (in this case, the mean). Display a map of the UK on the overhead projector or data projector, for students to copy into their books. Make A4 copies available for students to refer to. When commenting on patterns of loss, they should consider the whole of the UK, from north to south.

- Read Task 2 with students. Tell them that the percentage should be converted into a fraction. This is a good practice in multiplying fractions. Demonstrate on the board how to convert a percentage to a fraction and how to multiply fractions.

- **Let students do Task 2**. When they have worked out their fractions on paper, show them how to use the fraction button on their calculators to check their own answers.

- Let students work in pairs, as before, to **work together to do Task 3**, answering the questions in the honey-bee quiz.

- Read Task 4 with students. Distribute the data sheet, the honey bee map, and explain that the numbers in the corners show the numbers of flowers in that corner of the field. Make sure they have all located the hive in the top left of the field. Explain that the scale is one square for every 50 metres. Ask students what the length and width of the field is, in real life.

- Remind students that in question 2 they are asked for the total distance, so they should keep a running log of how many trips they make to and from the hive, and the length of each trip out and back.

- **Let students do Task 4**. Check that students using rulers that show both centimetres and inches are using the correct (centimetre) scale. Remind them that they do not have to collect all the pollen from each group of flowers at one time. They can adjust the numbers and make another trip to visit any remaining flowers. If appropriate, less able students could be asked to visit fewer areas on the map, or they could be paired with more able students.

Beginner *

- Read Task 5 with students. Ask them to show how big they think half an inch is. Remind them that an inch is approximately equivalent to 2.54 cm. Ask them how many millimetres there are to an inch. (Answer: 25.4) Distribute plain paper. Less able students may benefit from using paper with a pre-drawn scaled grid, such as 2 mm-squared paper. Remind students what **significant figures** are and give, as an example, 345 634 = 350 000 to two significant figures (2 sf).

- **Let students do Task 5**. Check they have correctly measured the length of the bee as $\frac{1}{2}$ inch or 12.7 mm (they can round to 13 mm if needed). If students are less confident about drawing, suggest that they use tracing paper to draw a grid and trace over the image of the bee, then transfer the dimensions to the squared paper they are using. If they use coloured pens, students' enlarged drawings would make a good wall display.

Plenary

- Ask students for examples of the speed at which a bee can fly. (Answer: Up to 43 mph (winter) or 47 mph (summer)). Ask again about the number of miles a bee covers in its lifetime. Ask who found the shortest route around the map on the data sheet. Write a list of the 10 best distances, in rank order. Ask the students whose distances ranked as first and tenth to explain how they tackled the problem. Did they work out the shortest routes and then collect as much pollen as they could on the route, or did they try to collect as much as possible from each group of plants, then return to the hive?

Outcomes

- Students will have used maths to identify and obtain the necessary information to find solutions.
- Students will have selected mathematics in an organised way to solve a problem.
- Students will have applied mathematics and used appropriate checking procedures.
- Students will have interpreted the solutions to their calculations and drawn conclusions.

*Beginner **

Answers

Task 1

1 a The average number of hives per beekeeper has increased. The number of beekeepers has also increased, so there should be more bees around.

b Students should produce charts (a simple example is shown below) and add suitable trend lines to show, for example, approximately 21 000 for 2010–11 and approximately 25 000 for 2011–12. They should comment that it is difficult to predict as the graph is not a simple straight line.

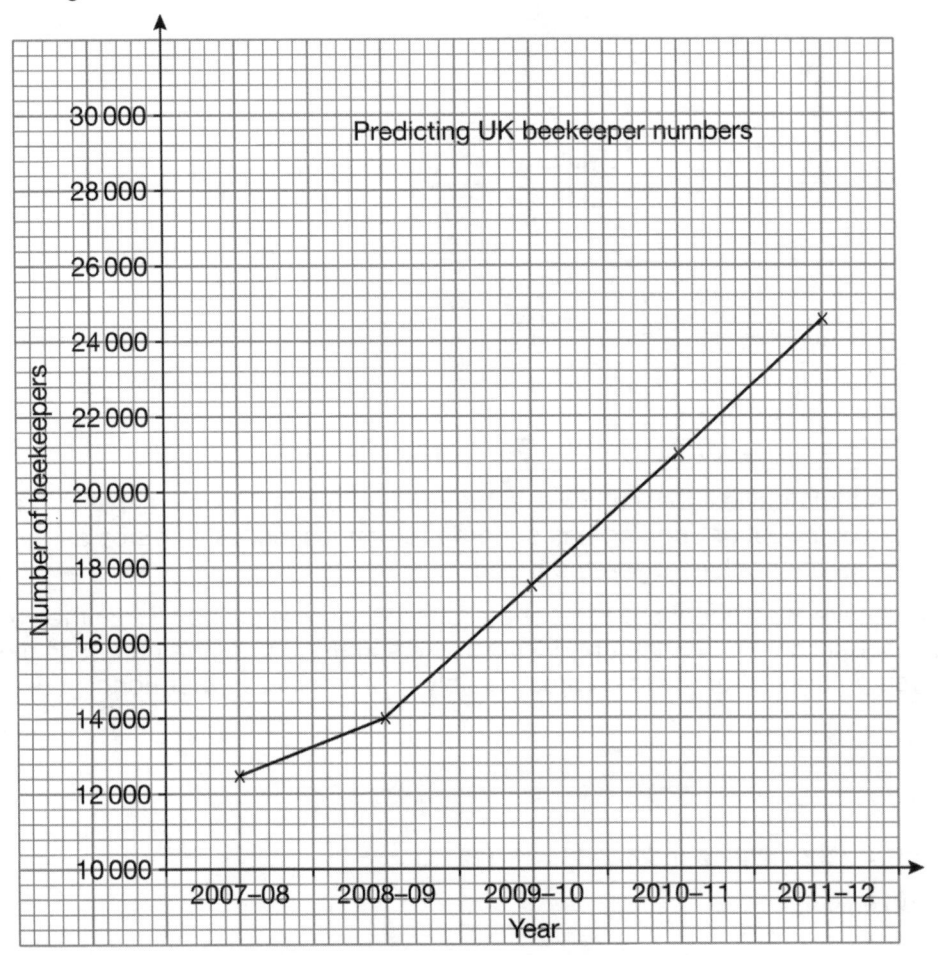

2 a 2007–08: 3.7 × 40 000 × 0.301 = 44 548 bees
2008–09: 3.9 × 40 000 × 0.192 = 29 952 bees
2009–10: 4.7 × 40 000 × 0.177 = 33 276 bees

b

	2007–08	2008–09	2009–10
Before loss	148 000	156 000	188 000
After loss	103 452	126 048	154 724

c 154 724 × 17 500 = 2 707 670 000

3 a (26 + 17.9 + 18.6 + 12.8 + 17 + 16.6 + 19.7) ÷ 7 = 128.6 ÷ 7 = 18.37%

The regional is higher than the national rate by 1.07%

*Beginner * *

b

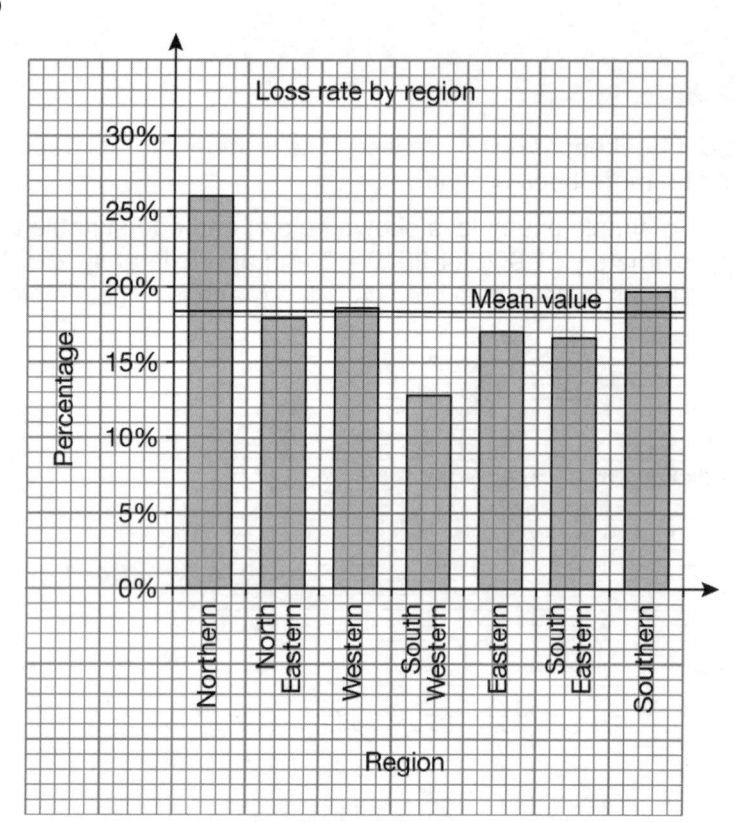

[Bar chart titled "Loss rate by region" showing percentages for Northern (~26%), North Eastern (~18%), Western (~19%), South Western (~13%), Eastern (~17%), South Eastern (~16%), Southern (~20%), with Mean value line at ~18%.]

The graph shows that heaviest losses occur in the north of England, well above average for the country. The southwest of England has suffered fewest losses, with figures as far below the mean as that for the north is above the mean.

c Students should have sketched the outline of the UK and roughly divided it into the six sections. They should comment that, apart from in the southern area, the pattern is that the further north you go the higher the loss rate, possibly as it's colder further north.

Task 2

1 $\frac{80}{100} \times \frac{1}{3} = \frac{4}{15} = 26.7\%$

2 Maximum 24 × 100 = 2400, minimum 24 × 50 = 1200

3 2400 × 35 = 84 000 flowers

*Beginner ***

Task 3

1 2 million

2 55 000 miles

3 A hexagon

4 Students should produce a pattern of tessellating regular hexagons.

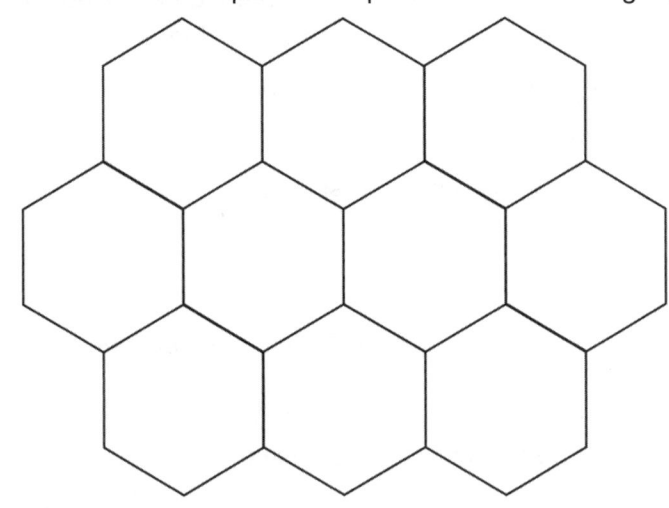

5 The answer depends on how much honey a student uses on their toast. For one teaspoon, the answer is 12 bees.

6 $0.218 : \frac{10}{1000} = 0.218 : 0.01$ or $218 : 10$; it only carries about a 20th of its own weight.

7 Students should calculate their own weight $\times \frac{10}{218}$, for example, $50 \text{ kg} \times \frac{10}{218} = \frac{500}{218} = \frac{250}{109} = 2.29 \text{ kg}$

Task 4

1 Students should have planned a route to visit all the flowers; routes will vary considerably. Bearing in mind the constraints of no more than 100 flowers per trip, and no more than 24 return trips per day, they should have worked out the number of days needed to collect all the nectar.

2 Students should have calculated the total distance travelled to collect all the nectar.

3 Students should have ranked their routes in order of distance.

Task 5

1 a $180 \times 60 = 10\,800 = 11\,000$

  b $180 \times 60 \times 60 \times 6 = 3\,888\,000 = 3\,900\,000$

2 a 1 inch = 2.54 cm, length of bee = 25.4 ÷ 2 = 12.7 mm

  b Students should have **drawn** scale versions of the bee, to the correct height : depth proportion.

  c Students should find that the wing span is 1.375 inches, the body is 0.375 inches wide and each wing is close to 0.5 inches long.

Beginner *

Money – making the world go round?

Learning objectives
- **Representing Level 1**: obtain the necessary information to tackle the problem; draw bar charts
- **Analysing Level 1**: solve problems requiring calculation, with common measures, including money, length and weight; work out areas of rectangles and calculate percentages
- **Interpreting Level 1**: extract and interpret information from tables; compare bar charts

APP
Evidence of Using and applying mathematics Level 4, Calculating Level 4, Shape, space and measure Level 4, Handling data Level 4

PLTS
Develops Independent enquirers, Creative thinkers, Self-managers, Effective participators.

Every child matters outcomes
Enjoy and achieve, Make a positive contribution, Achieve economic well-being

Cross-curricular links
Citizenship, Science, Economics, English

Underpinning maths
- Bar charts
- Calculating percentages
- Working with large numbers
- Areas of rectangles

Resources
- *Student book*, pages 38–41
- Calculators
- Internet access

Useful websites
- medlibrary.org/medwiki/British_One_Pound_coin#Designs

Context
Students are familiar with coins but may not know about the metals that are used in them.

Counterfeiting is common in many areas of everyday life, and coins are no exception.

Lesson plan
This activity takes one lesson. Task 5 (extension) could be set as homework.

Starter
- Discuss with students the current set of British coins and those used in other countries.

  We use coins with values of 1p, 2p, 5p, 10p, 20p and 50p as parts of £1.

  Similarly, the euro has coins of 1c, 2c, 5c, 10c, 20c and 50c.

- The USA dollar has coins of 1c, 5c, 10c, 25c and 50c and the Eastern Caribbean dollar has coins of 1c, 2c, 5c, 10c and 25c.

Beginner *

- Ask students to suggest the advantages and disadvantages of each system. They may suggest there are too many different values of coins. Alternatively, they may say that it takes too many coins to make a sum of money. For example, to make 99p you need six coins, but for 99c in the USA you need eight coins and in the Caribbean it takes seven coins. On the other hand, in the USA and Caribbean, 35c requires only two coins, whereas making up 35p requires three coins.
- To **extend the activity** at any point, students could be asked to choose a new set of values that might be better.

Main activity

- The number of coins in circulation is a staggering 28 billion. Write this number on the board, in full (28 000 000 000). Discuss with students why there are so many more coins of some values than others, for example, there are 11 billion pennies to 1.4 billion pound coins, which is about eight times as many. (Answer: Some coins get used more; to make any sum of money you never need more than one 5p, or one 10p, or one 50p, but you sometimes need two 2p coins or 20p coins. Also, many of us rarely use small change; it accumulates in our pockets and purses; some people save their small change, effectively taking it out of circulation.)
- Look at Task 1 with students. Suggest they could use a spreadsheet to complete it. This would enable them to input formulae to calculate the value of the coins as well as to draw the bar charts. Raise these points before they start the task:

  a   There is no need to include the totals on the bar charts.

  b   Although the figures are in millions, that does not make the calculations any more difficult – the answers will also be in millions.
- **Let students do Task 1**.
- Look at Task 2 with students. Discuss the metals used in making coins. Ask students to suggest the important characteristics of the metals used for coinage. The materials need to be cheaper than the coins' face value, otherwise people would melt them down, as has happened in the past. They need to be easily cleaned. They must be hardwearing, so the faces do not wear off. They must not rust or corrode.
- Ask if it would matter if the composition of the alloy were changed. (Answer: No.) Explain that, for example, 'copper' coins, 1p and 2p, produced after 1992 are made from copper-plated steel. Earlier coins were made from bronze. Steel is an alloy of iron and carbon and, because of the iron, recent 'coppers' are magnetic, whereas earlier coins were not. The important factor is maintaining the same weight, as many vending machines check coins by size and weight.
- **Let students do Task 2**. Simplify the percentages of zinc and nickel to 25% and 5% if necessary. Encourage students to look for the information they need, such as the number of £1 coins, in the previous table.
- Look at Task 3 with students. Using cheap metal keeps the actual value of the metal in a coin very small. Ask for advantages and disadvantages. (Answer: They are cheap to make, but it encourages counterfeiting.)
- Ask students to suggest other areas of counterfeiting. (Answer: CDs, watches, perfume, designer labels) Discuss the ethics: it is obviously illegal and makes large sums of money for the counterfeiters. In many cases though, the genuine goods are over-priced, so the practice is encouraged by buyers who often know they are buying counterfeit goods but want to be seen to be wearing something that looks exclusive or expensive.
- The Royal Mint knows how many £1 coins it makes but it doesn't know how many fakes are in circulation. Ask students how they think the estimate of 2.5% is made. (Answer: By sampling coins taken in to banks.) **Let students do Task 3**.

Beginner *

- Return to the topic of counterfeiting. Ask: 'Who loses out?' In the case of designer goods, the manufacturers might lose some sales, but most people who buy the cheap goods wouldn't buy them at full price. However, some people may buy unwittingly, and do not get what they think they are paying for, and so lose out. With CDs, the record companies lose genuine sales and the artists lose royalties. The buyer also might end up with goods of inferior sound quality. With coins, the individual – often the shopkeeper – loses out when they bank the money; if the bank spots the counterfeit, the shopkeeper loses.
- Look at Task 4 with students. Remind them how to find the area of a rectangle. Advise them, despite the large numbers, to leave answers in centimetres (cm) and square centimetres (cm^2). **Let students do Task 4**.
- Look at Task 5 (extension) with students. They are asked to research two different topics, for which they should use internet searches, if possible. **Let students do Task 5 (extension).**

Plenary

- Ask students why, with the ready availability of colour photocopiers, it is difficult to produce counterfeit notes. (Answer: The metallic strip and watermark cannot be reproduced by a photocopier. These features are built in during the papermaking process.)
- Explain that the UK used pound notes until 1983. Ask why, if notes are more difficult to counterfeit, we don't return to £1 notes. (Answer: As prices rose, the £1 note was used so much that it wore out quickly and had to be replaced frequently. The coin has a much longer life.)

Outcomes

- Students will have calculated with large numbers.
- Students will have drawn bar charts and compared charts.
- Students will have used a spreadsheet to make calculations and to produce graphs.
- Students will have calculated percentages of quantities and expressed one quantity as a percentage of another.
- Students will have rounded to a sensible degree of accuracy.
- Students will have calculated currency conversions and drawn conversion graphs.
- Students will have calculated areas of rectangles.

Answers

Task 1

1

Denomination	Number of coins (millions)	Value (£millions)	Rounded value (£millions)
£2	345	690	690
£1	1474	1474	1474
50 pence	845	422.5	423
20 pence	2473	494.6	495
10 pence	1651	165.1	165
5 pence	3774	188.7	189
2 pence	6664	133.28	133
1 penny	11 215	112.15	112
Total	**28 441**	**3680.33**	**3681**

*Beginner ***

2

[Bar chart: Number of pieces (m) vs Coin (£2, £1, 50 pence, 20 pence, 10 pence, 5 pence, 2 pence, 1 penny)]

3

[Bar chart: Face value (£m) vs Coin (£2, £1, 50 pence, 20 pence, 10 pence, 5 pence, 2 pence, 1 penny)]

4 The bar charts are almost reversed; the first shows that there are many more coins of smaller denominations, but the second shows that the value of the larger denominations is much greater than the smaller denominations.

Task 2

1 1474 million × 9.5 g = 14 003 million g = 14 003 tonnes

2 9802 tonnes of copper, 3431 tonnes of zinc and 770 tonnes of nickel.

Task 3

1 36.85 million   **2** £200   **3** £18

4

[Graph: Conversion between UK pounds and Lilangeni, straight line from origin, x-axis Pounds (0–20), y-axis Lilangeni (0–250)]

© HarperCollins*Publishers* 2010

49

Beginner *

Task 4

1	2250 cm or 22.5 m	**2**	5062.5 cm²	**3**	4000 cm²	**4**	79%
5	3.86 cm	**6**	3860 cm or 38.6 m	**7**	14 899.6 cm²		
8	11 700 cm²	**9**	78.5% – almost the same as in question 4				

Task 5

1 The reverse of the £1 coin goes through a five-year cycle, depicting the Royal Coat of Arms one year, then in successive years images based on Scotland, Wales, Northern Ireland and England.

Royal designs	Themed designs				
	Theme	**Scotland**	**Wales**	**Northern Ireland**	**England**
1983: Royal coat of arms	Plants	1984: Thistle	1985: Leek	1986: Flax	1987: Oak
1988: Crown over royal shield	Plants	1989: Thistle	1990: Leek	1991: Flax	1992: Oak
1993: Royal coat of arms	Regional symbols	1994: Lion Rampant	1995: Welsh dragon	1996: Celtic cross	1997: The three lions
1998: Royal coat of arms	Regional symbols	1999: Lion Rampant	2000: Welsh dragon	2001: Celtic cross	2002: The three lions
2003: Royal coat of arms	Bridges	2004: Forth Railway Bridge	2005: Menai Suspension Bridge	2006: MacNeill's Egyptian Arch	2007: Gateshead Millennium Bridge

The 2008 coins showed the royal coat of arms and in 2010 there were two designs minted, one showing the City of London coat of arms and the other the Belfast coat of arms.

All the designs can be found at the website listed above.

2 Apart from the undated 20p coin in the text, the other main rarity is the 1983 2p coin with the words 'NEW PENCE' on it. All 2p coins struck between 1971 and 1981 included the words 'NEW PENCE' as part of their reverse. In 1982 and in subsequent years the words 'NEW PENCE' were replaced with the word 'PENCE'. However, in 1983 a small number of 2p coins were mistakenly struck with the wording 'NEW PENCE' on the reverse. These coins were produced to 'brilliant uncirculated' quality – a standard higher than ordinary circulating coins – and were included in special sets intended for collectors.

Its value might be higher than the face value of 2p, but certainly not as valuable as the undated 20p.

Students could start their search on a reputable auction website, making sure that they look for coins that someone has bid on to indicate that someone is prepared to buy the item for sale.

Beginner *

Flags

Learning objectives
- **Representing Level 1**: understand simple problems in familiar and unfamiliar situations
- **Analysing Level 1**: use mathematics to obtain answers to simple practical problems
- **Interpreting Level 1**: interpret and communicate solutions to practical problems, drawing simple conclusions and giving explanations

APP
Evidence for Using and applying mathematics Level 5, Numbers and the number system Level 4, Calculating Level 5, Shape, space and measure Level 4/5

PLTS
Develops Independent enquirers, Creative thinkers, Reflective learners

Every child matters outcomes
Enjoy and achieve, Make a positive contribution

Cross-curricular links
Citizenship, Art, Science, English

Underpinning maths
- Symmetry
- Number patterns
- Measure
- Ratio
- Substitution
- Fractions

Resources
- *Student book*, pages 42–47
- Data sheet 1: Flags, semaphore alphabet
- Data sheet 2: Flags, flag templates
- A4 paper, rulers, metre rulers, set squares, protractors
- Calculator
- Internet access to explore flags from different countries (optional)

Useful websites
- www.astroflag.com/world-cup-flags/world-cup-flags.html

Context
Students will know what flags are, but may not be familiar with their meanings. This activity is about the design of flags for warnings on beaches or for representing countries, and the positioning of flags for communicating messages. It culminates in the open-ended task in which students use what they have learnt to design their own flags, including dimensions, and writing explanations of the positioning of flags to communicate messages.

Beginner *

Lesson plan
This activity takes two lessons. For those students working at Grade E, you may do it in one lesson by using Tasks 4 and 5 only. Task 7 would make a good homework exercise.

Starter
- Tell students that today they are going to be **vexillologists**. Vexillology is the study of flags, and a vexillogist is a person who studies them.
- Ask students where they have seen flags flying, and make a list. Then work through the list together, discussing each flag's meaning. For example, a country's flag may be used on the side of an aeroplane of the national airline. Alternatively, students may talk about flags that are used to communicate to athletes at sporting events, such as by linesmen at football matches, or in formula one racing.
- Work through the list again, discussing the designs. Ask students what they think is important in the design of a flag. Talk about the colours, so that they can be easily seen and recognised, and the symmetry, so that they can be understood even when moving. Remind students that:
  - a **line of symmetry** is a line that can be drawn so that one side of the line is the mirror image of the other side
  - a shape has **rotational symmetry** if it can be rotated about a point to look exactly the same in a new position
  - the **order of rotational symmetry** is the number of different positions in which the shape looks the same when it is rotated about a point.

Main activity
- If you have internet access, you could show students the flags of the nations who played in the World Cup 2010. (See the website listed above.)
- Alternatively, you could use flags as printed in an atlas, or draw the following flags, coloured appropriately.

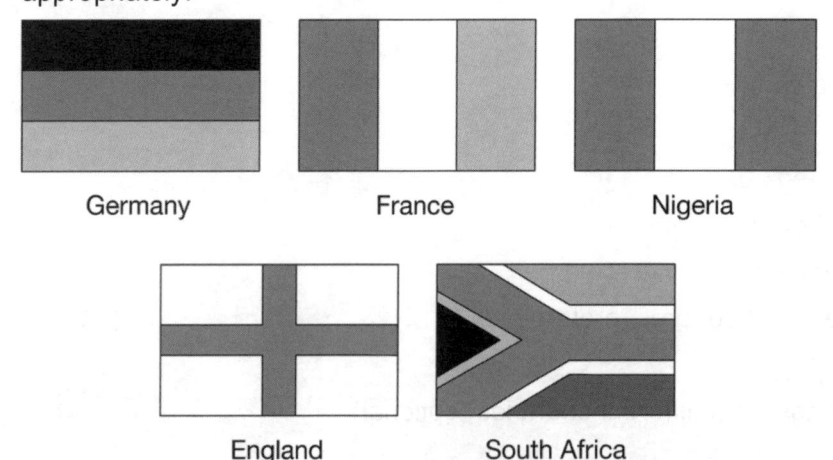

Germany   France   Nigeria

England   South Africa

- Ask students how many lines of symmetry each flag has and the order of rotational symmetry for each flag. (Answer: As in the table below.)

Country	Number of lines of symmetry	Order of rotational symmetry
Germany	1	1
France	1	1
Nigeria	2	2
England	2	2
South Africa	0	1

Beginner *

- Ask students to discuss with a partner whether the number of lines of symmetry or the order of rotational symmetry would change for any of these flags, if the flag were square rather than rectangular. (Answer: If square, then England's flag would have four lines of symmetry and order of rotational symmetry, four.)
- **Let students do Task 1**. Remind students to think about the shape of the flag, as well as its design. (You could read together the meanings of the beach flags, for example, checking students understand what 'prohibited' means.)
- Ask students if they have heard of **semaphore** – the system of using the positions of flags to signal. The word comes from the Ancient Greek *sêma*, meaning 'sign', and *phoros*, meaning 'bearing, bearer'. Explain that the signaller requires two flags, one held in each hand, which can be positioned to represent different letters of the alphabet. Ask students to imagine you have a flag in each hand and to watch carefully, as you send a message with your arms.
- Divide the class in half. As students watch again, ask half the class to count how many different positions your right arm takes and how many different positions your left arm takes. (Answer: Right four, left four)
- Ask students to discuss with a partner how many possible signals you could give with these different positions. (Answer: 16)
- Ask students how many more letters there are in the alphabet. (Answer: 10)
- Tell students you sent a plea for help. Tell them to watch a final time while you spell out each letter of your message: 'S', 'A', 'V', 'E', 'M', 'E'.
- **Let students do Task 2**. You may decide to do questions 4–9 together, as a whole class discussion.
- For Task 3 (extension), ask students to suggest how they may 'sketch' their message, for example, drawing only the positions of the flag poles, or using a stick figure. **Let students do Task 3 (extension)** and then ask them to swap their sketched messages, allowing their classmates to decipher them. (You may wish to remind students to keep their messages polite!)
- Ask students to look at the national flags for the UK, on data sheet 2. Explain that the normal proportions for these national flags are 3 : 5. Discuss with students what this means, drawing a rectangle 3 cm by 5 cm, to demonstrate 3 : 5.
- Now draw a rectangle 6 cm by 10 cm. Ask students if it has the same proportions. (Answer: Yes, because 6 : 10 simplifies to 3 : 5 when both sides are divided by two.)
- Draw a few more rectangles and ask students to work with a partner to decide if they also have the same proportion; for example, 12 cm by 20 cm (Answer: Yes), 27 cm by 40 cm (Answer: No).
- Give each student an A4 sheet of paper; ask them to measure the sides, in centimetres. (Answer: 21 cm by 29.7 cm)
- Now ask students to look at the diagrams for the national flags of the UK, and assume the dimensions are in centimetres. Ask whether one of the flags would fit on A4 paper. (Answer: No)

© HarperCollins*Publishers* 2010

Beginner *

- Tell students that an A3 sheet of paper is the same size as two A4 sheets of paper arranged like this.

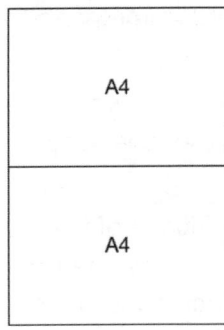

- Ask students the dimensions of an A3 sheet of paper (Answer: 29.7 cm by 42 cm) and whether a flag would fit on A3 paper. (Answer: No)
- Explain that an A2 sheet of paper is the same size as two A3 sheets, arranged like this.

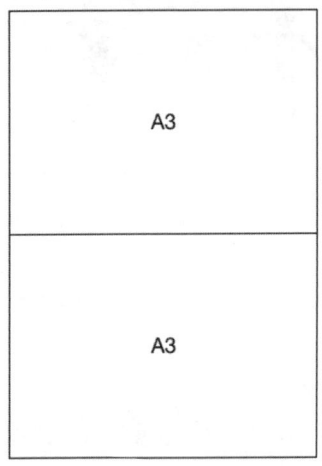

- Ask students the dimensions of an A2 sheet of paper (Answer: 42 cm by 59.4 cm) and whether a flag would fit on A2 paper. (Answer: Yes)
- Ask students to discuss with a partner how to find the size of an A5 sheet of paper. (Answer: Half of A4, 14.85 cm by 21 cm)
- Ask students what they could do if they really wanted to draw the flag to the correct dimensions, to fit on a sheet of A4 paper. How could they simply the ratio 30 : 50 to make the flag fit on the paper? Discuss the idea of dividing both sides by the same number. What number could they use? (Answer: Two to make the ratio 15 : 25)
- **Let students do Task 4**. Suggest they draw sketches of A2, A3, A4 and A5 paper, with dimensions, to help them.
- Read the introduction to Task 5 together. As you read, discuss the meaning of 'perpendicular' (at right angles or 90°); discuss the meaning of 'parallel'. If necessary, explain that parallel lines stay the same distance apart and never meet.
- Ask students to imagine they have measured a flagpole shadow and it is 4.2 m long, compared to the metre ruler shadow of 0.8 m. Ask students how they would use this formula to find the height of the flagpole, then introduce the formula:

$$\text{height of flagpole} = \text{length of flagpole's shadow} \times \frac{\text{height of ruler}}{\text{length of shadow of ruler}}$$

- Remind students about substitution:

$$\text{height of flagpole} = 4.2 \times \frac{1}{0.8} \quad \text{(Answer: 5.25 m)}$$

Beginner ⋆

- Ask students if they understand the term 'flying the flag at half-mast'. Tell students that, in fact, it does not mean flying the flag halfway up the flagpole, but two-thirds of the way up.
- Ask students how they would work out the height of half-mast on a flagpole of height 5.25 m. (Answer: Divide by three to find one-third and then multiply by two to find two-thirds, 5.25 ÷ 3 × 2 = 3.5 m.)
- **Let students do Task 5**. Encourage them to look at their answers and check if they seem sensible, by asking the question: 'Does this seem like an appropriate height for a flagpole?'
- For Task 6 (extension), ask students to draw a sketch of the flag at the top of a flagpole and at half-mast. Discuss with students the dimensions they should include: the dimensions of the flag, and the distance up the flagpole it flies when at full-mast and at half-mast; also the distance above the flag when flying at half-mast. **Let students do Task 6 (extension)**.
- Ask students what they would need to think about if they were designing a flag to be flown at the top of a flagpole. Students should mention colour, symmetry, size, height of flagpole.
- **Let students do Task 7**.

Plenary

- Ask students what mathematics they have used in their study of flags.
- Ask students what words they had forgotten, but were reminded of, by doing this activity, or that were new to them. Students may mention the words 'symmetry', 'proportional', 'perpendicular', 'parallel', 'vexillology', 'semaphore'.

Outcomes

- Students will have used mathematics to gain insight into the study of flags.
- Students will have been reminded of – or learnt new – mathematical language, such as 'symmetry', 'proportion', 'parallel' and 'perpendicular'.

Answers

Task 1

1. a Flag 1: 1; Flag 2: 0; Flag 3: 2; Flag 4: 0; Flag 5: 0; Flag 6: 1; Flag 7: 1
   b Flag 1: 1; Flag 2: 2; Flag 3: 2; Flag 4: 2; Flag 5: 1; Flag 6: 1; Flag 7: 1
2. a Flag 1: yes; Flag 2: no; Flag 3: no; Flag 4: no; Flag 5: yes
   b Flags that look the same upside down have order of rotational symmetry 2.
3. Students should note that it has 0 lines of symmetry and order of rotational symmetry 1. Students may state that it is a bad design for a flag, because it does not use bright colours or symmetry. It would be difficult to recognise from a distance or when blowing in the wind.

*Beginner *

Task 2

1. **a** 4 **b** 22
2. **a** 6 **b** 20
3. **a** 8 **b** 18
   c Number of possible signals = number of right positions × number of left positions
4. 5
5. 4
6. 20
7. Students should make sensible suggestions for signalling the remaining six letters.
8. The signaller holds one flag across the body so both flags are on the same side.
9. Students should provide sensible comments, giving reasons for their opinions.

Task 3 (extension)

Students should sketch a clear, short message.

Task 4

1. **a** 2 **b**

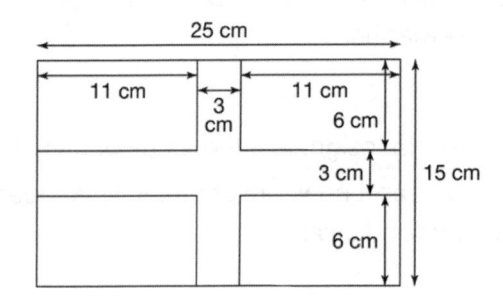

2. **a** 3 or 4 **b** Divide by 3:   or divide by 4:

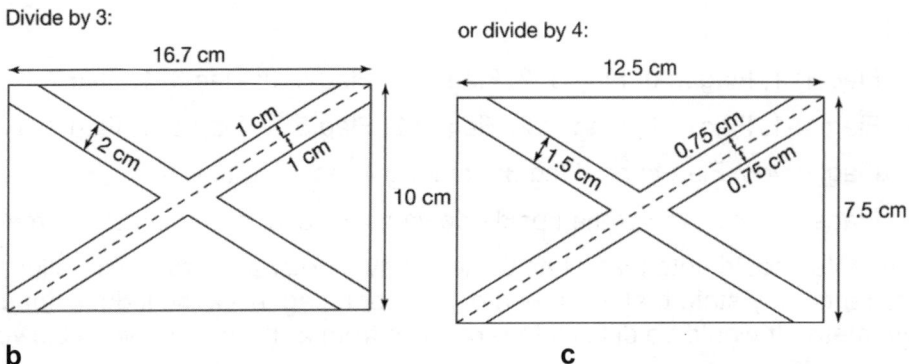

3. **a** 31° **b**   **c**

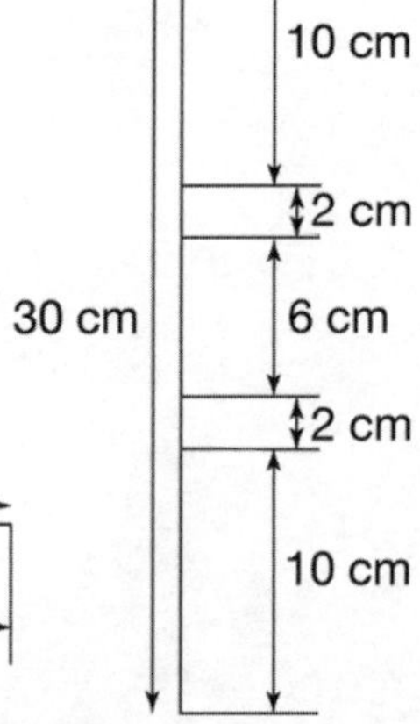

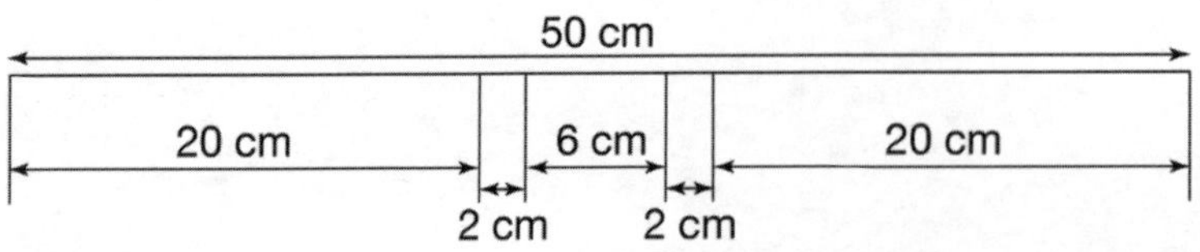

Beginner *

4   × 5 so flag dimensions are 30 cm × 50 cm, fitting A2 paper 42 cm × 59.4 cm

5

Country	Number of lines of symmetry	Order of rotational symmetry
England	2	2
Scotland	2	2
Wales	0	1
Union flag	0	2

Students should provide sensible comments on the design of each flag, giving reasons for their opinions.

Task 5

1   Flagpole 1: 4.5 m; Flagpole 2: 6 m; Flagpole 3: 4.2 m; Flagpole 4: 5.2 m

2   Flagpole 1: 3 m; Flagpole 2: 4 m; Flagpole 3: 2.8 m; Flagpole 4: 3.5 m (1 dp)

Task 6 (extension)

Depending on which bamboo cane (flagpole) the student decides for which flag:

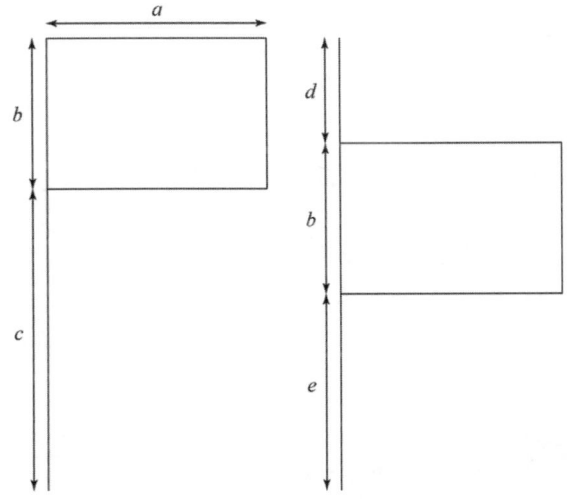

Flagpole	1 At the top	2 Half-mast
60 cm	Ella: a = 25 cm; b = 15 cm; c = 45 cm Lily: a = 16.7 cm; b = 10 cm; c = 50 cm or: a = 12.5 cm; b = 7.5 cm; c = 52.5 cm Mandy: a = 50 cm; b = 30 cm; c = 30 cm	Ella: d = 20 cm; e = 25 cm Lily: d = 20 cm; e = 30 cm or: d = 20 cm; e = 32.5 cm Mandy: d = 20 cm; e = 10 cm
90 cm	Ella: a = 25 cm; b = 15 cm; c = 75 cm Lily: a = 16.7 cm; b = 10 cm; c = 80 cm or: a = 12.5 cm; b = 7.5 cm = 82.5 cm Mandy: a = 50 cm; b = 30 cm; c = 60 cm	Ella: d = 30 cm; e = 45 cm Lily: d = 30 cm; e = 50 cm or: d = 30 cm; e = 52.5 cm Mandy: d = 30 cm; e = 30 cm
150 cm	Ella: a = 25 cm; b = 15 cm; c = 135 cm Lily: a = 16.7 cm; b = 10 cm; c = 140 cm or: a = 12.5 cm; b = 7.5 cm; c = 142.5 cm Mandy: a = 50 cm; b = 30 cm; c = 120 cm	Ella: d = 50 cm; e = 85 cm Lily: d = 50 cm; e = 90 cm or: d = 50 cm; e = 92.5 cm Mandy: d = 50 cm; e = 70 cm

Task 7

Students should take account of colour and symmetry when designing their flag. When they describe the position, they should use mathematical language (e.g. dimensions or fraction of height of the flagpole).

Beginner *

Commuting

Learning objectives
- **Representing Level 1**: obtain information from tables and the internet to tackle the problem
- **Analysing Level 1**: apply mathematics in an organised way
- **Interpreting Level 1**: interpret results in the form of graphs and charts, giving a simple explanation

APP
Evidence for Using and applying mathematics Level 4, Numbers and the number system Level 3, Calculating Level 4, Handling data Level 3

PLTS
Independent enquirers, Creative thinkers, Team workers

Every child matters outcomes
Enjoy and achieve, Achieve economic well-being

Cross-curricular links
Geography, ICT

Underpinning maths
- Extracting information from tables
- Using percentages
- Displaying data graphically

Resources
- *Student book*, pages 48–51
- Data sheet 1: Commuting time by occupation
- Data sheet 2: Commuting to London
- Graph paper, coloured pencils
- Calculators
- Internet access

Useful websites
- www.eurotunnel.com/ukcP3Main/ukcPassengers/ukcTickets
- www.directferries.co.uk/dover_calais_ferry.htm
- www.thetrainline.com
- ojp.nationalrail.co.uk

Context
All students are likely to be familiar with the term commuting and the different methods people use to get to work. Depending on their geographical location, students may be more familiar with commuting times in and around London rather than in less densely populated areas of the country. In this activity, students will think about commuting in London and the UK.

Beginner *

Lesson plan

This activity takes two lessons. It could be done in one lesson by concentrating on Tasks 1 and 3. Task 4 (extension) could be done as homework.

Starter

- Ask students what they understand by the term **commuting**. Explain the term **mode of travel** as a useful way of grouping different means of travel, such as by car, bus, coach, mainline railways and London Underground. Say that, as more people choose to travel to work by car, large cities charge people to drive into the city centre, in an attempt to reduce congestion and emission of harmful exhaust gases. This is known as a **congestion charge**. Less densely populated areas of the country may have little or no congestion, so commuting times may be shorter.

Main activity

- Discuss with students how commuting times vary around the world. In 2005, Thailand had the longest average commuting time of 2 hours each way, to and from work.
- Read Task 1 with students. Explain that the numbers in the table are percentages, except for those in the last row, which give the total number of people in each column. Show that the percentages in each column add up to 100%. Discuss with the class which modes of travel count as public transport.
- **Let students do Task 1**. Check that they have identified the correct percentages to find the number of people using public transport and that they use the value for central London. If necessary, review how to find a percentage of an amount. If computers are available, students could use spreadsheet software to first find the number of people using each mode of transport, then use their results to produce their pie charts. Remind students that the number of people in the table is given in millions.
- Read Task 2 with students. Explain that people are not usually paid for commuting time. Employees usually have to pay their own travel costs, and commuting also has a cost in terms of time. This time can be given a value by considering how much it would cost if commuters were paid for this time at their usual hourly rate.
- **Let students do Task 2**. Remind students that the **average pay** is per hour but commuting time is in minutes, so they will need to divide the average commuting time by 60 to convert it to hours.
- Read Task 3 with students. Make sure they know how to use a mileage chart and remind them of the relationship between speed, distance and time. Discuss with students how to find the amount of fuel they will need. (Answer: Find the number of gallons needed and note that 1 gallon is equivalent to 4.55 litres.)
- **Let students do Task 3**. Help less able students to find the cost of fuel, working through the first part of question 1c on the board. Alternatively, let them work in mixed-ability groups. Let students copy the work into their exercise books, as an example to follow. Students could present their answers to question 2 graphically, for example using comparative bar charts. Remind them to compare return journeys for both car and train. **Extend the task** by asking more able students to use internet searches to find the cheapest options for fares, including the use of railcards and special terms.
- Read Task 4 (extension) with students, Explain that house prices in France (outside Paris) are much lower than in the south of England. Some people have moved to France and commute each day, via Eurotunnel, or fly to London on Mondays and stay in a hotel, returning to France on Thursdays. **Let students do Task 4 (extension)**. They should investigate the cost of using

© HarperCollins*Publishers* 2010

Beginner *

Eurotunnel. They should compare the cost of living in the north of England and commuting to London with that of commuting from France. Appropriate websites are listed above.

Plenary

- Ask students if they were surprised at how long people spend commuting in other countries. Did they expect the British to spend as much time as they do commuting to work? Ask for a show of hands on how their parents and carers travel to work. Comment on any trends; for example, most drive or most use public transport. Tell students that, years ago, most people would walk, go by bus or bicycle as they lived in smaller communities and worked in the same town or village. Ask how many students would like to live in France and work in the UK, and ask for any pros and cons they can think of in doing this.

Outcomes

- Students will have used maths to identify a situation and obtained the information needed to find solutions.
- Students will have selected maths in an organised way to find a solution.
- Students will have interpreted the results of their calculations and graphs.
- Students will have drawn conclusions from their results and provided simple explanations.

Answers

Task 1

1 a 12 + 40 + 27 = 79% **b** 1 110 000 × 0.79 = 876 900 people

2 a

How people commute to work in 'All London'

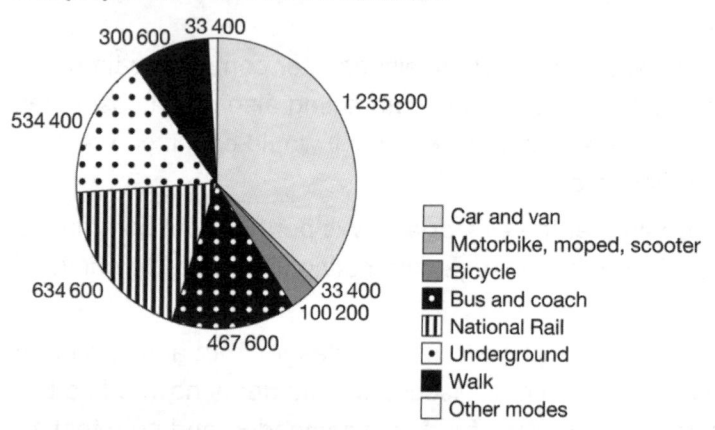

b

Main mode	All London
Car and van	1 235 800
Motorbike, moped, scooter	33 400
Bicycle	100 200
Bus and coach	467 600
National Rail	634 600
Underground	534 400
Walk	300 600
Other modes	33 400

c

How people commute to work in 'Rest of Great Britain'

Car and van	16 324 800
Motorbike, moped, scooter	214 800
Bicycle	429 600
Bus and coach	1 503 600
National Rail	429 600
Underground	
Walk	2 362 800
Other modes	214 800

60 © HarperCollins*Publishers* 2010

Comment: There is less use of cars and vans in London; travel by cars and vans dominates commuting in the rest of the UK; London may have better public transport and there is a more even spread of modes of travel for public transport.

Task 2

1 52 × 5 working days per week = 260, 260 − 28 − 8 = 224 days per year. Answers in column 4 (Commuting time per year (hours))

Occupation	Average commute time (minutes)	Average pay per hour (£)	Commuting time per year (hours)	Cost per year (£)
Managers and senior officials	68.6	21.75	256.1	5570.18
Professional occupations	61.4	21.15	229.2	4847.58
Associate professional and technical	58.8	15.21	219.5	3338.60
Administrative and secretarial	50.6	10.25	188.9	1936.23
Skilled trades occupations	53.6	11.21	200.1	2243.12
Personal service occupations	38.4	8.63	143.4	1237.54
Sales and customer service occupations	41.4	7.51	154.6	1161.05
Process plant and machine operatives	44.6	9.89	166.5	1646.69
Elementary occupations (e.g. cleaners and labourers)	40.4	7.81	150.8	1177.75

2 a See 1 column 5 (Cost per year)

b 21.8 million = 21 800 000 × £13.90 = 303 020 000 = £303 million

Task 3

1 a Luton to London: 35 miles
Birmingham to London: 113 miles
Manchester to London: 193 miles
Norwich to London: 111 miles
Newcastle to London: 273 miles

b Luton: 0.7 hours = 42 minutes
Birmingham: 2.26 hours = 2 hours 16 minutes
Manchester: 3.86 hours = 3 hours 52 minutes
Norwich: 2.22 hours = 2 hours 13 minutes
Newcastle: 5.46 hours = 5 hours 28 minutes

c Luton: 35 ÷ 45 = 0.777... gallons, 0.777... × 4.55 = 3.538... litres, 3. 538... × £1.20 = £4.25
Birmingham: 113 ÷ 45 = 2.511... gallons, 2.511... × 4.55 = 11.425... litres, 11.425... × £1.20 = £13.71
Manchester: 193 ÷ 45 = 4.288... gallons, 4.288... × 4.55 = 19.514... litres, 19.514... × £1.20 = £23.42
Norwich: 111 ÷ 45 = 2.466... gallons, 2.466... × 4.55 = 11.223... litres, 11.223... × £1.20 = £13.47
Newcastle: 273 ÷ 45 = 6.066... gallons, 6.066... × 4.55 = 27.603... litres, 27.603... × £1.20 = £33.12

Beginner *

2 Students compare the time and cost of commuting by car and train. They may present the following data graphically, for example in a comparative bar chart.

	Cost of return journey		Time for return journey	
	Car	**Train**	**Car**	**Train**
Luton	£8.50	£22.40	1 hour 24 min	1 hour
Birmingham	£27.42	£140.00	4 hours 32 min	2 hours 46 min
Manchester	£46.84	£131.00	7 hours 44 min	4 hours 6 min
Norwich	£26.94	£52.80	4 hours 26 min	3 hours 50 min
Newcastle	£66.24	£266.00	10 hours 56 min	5 hours 55 min

They are likely to conclude that travel by car appears to be significantly cheaper than travel by train (ignoring costs of car and maintenance). The difference may be less if ticket deals and/or railcards are taken into account. Train travel, however, is generally quicker (although time must also be allowed for the journey between home and the station, and between the London terminal and place of work).

Task 4

1 a Students should use the Eurotunnel website to find up-to-date costs of return fares, and also cross-channel ferry fares.

b Students should compare costs of travelling via tunnel and ferry to results from Task 3 and make appropriate comments, drawing suitable conclusions. More able students will factor in that cheaper houses and lower cost of living in France would allow more money for travel costs. Hotel costs may also need to be taken into account.

2 Students should use budget airline websites and find prices of travel to airports in northern France. Students may find some low-cost flights but must add on hidden charges and also understand that the cost of a flight varies according to the season. Students should use the data they have researched to help them to express a preference about where to live.

Beginner

Website design

Learning objectives
- **Representing Level 1**: understand an unfamiliar problem and select appropriate mathematics to find solutions
- **Analysing Level 1**: apply mathematics to find straightforward solutions
- **Interpreting Level 1**: interpret findings and draw conclusions, giving an explanation

APP
Evidence for Using and applying mathematics Level 3, Algebra Level 4, Calculating Level 4, Number and the number system Level 3, Shape, space and measure Level 2

PLTS
Independent enquirers, Creative thinkers

Every child matters outcomes
Achieve economic well-being, Make a positive contribution, Enjoy and achieve

Cross-curricular links
ICT, English, Media studies, Business studies

Underpinning maths
- Shape and space
- Generate and use a formula
- Working with currency
- Accurate measurements
- Converting between imperial and metric
- Calculating percentages

Resources
- *Student Book*, pages 52–54
- Data sheet 1: Glossary of terms
- Data sheet 2: Charges for hosting a website
- Data sheet 3: Planning a home page
- Calculators, graph paper, tape measures
- Internet access

Useful websites
- www.cyberindian.com/web-designing/8-tips-for-great-website.php
- www.jessett.com

Context
All students should be familiar with websites and the global market that the internet reaches. Students will probably not have given much thought to what makes a good website and how a website gets onto the internet. In this activity, they will look at how to plan a website and will find the cost associated with producing a website, using a range of options.

© HarperCollins*Publishers* 2010

Beginner *

Lesson plan
This activity takes one or two lessons. To reduce it to one lesson, Task 4 (extension) could be set as homework.

Starter
- Ask students what sort of websites they look at and if they find them easy to navigate. Explain that a website is simply a collection of pages that have been linked together, and are accessed from a home page, rather like the contents page of a magazine, to find the topic you want to read about. Read through the glossary of terms on data sheet 1 with the students and make sure they understand the terms.

- Explain that a website is like a text document, with pictures, that they might produce in a word-processing program, but it has to be converted so that it can appear on the internet. Tell students that they don't necessarily have to use expensive software to make their own website, they can use a word-processor and save it as a website, if the option is available. Alternatively, they could use a template in a page-layout application, although the result might not be as professional.

Main activity
- Discuss how a small company might plan website, how many pages it might need and what would appear on each page. Remind students that there is usually different information on each page, for example, 'About us', 'Products or services', 'Contact us'.

- Distribute data sheet 1 and read through the definitions of important terms with students.

- Read Task 1 with students. Explain that they, as a hypothetical small business, would need to have the website designed and then they would need to pay a company to host it on the internet. Remind students how to generate a formula and to remember BIDMAS/BODMAS when a formula comprises more than one process.

- **Let students do Task 1**. Encourage them to be creative with their website ideas. Distribute copies of data sheet 2: Charges for hosting a website. Let students work in pairs to calculate the yearly cost of each package. Make sure students are using their own numbers of pages for question **2b**. Check that students have generated the correct formula and, if necessary, go through how to derive it on the board, with the class. Encourage students to compare their two answers.

- Explain to the class that, instead of paying someone else, they might want to try to build their own website. They are likely to need software that is more refined than a standard word-processing package. Ask students to suggest any benefits of building their own websites. (Answer: You get exactly what you want, it can be cheaper in the long run, and you can update it with price changes, special offers, etc. whenever you like, without having to pay someone more money to make these changes.)

- Read through Task 2, explaining that computer screen sizes are generally measured in imperial units of inches. Demonstrate that an inch is approximately the width of an adult thumb and is about 2.5 cm. Encourage students to use 2.54 cm as a conversion for an inch in real-life situations, especially when larger distances are to be measured. Give the example of fitting an outside tap at the end of a garden that is 35 feet long. Remind students there are 12 inches in one foot. On the board, show: 35 × 12 × 2.5 = 1050, but 35 × 12 × 2.54 = 1066.8. Ask how they plan to get the water to travel 16.8 cm without a pipe (1066.8 − 1050) − a good example of functional mathematics in action.

- **Let students do Task 2**. They could work in pairs on question 1a. Tell students they are being asked to convert centimetres to pixels for their length and height. Note that the ratio of the length to the height of A3 paper, in landscape orientation, is close enough to 4 : 3 to give a good representation of the computer screen. Drawing the diagonal first, and measuring 15 inches along it, will allow students to plan their layouts almost full size. Remind them of the idea of tessellation, which is how shapes fit together without any gaps. Stress that shapes can be rotated. Distribute centimetre-squared paper, or use data sheet 3, which shows a grid, border and shapes they should use. Suggest that students find the area covered by one of each type of shape, when finding the fraction of the whole area covered by each type of shape.

- Read Task 3 with students. Remind them they will need to add VAT. Remind them of the current rate (20%) and show them how to find 20% of an amount. (Answer: Find $\frac{20}{100}$ or divide the amount by 5.)

- **Let students do Task 3**. Let them decide how long they would advertise in a local newspaper. Encourage students to think about which method is more cost effective in the long term. **Extend the task** for more able students, encouraging them to find out how many days they could advertise in the local newspaper for the same cost as paying for the signwriting on the car.

- Read Task 4 with students, Ask them to highlight or circle their answers to previous parts of the activity, to help calculate the cost of designing and hosting a website.

- **Let students do Task 4 (extension)**. Remind them that they shouldn't be adding all their costs together but need to make decisions about which method they will use at different stages; for example, they might decide to design the website themselves or pay to have it designed.

Plenary

- Ask students for examples of a good website they have used in this task. What did they think made it a good website? Ask who had the cheapest total costs for building and hosting a website and who had the most expensive. Ask these two students to explain why they chose to do it the way they did. Tell students that a large national company used to charge £1000 to design and host a six-page website for a year, including advertising in search engines. Was this a good deal?

Outcomes

○ Students will have used mathematics to identify a situation and will have identified the methods needed to find solutions.

○ Students will have used found information to help solve problems.

○ Students will have interpreted the solutions to their calculations and drawn conclusions.

Answers

Task 1

1 a   Including but not limited to: home, about us, products, offers, services, useful links, contact us

   b   Students' flowcharts should be similar to this one. All pages should link back to the home page.

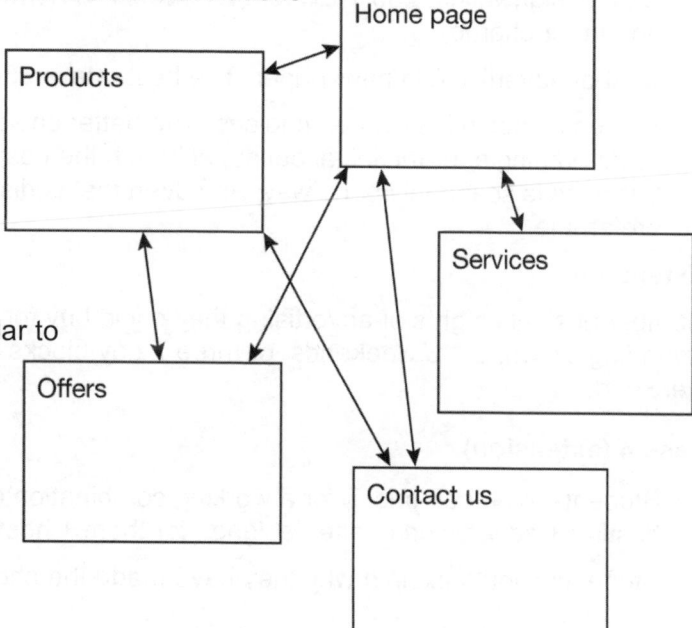

Beginner *

2 a

Company	Package	Cost per month	Special offers	Cost per year
Fasthosts	Home Website Hosting	£4.99	–	£59.88
Fasthosts	Developer Web Hosting	£8.99	–	£107.88
Fasthosts	Business Website Hosting	£15.99	–	£191.88
Virtual Servers	Business Website Hosting	£20.50	15% discount	£209.10
1and1 Internet	Beginner Website Hosting	£1.99	–	£23.88
1and1 Internet	Home Website Hosting	£4.99	–	£59.88
1and1 Internet	Business Website Hosting	£8.99	3 months free	£80.91
1and1 Internet	Business Pro Website Hosting	£14.99	3 months free	£134.91
1and1 Internet	Developers Website Hosting	£24.99	3 months free	£224.91
eUKhost	Copper, Website Hosting	£1.91	–	£22.92
eUKhost	Bronze, Website Hosting	£2.50	–	£30.00
eUKhost	Silver, Website Hosting	£3.17	–	£38.04
eUKhost	Gold, Website Hosting	£4.58	£25 off per year	£29.96
eUKhost	Platinum, Website Hosting	£5.84	–	£70.08

    b Uses their number of pages, i.e. 5, 1 × £390 + 1 × £130 = £520

Task 2

1 a 15 × 2.54 = 38.1 cm. Students should complete the task to produce a rectangle with diagonal of 38.1 cm.

   b Their length × 59 = length in pixels, their height × 59 = height in pixels

   c Divide the height by 3 then multiply by 4 and compare this answer to the calculated length. If it is close, the ratio is 4 : 3; otherwise try dividing the height by 9 and multiplying by 16.

2 a Students should rotate and tessellate shapes to fill the large rectangle.

   b Students need to calculate the area covered by small triangles and put it over the area of the whole grid, to form a fraction, and cancel. Then repeat for all the other shapes.

Task 3

1 Cost of signwriting: £99 + £75.5 = £174.50 + VAT, works out £165.50 + 20% = £198.60, then no further charge.

Cost of advertising in newspaper: The best rate is £50 for seven days, repeated every week.

2 Students should justify their choices. The better choice may be signwriting on a car, as this costs nothing after the initial outlay, although the cost of this is high. Alternatively, if the business is seasonal in any way, an advert that is displayed for a month at a time might be preferable.

Extension

Number of single nights of advertising they could buy for £198.60 = 198.6 ÷ 10 = 19 nights (rounding down), or 13 weekends, or three 7-day blocks and £48.60 left over gives three weekends.

Task 4 (extension)

1 Students total their prices for a working combination of: self-design + software + computer + hosting + advertising or site designed for them + hosting + advertising

2 Students should explain why they have made the choices that they have.

Improver **

Eat well, live longer?

Learning objectives
- **Representing Level 1/2**: find required information from appropriate tables and choose from a range of mathematics to find solutions
- **Analysing Level 1/2**: work through calculations for mean and range, calculate percentages and use appropriate checking procedures to see that answers make sense
- **Interpreting Level 1/2**: use results to produce charts, explain findings and draw conclusions

APP
Evidence for Using and applying mathematics Level 5, Calculating Level 5, Algebra Level 4, Handling data Level 4

PLTS
Develops Independent enquirers, Creative thinkers, Effective participators

Every child matters outcomes
Make a positive contribution, Be healthy

Cross-curricular links
Science, Geography, English, Media studies, ICT

Underpinning maths
- Calculating mean
- Calculating percentages
- Working with fractions and decimals
- Working to a given level of accuracy and rounding
- Using formulae
- Producing charts and diagrams

Resources
- *Student Book* page 55–57
- Data sheet 1: Life expectancy
- Data sheet 2: Monitoring portion size
- Coloured pencils
- Graph paper, plain paper, sticky notes or scrap paper
- Calculators
- Access to computers with software to construct bar charts or use formulae (optional)

Context
Students should be familiar with classifying foods as 'healthy' or 'unhealthy'. In this activity, they will look at birth rates, death rates, changes in population and typical life expectancies across various countries. Finally, they will consider what a balanced diet should include.

Lesson plan
This activity takes one or two lessons. Task 3 (extension) may be started and finished in class, with research completed as homework, unless internet access is available within the classroom.

Improver **

Starter
- Ask students what comprises a well-balanced diet, and whether they think they follow healthy choices. Write a list of foods on the board, using the headings 'Healthy' and 'Junk'.
- Make sure that students understand the term 'life expectancy'. (Answer: The number of years someone can expect to live.) Ask students to suggest reasons why people living in some countries have a higher life expectancy than those in others. Ask students what significance there might be in people's diet.

Main activity
- Discuss with students the fact that, worldwide, population figures are rising. Briefly discuss any problems that might be associated with this.
- Read Task 1 with students. Remind the class how to find a percentage increase or decrease of an amount and refer them to the formula in the *Student book*. Stress that is it important to use the correct number as the original value. When completing the table in question 1, they need to take as the original value the figure for 1975. Remind students to make sure the table they draw is large enough and to set it out neatly. Remind students how to round a number to the first decimal place. (Examples: 1.349 rounds to 1.3, 12.501 rounds to 12.5, 23.993 rounds to 24.0.)
- **Let students do Task 1**. Where necessary, help students to set out their tables and check that they are using the formula correctly. Encourage students who are less confident to write down the formula and then substitute their values. Move around the class, checking answers and giving feedback and praise for those with correct tables of values. Encourage students to answer questions 2 and 3 with full sentences. If computers are available, students could use formulae in spreadsheet software to do the calculations.
- Read Task 2 with students. Distribute sticky notes or scrap paper and ask students to write down how long they expect to live and how long they expect their parents or carers to live. Ask them to write down how long they expect a young person of their age in Africa to live. Ask four students to read out their answers and write them on the board. If all answers are very similar, use some figures you have researched yourself, or take some from the table for this task on data sheet 1. Ask students to suggest reasons why the ages may be different. Reinforce correct answers that refer to different levels of food available, medical care, clean water and sanitation. If students query why life expectancy is different for men and women, explain that, in the UK at least, life expectancy is lower for men because traditionally they have labour-intensive jobs. In addition, men used to retire at 65, whereas women retired at 60 years of age. Figures for other countries may not follow the same pattern. Students may discuss why this is the case. Distribute data sheet 1 and graph paper.
- **Let students do Task 2**. Ensure that students try to estimate life expectancies before they refer to the table. Make sure students answer question 2 by justifying their answer with numerical data (e.g. my guess was close, with a difference of only 2.3 years). Remind students not to do a stacked comparative bar chart. **Extend the activity** for more able students by asking them to complete the bar chart for all the countries listed in the table on data sheet 1.
- Look at Task 3 with students. Ask them to look at the food pyramid and to give examples for each food group listed. Draw a simple triangle on the board and add their foods to the diagram.
- **Let students do Task 3**. If necessary, have coloured pens available so that students can show different food types in different colours in their food pyramids. Distribute data sheet 2, as a background resource. Students could use internet searches to extend the table, and suitable computer software to produce their own versions. This part of the activity could be completed as homework.

Improver **

- Assign students to appropriate groups of four and distribute plain paper for cartoon storyboards. Allow enough time for them to complete their storyboards or presentations. Ask each group to elect one person to report back to the rest of the class.

Plenary

- Ask students for ways they can stay healthy and what factors affect the health of people in other countries around the world.
- Ask students how the population in different countries is changing. Why are their figures for the increase in population much higher than the published figure for 2009, i.e. of 1.133%? (Answer: For example, this does not take into account the age at which people die, it does not include all countries around the world.)
- Ask them to describe the differences have they seen between developed and developing countries.

Outcomes

o Students will have identified appropriate information from a table or diagram and identified the methods needed to find solutions.
o Students will have carried out calculations correctly.
o Students will have interpreted the solutions to their calculations, presenting their findings in a suitable way and drawn conclusions.

Answers

Task 1

1

Country	Difference in birth rate (%)	Difference in death rate (%)	Population difference per 1000 in 1975	Population difference per 1000 in 2007
Australia	−29.0	−3.8	9	4.4
Belgium	−15.6	−15.6	0	0
Czech Republic	−54.1	−7.8	8.1	−1.6
Greece	−38.9	15.7	6.8	−0.7
Israel	−37.2	−12.7	2.11	11.5
UK	−14.4	−15.1	0.6	0.6
USA	1.4	−6.7	5.1	5.9

2 Negative values occur when, for example, the birth rate fell from 1975 to 2007. For population difference, a negative value represents a reduction in the population, a positive value shows an increase in population.

3 Both the birth rate and the death rate are decreasing. This means that people are living longer and the younger generation is decreasing in size, so there will be fewer people working to support pension and healthcare payments for the elderly.

Task 2

1 This will vary from student to student but should be around 65 to 80.

2 Look for reasonable answers that must be backed up mathematically, such as: 'I was close to the actual value, I was only 3.65 years out.'

Improver **

3 The graph shows the data for all the countries listed in the table on data sheet 1.

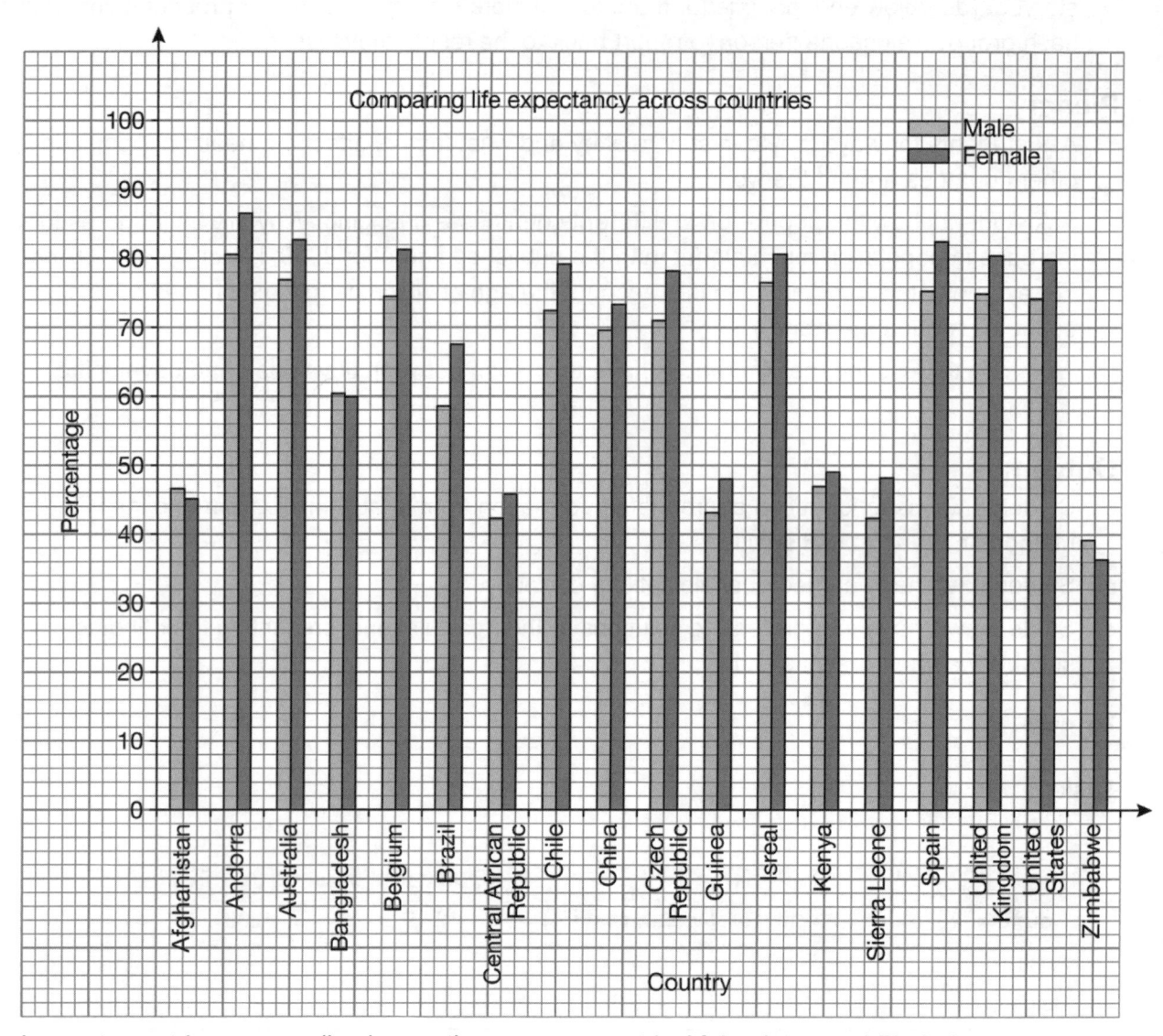

[Graph: Comparing life expectancy across countries — bar chart showing Male and Female percentages for: Afghanistan, Andorra, Australia, Bangladesh, Belgium, Brazil, Central African Republic, Chile, China, Czech Republic, Guinea, Isreal, Kenya, Sierra Leone, Spain, United Kingdom, United States, Zimbabwe]

4 In most countries, women live longer than men, except in Afghanistan and Zimbabwe.

Extension

See the graph in answer 3 above.

Task 3

1 Total number of servings of all foods = 2 + 3 + 2 + 2 + 6 = 15, dairy = $\frac{2}{15}$, protein = $\frac{2}{15}$, vegetable = $\frac{3}{15} = \frac{1}{5}$, fruit = $\frac{2}{15}$, bread/grain = $\frac{6}{15} = \frac{2}{5}$

2 a Minimum value 15 × 80 g = 1200 g or 1.2 kg

b Maximum value 26 × 80 g = 2080 g or 2.08 kg

3 Students should produce their own food pyramids, similar to the one in the student book.

4 Answers will vary between students. They should use principles already developed.

5 Students should produce the results of their investigations in an interesting way. Some students may also cover wider topics, such as obesity and anorexia.

Improver **

Coastguard search

Learning objectives
- **Representing Level 1/2**: look at data and draw conclusions, using different types of graph
- **Analysing Level 1/2**: analyse situations mathematically to find the most efficient way of solving problems
- **Interpreting Level 1/2**: interpret and communicate solutions to multistage problems in familiar and unfamiliar contexts and situations

APP
Evidence for Using and applying maths Level 5, Numbers and the number system Level 5, Calculating Level 5, Shape, space and measure Level 7, Handling data Level 5

PLTS
Develops Creative thinkers, Independent enquirers, Reflective learners

Every child matters outcome
Be safe, Enjoy and achieve

Cross-curricular links
English, PHSE, Geography, Economics

Underpinning maths
- Drawing and interpreting graphs
- Percentages
- Area
- Pythagoras' theorem

Resources
- *Student book*, pages 58–61
- Data sheet: Watersport participation
- Highlighter pens, pencils, squared paper, hexagonal grid paper
- Calculators

Context
Many people like to visit the coast, whether for a day trip or for their holiday. Some people just want to sit on the sand and dip their feet in the water; others like to take part in water sports. People interested in the natural world go to watch the wildlife that lives on the coast. However, no matter what visitors do or how favourable the weather and tide conditions, there are always risks associated with the coast.

Lesson plan
This activity takes two lessons.

Improver **

Starter
- Ask students, in pairs, to answer one of these questions.
  - How many water sports can you name?
  - List the non-water sports activities you think people can do around the coasts, in the sea.
  - List the wildlife you might find on the coast.
  - List the types of watercraft you might see around the coast.
  - List the types of building and other structures you see when you visit the seaside but that you don't see inland.
- After two or three minutes, collate answers.

Main activity
- Ask students to give examples of the types of incident to which coastguards might have to respond. Record their first six suggestions on the board.
- Look at Task 1 with students, which is about trends in the type of coastal incident. Refer them to the table. Ask them to match their suggestions to the types of incident listed.
- Discuss the categories below to make sure they understand them.

Type of incident
Leisure diving: Looking at sea life, old wrecks, for fun
Diving–medical: Incidents that involve a medical emergency resulting from diving, for example, a diver with the bends, a jellyfish sting, collision with a boat
Water sports: Swimming, water skiing, jet ski, windsurfing
Inshore vessel: Yachting, speedboats, small craft, dinghies
Commercial vessel: Any craft involved in money-making activities not covered in any other section, for example, ferries, day-trip and sightseeing boats, rig supply vessels
Fishing vessels: Fishing boats, including shrimp, oyster, lobster, crab-fishing
Commercial diving: Includes repairing rigs, salvage operations, pipeline inspections
Shore-side: Incidents that are not beach incidents, for example, cliff falls, people stranded on islands cut off by tide
Beach incidents: Anything that happens on beaches

- **Let students do Task 1**.
- Discuss reasons for the fluctuation in numbers of incidents. (Answer: As well as the change in participation figures, weather plays an important part.) Remind students that the incidents described are those based in the UK Search and Rescue area. The increase in numbers of water-sport incidents may be a result of the recession, leading to more people holidaying in the UK rather than abroad.
- Read through the data sheet with students, ensuring they understand the terms used.
  - Total population: Everyone in the UK who takes part in the activity.
  - Population participating in UK: those members of the total population who take part in the activity in the UK rather than abroad.
  - UK coastal population (SAR area): Those who take part in a coastal (Search and Rescue) area rather than inland.
  - Number of coastal events: how many events are organised at the coast.
    Number of inland events: how many events took place inland

Improver **

(These two figures are used to estimate the UK coastal population (SAR area) from the 'population participating in the UK' figure.)
- o The next five columns (participants) relate to the total population.
- o The last four columns refer only to the UK coastal population (SAR area); the 16 deaths per million for kite surfing is based on one death out of 62 000 incidents.

- Explain that deaths are very rare, which is why they are recorded as deaths per million rather than as percentages.
- **Let students do Task 2**.
- Discuss how helicopters might search for people in the sea. If they have a rough idea of where the person is, for example, having fallen from a boat, the rescue team might start there and spiral outwards. Whatever approach they take, they need to be systematic.
- Explain how, in mathematics, we often use a model and then refine it to find a better one. Suggest that a hexagon is a better approximation for a circle than a square is and ask why this is the case. (Answer: Helicopters can move in six directions rather than just four; there is less difference between maximum and minimum 'diameters'.)
- Look at Task 3 with students. This introduces search patterns. Distribute squared paper and highlighter pens, if necessary.
- **Let students do Task 3**. Encourage them to find an algebraic rule for the searches, in terms of squares covered. Some may need prompting or support, either before they start or during the activity.
- **Let students do Task 4**. Distribute hexagonal-grid paper. Students may need some support with question 2. The following suggestions may help.
  - o Draw the major diagonals on a hexagon. What shapes do you make? (Six congruent equilateral triangles)
  - o What is the side length of each equilateral triangle? (50 m)
  - o Split an equilateral triangle into two equal pieces. What shapes have you got? (Right-angled triangles)
  - o Which side lengths do you know? (Hypotenuse = 50 m, base = 25 m)
  - o How could you find the height? (Pythagoras' theorem; 43.3 m)
  - o What is the area of each equilateral triangle? (1082.5 m)
- Read Task 5 with students. Discuss what equipment might be used for a helicopter search. (Answer: lights, radar). Explain that *Sea King* helicopters are equipped with radar.
- **Let students do Task 5**. Make sure they understand the diagrams before they begin.

Plenary
- The SAR helicopter diagram shows a 30°, 60°, 90° triangle ABC. Students could be encouraged to explain why AC = 2000 m (by thinking of the triangle ABC as half of an equilateral triangle). They could use Pythagoras' theorem to check the length given for BC.
- The last task demonstrates that enlarging the trapezium with a scale factor of two results in an area four times that of the original. Discuss this further; if, for some reason, the helicopter had to drop to 500 m, what area would it cover then? (Answer: A quarter of the original area, 178 736 m^2)

Outcomes
- o Students will have drawn bar charts.
- o Students will have investigated spatial arrangements, searching for optimum solutions.

Improver **

- Students will have found formulae to fit a mathematical model.
- Students will have carried out complex calculations by breaking them down into more manageable tasks (area of a hexagon).
- Students will have applied Pythagoras' theorem.
- Students will have understood the effect on area of an enlargement.

Answers

Task 1

1

Type of incident	Year 1	Year 2	Year 3	% increase
Leisure diving	39	38	40	2.6
Diving – medical	54	101	102	88.9
Water sports	270	612	753	178.9
Inshore vessel	561	823	738	31.6
Commercial vessel	830	550	582	–29.9
Fishing vessels	521	628	360	–30.9
Commercial diving	131	121	90	–31.3
Shore-side	744	512	591	–20.6
Beach Incidents	672	604	705	4.9
Other medical assistance	481	431	458	–4.8
Total	4303	4420	4419	2.7

2 There has been a decline in the fishing industry.

3 There has been an increase in the number of people taking up water sports.

Task 2

1 a More people participate in power boating than rowing. **True** (350 000 to 332 000)

  b Coastal walking is the only activity with more female than male participants. **False** (The beach is the other)

  c 87% of shore anglers are male. **False** (88.6%)

  d More than half of the canoeists are aged between 16 and 34. **True** (50.6%)

  e More than half of the windsurfers are aged between 35 and 54. **False** (48.1%)

2 a Coastal walking and beach activities are the most popular

  b In the UK, coastal walking: 94%, beach activities: 46%

3 a The least popular are kite surfing and yacht racing.

  b Their relative lack of popularity is probably due to a number of factors including cost, danger, and fewer organised events.

4 a

Bar chart: People taking part in waterskiing activity

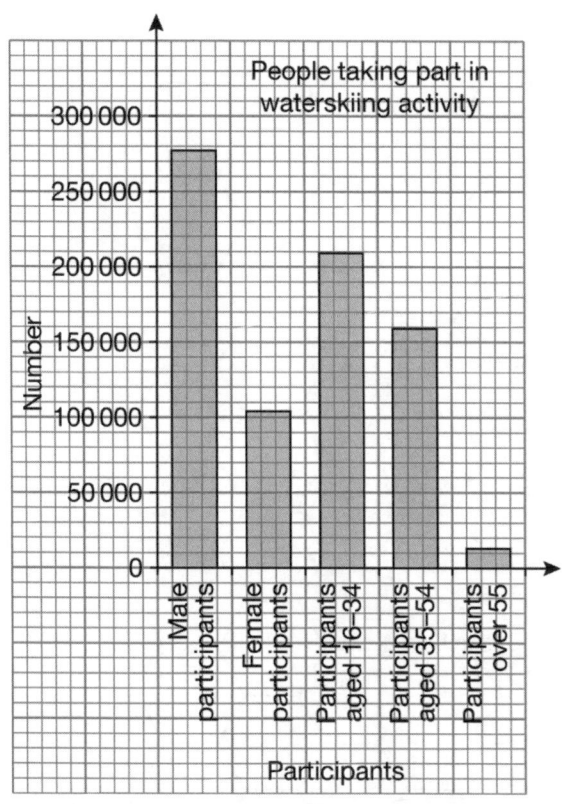

Categories (x-axis): Male participants (~275,000), Female participants (~105,000), Participants aged 16–34 (~210,000), Participants aged 35–54 (~160,000), Participants over 55 (~10,000). Y-axis: Number (0 to 300,000).

b Main differences include the following.

Waterskiing has fewer participants.

Waterskiing is largely a male activity, whereas coastal walking has slightly more females.

Waterskiing is enjoyed by the younger age group with few over 55s participating. Coastal walking has fewer young participants than either of the other age groups.

5 There were 61 deaths (once the repeated figures have been removed) out of 15 232 000, which is 4.0 deaths per million.

Task 3

1

21	22	23	24	25	26	27	28	29
20								
19								
18			1	2	3	4	5	
17							6	
16							7	
15	14	13	12	11	10	9	8	

2 3

(h)	(n)	Area (km^2)
1	9	0.09
2	12	0.12
3	15	0.15
4	18	0.18
5	21	0.21
6	24	0.24
7	27	0.27
8	30	0.30
9	33	0.33

4 $n = 3h + 6$

Improver **

Task 4

1

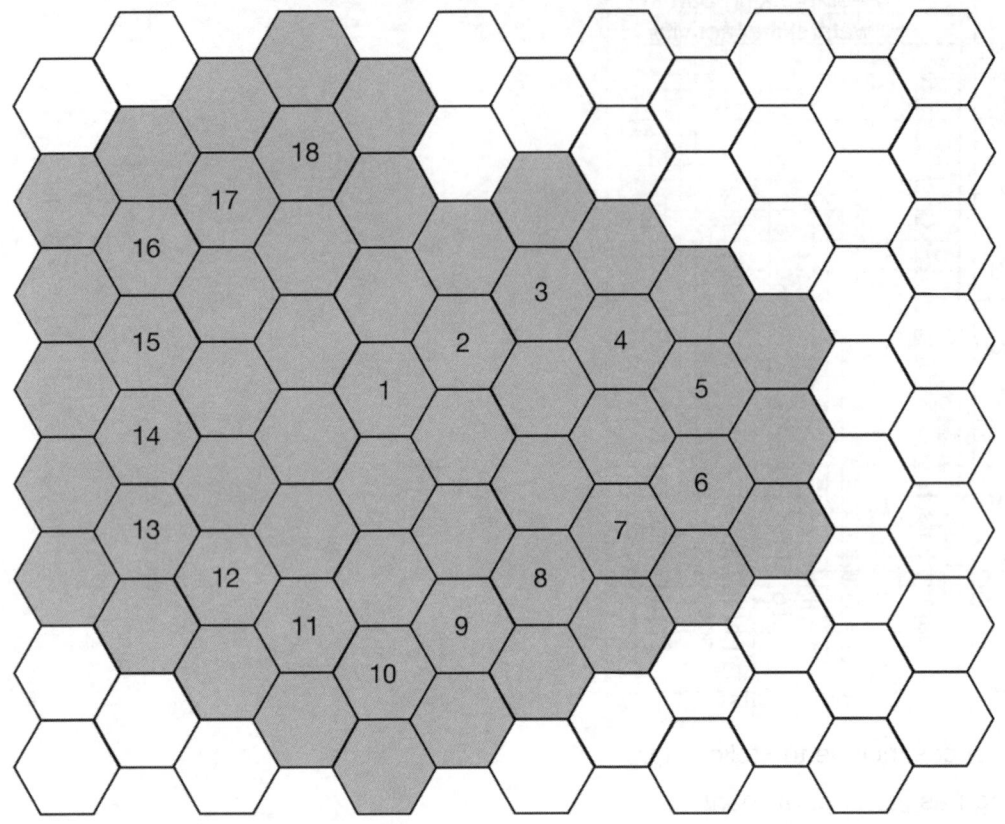

The most economical spiral arrangement is more difficult to find.

(h)	(n)
1	7
2	10
3	13
4	16
5	19
6	22
7	25
8	28
9	31

$n = 3h + 4$

2 The diagonal is 100 m.

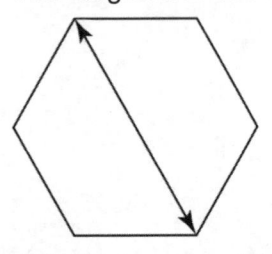

Split the hexagon into six equilateral triangles with sides of 50 m.

Improver **

Split one into two right-angled triangles with base of 25 m and hypotenuse of 50 m.

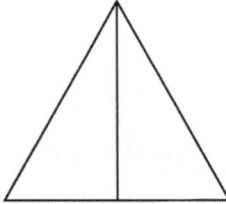

By Pythagoras' theorem, height = $\sqrt{50^2 - 25^2}$ m = 43.3 m

3 Area of hexagon = 6 × area of equilateral triangle = 6 × 25 × 43.3 = 6495 m²

Task 5

1 $\dfrac{(310+928) \times 1155}{2}$ m² = 714 945 m² or 0.71 km²

2 By Pythagoras' theorem, $\sqrt{2000^2 + 464^2}$ = 2053 m = 2.053 km

3 $\dfrac{(620+1856) \times 2310}{2}$ = 2 859 780 m² or 2.86 km²

4 Although the area scanned will be larger, the 'image' viewed by the crew will be proportionately less clearly defined.

Improver **

Photography: past, present and future

Learning objectives
- **Representing Level 1/2**: identify the problem and find information needed to solve it, using appropriate mathematical methods
- **Analysing Level 1/2**: apply a range of mathematics to find solutions and check that answers make sense
- **Interpreting Level 1/2**: use results to produce graphs and charts, explain what has been found and draw conclusions to justify answers

APP
Evidence for Using and applying mathematics Level 6, Numbers and the number system Level 6, Calculating Level 7, Handling data Level 5

PLTS
Develops Independent enquirers, Creative thinkers

Every child matters outcomes
Make a positive contribution, Achieve economic well-being, Enjoy and achieve

Cross-curricular links
ICT, English, Media studies, Science, History

Underpinning maths
- Converting between units of measure
- Understanding ratios
- Extracting information
- Producing charts
- Working with capacity

Resources
- *Student book*, pages 62–65
- Graph paper
- Tracing paper, rulers
- Calculators
- Internet access (optional)

Context
All students should be familiar with photography and most will understand the term 'megapixel', at least in relation to 'the greater the number, the better the quality of the photograph'. Not many students will be familiar with a film-loaded camera. This topic is about the development of photography and will give students an understanding of how to use and process film.

Lesson plan
This activity takes one lesson. Task 3 could be set as homework.

Improver **

Starter
- Ask students if anyone has a film-loaded camera at home. Also ask how many of them own a digital camera and how many of them have a good-quality (high resolution) camera on their mobile phone. Take a show of hands for the quality of camera on their phones, from 2 megapixels up to 8 megapixels.
- Explain that, not so many years ago, many people used to develop their own films, at home in a special room called a darkroom. Explain that no visible external light could enter the room but a low-wattage red light bulb provided some light, so that the person working in the room could see what they were doing, without damaging the film. Because the film captures small amounts of light, exposure to a light source during the developing process would simply produce an over-exposed or a white photograph.

Main activity
- Ask students how many of them print photos at home, on either a normal colour printer or a dedicated photo printer. Ask if they have worked out the cost per photograph.
- Read Task 1 with students. Remind them that they will sometimes need to interpret information that has not been put into a list format and extract relevant information. This is a good skill to develop. Remind students that there are 1000 millilitres (ml) in a litre.
- **Let students do Task 1**. Remind them that, when working with ratio, they should divide the total volume by the total number of parts, to find out how much of each chemical is needed. Remind students they would need to buy enough of each chemical, so they should round up rather than down and choose the appropriate pack size.
- Read Task 2 with the students. Explain that ink cartridges for photo printers cost more than general printer cartridges because they give a better finish and won't easily come off on your hands. Say that few printer manufacturers publish figures giving a cost per photo, as this varies, depending on the depth of colour – or number of colours – in the photo. Explain that seascape photographs use more blue and yellow than pictures of poppy fields, which use more red tones. However, it is possible to state the average number of photos that can be printed by one cartridge (as in the information box). In this task, they will not just be calculating general printing costs, but also taking into account the initial outlay (the printer).
- **Let students do Task 2**. Make sure they realise that the price of photos changes in steps (every time new paper or ink is needed) so their graph will not be a straight line or curve but a series of straight lines. When they are answering question 2, suggest that students add the cost of high street printing and developing photos in a dark room to their graph. Encourage them to consider whether factors other than cost might affect the decision of which method of printing to choose.
- Read through Task 3 and show students how to use the rule of thirds to divide a photograph into threes, horizontally and vertically. Distribute tracing paper and encourage students to draw the grids on this and then lay them over the photographs.
- **Let students do Task 3**, perhaps in pairs. Encourage them to discuss what they notice.

Plenary
- Ask students if they were surprised by the cost of printing their own photographs. If they had a darkroom, would they like to try to develop their own photographs? Ask students which type of printer was most cost effective for printing photographs. Discuss students' observations about the rule of thirds.

Improver **

Outcomes

- Students will have used maths to identify a situation and the methods needed to find solutions.
- Students will have used appropriate checking procedures.
- Students will have interpreted the solutions to their calculations and justified their answers.

Answers

Task 1

1 a 4.55 × 1000 = 4550 ml in a gallon

Developer 4550 ÷ 4 = 1137.5 ml, stopbath 4550 ÷ 64 = 71 ml, fixer 4550 ÷ 5 = 910 ml, rinsing aid 4550 ÷ 401 = 11.3 ml

b $\frac{1}{4} \times \frac{1}{8} = \frac{1}{32}$

4550 ÷ 32 = 142 ml

2 a 2 litres developer = £14.98, 1 litre stopbath = £3.49, 1 litre fixer = £3.49, 300 ml rinsing aid = £4.58, 500 g hypo-cleaning agent = £5.42

Total = £31.96

b £31.96 ÷ 48 = 67p each

Task 2

1 a

		Number of photos						
		0-150	151-300	301-450	451-600	601-750	751-900	901-1050
Cost (£)	Printer	149.99						
	Paper	39.85	39.85	39.85	39.85	39.85	39.85	39.85
	Black ink	19.99				19.99		
	Tri-colour ink	26.99		26.99		26.99		26.99
	Total	236.82	276.67	343.51	383.36	470.19	510.04	576.88
	Per photo	1.58	0.92	0.76	0.64	0.63	0.57	0.55

		Number of photos						
		1051-1200	1201-1350	1351-1500	1501-1650	1651-1800	1801-1950	1951-2100
Cost (£)	Printer							
	Paper	39.85	39.85	39.85	39.85	39.85	39.85	39.85
	Black ink		19.99				19.99	
	Tri-colour ink		26.99		26.99		26.99	
	Total	616.73	703.56	743.41	810.25	850.1	936.93	976.78
	Per photo	0.51	0.52	0.50	0.49	0.47	0.48	0.47

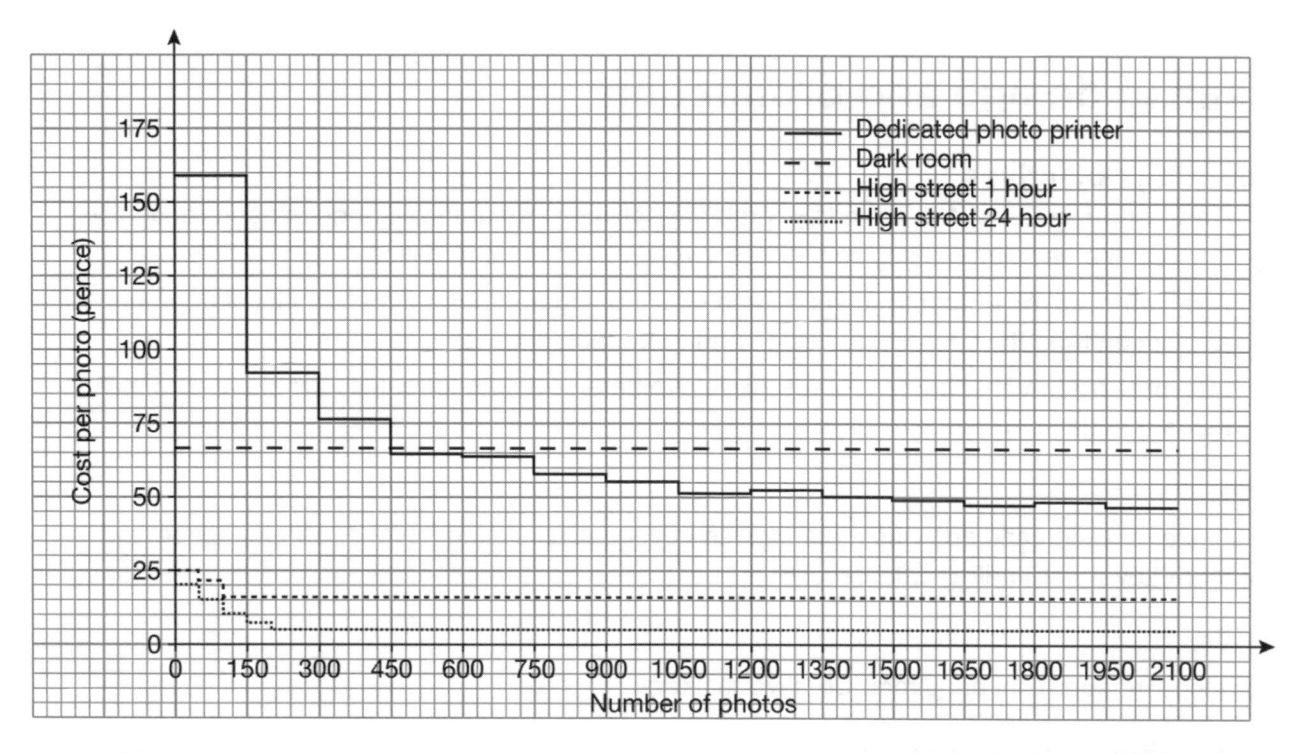

b The cost of using a dedicated printer levels out at about 600 photos. (Disregarding the cost of the printer, every 600 photos costs (4 × £39.85) + £19.99 + (2 × £26.99) = £233.37, so £233.37 ÷ 600 = 39p per photo.) Students should conclude that having photos printed on the high street is significantly cheaper than either of the other methods, even taking into account that you would probably print the photos in separate batches over time, meaning that, for example, 1000 photos might cost £0.25 × 1000 = £250 rather than £0.16 × 1000 = £160 (1000 photos using a dedicated printer costs £576.88; developing 1000 photos in a dark room costs £0.67 × 1000 = £670). Developing film at home is cheaper than having photos printed on the high street up to 450 photos, and then becomes slightly more expensive (more able students may have realised that the answer to Task 1 question **2b** does not take into account the savings possible by buying the chemicals in bulk, e.g. 5 litre packs of developer). Other factors that might affect the decision of which method to use include convenience and the artistic element of developing your own film.

Task 3

1 a Students should notice that the rule of thirds can be seen in all the photos, but that the images do not follow it exactly. For example, in the photograph of trees on the horizon, the trees extend just above the bottom third of the photograph. They should notice that in the photograph of the runners, the man is in the left two-thirds and the woman in the top two-thirds of the right-hand third; their heads are in the top third. In the photograph of the building, they may find it interesting to further divide the nine sections according to the rule of thirds as well.

b Students find and consider further photographs.

Improver **

Teabag design and production

Learning objectives
- **Representing Level 1/2:** undertake problem-solving in an unfamiliar context and recognise that real-life decision-making sometimes involves using mathematics
- **Analysing Level 1/2:** analyse shape and costs, using appropriate mathematical approaches and understand their impact on design and manufacturing
- **Interpreting Level 1/2:** interpret results to evaluate solutions to real-life problems and make recommendations

APP
Evidence for Using and applying mathematics Level 6, Calculating Level 7, Shape, space and measure Level 5, Handling data Level 6

PLTS
Develops Independent enquirers, Creative thinkers

Every child matters outcome
Be healthy

Cross-curricular links
Design and technology, English, Economics, Science

Underpinning maths
- Nets
- Perimeter
- Circumference of a circle
- Conversion between metric units
- Using sketches for mathematical visualisation
- Calculating to solve real-life problems
- Conducting surveys

Resources
- *Student book*, page 66–69
- Calculator
- Selection of teabags (optional)

Context
- All students should be familiar with teabags and the various shapes in which they are available.
- In this activity, students investigate shape and design for the efficient use of materials and costs in the production of teabags.

Lesson plan
This activity takes two lessons. You may do it in one lesson by using only Tasks 1 and 2 and focusing on shape. Task 5 (extension) would make a good homework activity.

Improver**

Starter

- Conduct a quick survey, asking each student how many cups of tea, on average, they drink each day. Keep a tally for the whole class and work out how many cups of tea the students drink altogether in a day.

- Ask students to read this large number aloud: 165 000 000. (Answer: One hundred and sixty-five million) Explain that this is the number of cups of tea drunk daily in Great Britain – and that this makes teabag production big business! Ask students to use their calculators to work out how many cups of tea each person drinks per day, if the population of Great Britain is rounded to 60 million. (Answer: 2.75 cups) Compare this answer to the results of the class survey.

- Ask students what shapes of teabag they use in their homes. Make a list of the shapes.

Main activity

- Based on the discussion of teabag shapes, discuss with students how they think teabags are made. (Answer: 3D teabags: from nets of filter paper, filled with dried tea leaves, and sealed along the edges; 2D teabags: from tea sandwiched between two large rolls of filter paper, heat-sealed and cut into the teabag shape) You could pass real teabags around the class to help students answer this question.

- Read Task 1 with the students. Remind them that a **net** is a flat shape that can be folded into a 3D shape. Discuss with students what is meant by **sketch** in question 1: an accurate scale drawing is not required.

- **Let students do Task 1.** Encourage them to think about where each teabag is sealed. (**Note**: Those made from nets will not require sealing along every edge.) If necessary, remind students of the radius, diameter and circumference of a circle (circumference = $\pi \times$ diameter or $\pi \times 2 \times$ radius).

- Ask students to look at the dimensions of the teabags and then read the first sentence of Task 2. Ask them what they notice about the measurements. (Answer: The teabags are measured in centimetres, while the roll of filter paper has width in millimetres and length in metres.) Discuss with students the need to use the same measure for their calculations and what the most sensible measure might be. Remind them of the conversions:

    10 mm = 1 cm and 1 m = 100 cm

- **Let students do Task 2.** Remind them how teabags are made and, in particular, how the two rolls of filter paper will be used for each shape of teabag: the two sides of the square, rectangular and circular teabags can be cut from different rolls, but nets for the tetrahedral and pyramidal teabags must be made in one piece, from the same single roll. Encourage students to use sketches to help them visualise how each teabag shape will be cut from the filter paper.

- Read question 1 of Task 3 with the students. Ask them what calculation they need to do. (Answer: Number of teabags, as found in Task 2, × number of grams) The question asks for answers in kilograms. Ask students what this tells them about the number of grams of tea that may be required. (Answer: Over 1000 g, so more than 1 kg)

- **Let students do Task 3.** Encourage them to think about the calculations they need to do and the conversion between units. (1000 g = 1 kg and 100p = £1)

- Look at Task 4 with students. Discuss the information and calculations required. (Answer for question 1: Each cost as calculated in Task 3, question 2 + cost calculated in Task 3, question 3; for question 2: total cost divided by number of teabags) **Let students do Task 4.**

- Ask students to work in pairs to consider their answers to Tasks 1–4 and determine which shape of teabag is the cheapest to make. (Answer: Tetrahedron) Ask which is the most expensive to make. (Answer: Circular) Discuss as a class.

© HarperCollins*Publishers* 2010

Improver **

- Look at Task 5 (extension) with students. Discuss how they might conduct their survey of the sale price of different shaped teabags, and what they might do with the information. For example, you might ask them to think about the number of teabags that come in a box, and how they will compare the price of a box of 80 teabags with their answer to Task 4, question 2. **Let students do Task 5 (extension).**

Plenary

- Ask students if they are surprised by the difference in the cost of making teabags of different shapes.
- Ask what other products students can think of that come in different shapes and sizes. What mathematical analysis might they do in order to make comparisons in the manufacture and design of these products?

Outcomes

- Students will have used mathematics to gain insight into a real-life problem.
- Students will have used shape and chosen the correct calculations in order to make comparisons and draw conclusions.

Answers

Task 1

1 a b

2 Length of seals for:
square = 24.4 cm
rectangle = 24.2 cm
pyramid = 20.8 cm
tetrahedron = 12.3 cm
circle = 23 cm
The square requires the most seal; the tetrahedron requires the least seal.

Task 2

1 a 2   b   327   c   654
2 a 2 (one arranged landscape, one arranged portrait)   b   363 + 303 = 666
3 320
4 1124
5 420

Improver**

Task 3

1 a 654 × 3 = 1962 g = 1.96 kg (2 dp)
   b 666 × 3.3 = 2197.8 g = 2.20 kg (2 dp)
   c 320 × 3.2 = 1024 g = 1.02 kg (2 dp)
   d 1124 × 2.6 = 2922.4 g = 2.92 kg (2 dp)
   e 420 × 2.8 = 1176 g = 1.18 kg (2 dp)

2 a 1960 g × 0.2p = £3.92   **b** 2200 g × 0.2p = £4.40   **c** 1020 g × 0.2p = £2.04
   d 2920 g × 0.2p = £5.84   **e** 1180 g × 0.2p = £2.36

3 £1.30

Task 4

1 a 654, £5.22   **b** 666, £5.70   **c** 320, £3.34
   d 1124, £7.14   **e** 420, £3.66

2 a 1 square teabag costs 522 ÷ 654 = 0.80p (2 dp)
   b 1 rectangular teabag costs 570 ÷ 666 = 0.86p (2 dp)
   c 1 circular teabag costs 334 ÷ 320 = 1.04p (2 dp)
   d 1 tetrahedral teabag costs 714 ÷ 1124 = 0.64p (2 dp)
   e 1 pyramidal teabag costs 336 ÷ 420 = 0.8p (2 dp)

Task 5

Students' board reports should provide evidence of a sound approach to conducting a survey and include sensible calculations to enable comparisons. (For example, they should examine the price of more than one brand of teabag for each shape, and calculate the sale price per single teabag: the cost of a box divided by the number of teabags in the box.) They should compare this data with their answer to Task 4, question 2.

The most likely outcome is that students' surveys reveal that pyramidal and tetrahedral teabags tend to have a higher sale price, and their calculations show that these teabags (along with those that are square) are the cheapest to produce. Students' board reports may draw on these facts to recommend that the teabag manufacturer makes tetrahedral and pyramidal teabags.

Improver **

Small-scale farming

Learning objectives
- **Representing Level 1/2**: find information needed to solve the problem and use appropriate methods to solve it
- **Analysing Level 1/2**: work through the calculations and check that answers make sense
- **Interpreting Level 1/2**: use results to produce graphs, explain findings and draw conclusions

APP
Evidence for Using and applying mathematics Level 4, Numbers and the number system Level 5, Calculating Level 6, Algebra Level 4, Handling data Level 3

PLTS
Develops Independent enquirers

Every child matters outcomes
Make a positive contribution, Achieve economic well-being, Enjoy and achieve

Cross-curricular links
Science, Geography, Business studies, Media studies

Underpinning maths
- Calculating income and expenditure
- Converting units of measure between different systems
- Calculating mean
- Writing numbers in standard form
- Shape and space
- Working with percentages
- Using formula
- Using ratio and proportion

Resources
- *Student book*, page 70–72
- Scientific calculators, graph paper
- Internet access

Context
Most students will know something about farming and know the terms **arable** and **livestock**. The focus of this activity is small-scale farming. However, the principles could be extended to a study of intensive farming if desired. The activity is intended to widen the students' views of farming and help them develop an appreciation of the costs associated with food production.

Lesson plan
This activity takes two lessons. It could be done in one lesson by doing only Task 1 and either Task 2 or Task 3. Task 4 (extension) could be done as homework.

Improver **

Starter
- Ask students to name as many different foodstuffs and crops that they think are produced on UK farms. Explain that many farms grow crops for collection by local food industries. Give the example of frozen peas, which go from the field to being frozen in less than 12 hours; therefore, the fields need to be near the factory. Discuss transport costs for crops.

Main activity
- Explain that, although they will not be looking at transport costs, students will need to remember that an increase in VAT or fuel prices, for example, affects the price of all foods. Explain that an **acre** is an imperial unit of measure for large areas, such as fields. It would not be sensible to talk about land in terms of square metres, but there has not yet been a serious move in the UK to refer to land in **hectares** (10 000 square metres, m^2) or **square kilometres** (km^2).

- Read Task 1 with students. Remind them that, when planning how many potatoes they can plant, they need to allow enough space at the edges of the field as well as between potatoes (half the space required between potatoes/rows is sufficient). Ask students how many centimetres there are in an inch and write it on the board. Use the conversion 2.54 cm ≈ 1 inch. Explain that a **seed potato** is a potato that has started to grow and will form one plant.

- Discuss with students how Robert and Helen can sensibly estimate the total expected yield. (Answer: use the mean yield for one plant, (9 + 15) ÷ 2 = 12) Remind students, if necessary, of what VAT is, and of the current rate at which it is levied. Answers are based on 20%.

- **Let students do Task 1**. Encourage them to draw a sketch of the field to help them calculate the number of potatoes.

- Read Task 2 with students. Explain that all the information they need is in Helen's notes and remind them they will need to find a percentage of an amount. Discuss strategies for finding Helen's profit or loss. **Let students do Task 2**.

- Read Task 3 with students. Explain how to draw a break-even chart. Make sure they have the information for the fixed costs. They could use a computer spreadsheet package to draw the line for income from milk and add the fixed costs manually.

- **Let students do Task 3**. Make sure they understand what 'break even' means. Explain that the interest rate of 5% means the total amount to be repaid (over two years) is £100 000 × 1.05.

- Read through Task 4 with students. Explain that a stall is the area where the cow stands, to be milked. Once they are used to the process cows like being milked as excessive amounts of milk are heavy and become uncomfortable so a cow will enter the milking parlour by itself to be milked. The frequency of milking is the number of times a cow is milked per day, usually twice but sometimes three times a day, depending on the amount of milk they are producing.

- **Let students do Task 4**. Help less able students to understand how the formulae work and that they need to use the answer to the first formula in the second formula.

Plenary
- Discuss how Helen and Robert's fixed and variable costs will change over time. Is there anything they haven't included in their budget? For example, their profit will increase as there is no need to buy more cows. They haven't included vet bills. Milk prices go up and down, as do fixed costs such as heating and electricity.

Outcomes
- Students will have used maths to identify a situation and identified the methods needed to find solutions.

Improver **

- Students will have used appropriate checking procedures.
- Students will have interpreted the solutions to their calculations and drawn conclusions.

Answers

Task 1

1 a 140^2 = 19 600 m², 19 600 ÷ 4046.86 = 4.8 acres

b 9 inches = 22.86 cm, 24 inches = 60.96 cm

Potatoes per row = 14 000 ÷ 22.86 = 612.42 → 612 potatoes

Number of rows = 14 000 ÷ 60.96 = 229.67 → 229 rows (round down to ensure space at the edge of the field)

612 × 229 = 140 148 potatoes

c 140 148 seed potatoes produce average yield of 140 148 × 12 = 1 681 776 potatoes

1 681 776 ÷ 3000 = 560.592 tonnes

Crop fetches 560.592 × £207 = £116 042.54

140 148 seed potatoes cost 140 148 ÷ 3000 = 46.716 tonnes

Cost 46.716 × £100 = £4671.60

Basic profit = £116 042.54 − £4671.60 = £111 370.94

2 a 32 ÷ (6 + 6 + 12) = 32 ÷ 24 = 1.33...; N = 8 litres, P = 8 litres, K = 16 litres

b N: 8 × (£11.50 × 1.2) = £110.40, P: 8 × (£22.75 × 1.2) = £218.40, K: 16 × (£22.75 × 1.2) = £436.80 dilutes up to 1000 litres

Cost per 1000 litre mix = £765.60.

19 600 m² ÷ 1000 = 20 lots of 1000 litres needed.

20 × £765.60 = £15 312

3 Profit = £111 370.94 − £15 312 − (£1070 + £14 250 + £10 500) = £70 238.94

Helen and Robert have made a profit.

Task 2

1 20 × 0.87 × 7.9 × 365 = 50 172.9 litres of milk per year

50 172.9 × £0.2408 = £12 081.63

2 0.28 × 20 × 365 = £2044, £940 × 12 = £11 280

£12 081.63 − (£2044 + £11 280) = −£1242.37. She made a loss.

Task 3

1 a £98 000 + (£650 × 52) + (£0.38 × 170 × 365) = £155 379

£155 379 ÷ £0.2408 = 645 262 litres = 6.5 × 10^5 litres

b 170 × 0.87 × 26.4 × 365 = 1 425 164.4 = 1.4 × 10^6

c 1.4 × 10^6 − 6.5 × 10^5 = 750 000 litres; 750 000 × £0.2408 = £180 600

2 £105 000 to repay ÷ 2 = £52 500 in her first year.

Break-even figure increases: £155 379 + £52 500 = £207 879

Task 4

170 × 0.87 × 2 = 95.8 → 296 milkings needed

296 ÷ 6 = 49.3 → 50 milkings per hour

Total number of stalls = 50 ÷ 4.5 = 11.11 → 12 stalls

Improver **

Coastguard rescue

Learning objectives
- **Representing Level 1/2**: interpret the situation or problem and identify the mathematical methods needed to solve them
- **Analysing Level 1/2**: use appropriate checking procedures and evaluate their effectiveness at each stage
- **Interpreting Level 1/2**: interpret and communicate solutions to practical problems, drawing simple conclusions and giving explanations

APP
Evidence for Using and applying mathematics Level 5, Numbers and the number system Level 5, Shape, space and measures Level 7

PLTS
Develops Creative thinkers, Independent enquirers, Reflective learners

Every child matters outcomes
Be healthy, Be safe, Enjoy and achieve

Cross-curricular links
English, PHSE, Geography, Economics, Drama

Underpinning maths
- Map scales
- Time, distance and speed
- Working with money

Resources
- *Student book*, pages 73–75
- Data sheet 1: Sites and helicopters available
- Data sheet 2a: Map of the UK (A3 size – to print the map at the correct scale, ensure page scaling is set to 'None' in print options)
- Data sheets 2b and 2c: Map of the UK (A4 size, in case you do not have access to an A3 printer. To print the map at the correct scale, ensure page scaling is set to 'None' in print options. Stick the printed A4 maps together to create an A3 map. This can now be photocopied and handed out to the class)
- Data sheet 3: Key to incidents
- Task 2 sample typical answers
- Pencils, rulers, paper
- Calculators

Useful websites
- maps.google.co.uk (Google maps)

Improver **

Context
Although we often hear about the emergency services rescuing people, we rarely hear about the cost involved, or the problems of responding to a number of incidents simultaneously. This activity puts students in the position of planning responses and then having to modify plans according to further developments.

Lesson plan
Ideally, this activity should follow the activity Coastguard search. It takes one to two lessons. Tasks 1 and 2 could be done in one lesson, with Task 3 (extension) set as homework.

Starter
- Recap from Coastguard search; review and revise the investigations of different incidents to which coastguards may need to respond.

Main activity
- Discuss coastguard rescue facilities. Ask students if they know of any places where the rescue helicopters are based. (Answer: Coastguard helicopters are sited at Stornaway, Portsmouth and Brixham; the RAF has rescue helicopters at Chivenor, Wattisham, RAF Valley, RAF Boulmer, RAF Lossiemouth and Leconfield.)
- Read Task 1 with students. This relates to allocation of resources. Distribute data sheet 1, which lists the nine places named above, the number and types of helicopter at each place, and information about each type of helicopter. Ensure that students understand the information.
    - The **range** is how far the helicopter can travel without refuelling.
    - **Endurance** is how many hours the helicopter can stay in the air, including travel to and from the location, and hovering at the site, for example.
    - The **cost per hour** takes into account crew, fuel, maintenance and depreciation of the asset (the helicopter).
- Discuss the locations of the nine places around the British Isles. Distribute data sheet 2, which is an A3 map of the UK. Make sure students can identify the nine places. When they have correctly located them, suggest they highlight them, in red. Point out the scale on the map. Ask if these nine places are evenly distributed around the British Isles. (Answer: There is little cover around the west coast of Scotland and Northern England.) Distribute data sheet 3, which gives a list of typical incidents.
- **Let students do Task 1**. Make sure that they have paper, pencils and rulers available. Check that students understand the task. The incident considered in questions 1–4 is incident Z on data sheet 3. Ask what assumptions they have made. (Answer: For example, that the helicopter always achieves maximum speed. In reality, this would not be the case, so rescues take longer than might be expected.)
- Question 5 leads students to think about a situation in which more than one helicopter is needed. It may be cheaper for one helicopter to make more than one run, but is this the best way to proceed? For example, the cheapest way to deal with incident E is for a helicopter to rescue seven people, take them to hospital and then return for the last one. However, it may be better to send two helicopters, since time is more important than cost when lives are at risk.
- Read Task 2 with students. This is about organising resources. Suggest that students work in groups of two to four. Explain that emergency calls are often 'bunched'. Statistics suggest there are about 4500 incidents over a year, giving an average of 12 per day.

Improver **

- Give each group a different set of five incidents to which they must respond. The table gives some suggested sets.

Group	Incidents	Points students should notice
Group 1	A, K, O, P, R	Can go from Wattisham to P then on to O
Group 2	B, O, P, R, Z	Can go from Wattisham to O, then P, then Z
Group 3	C, J, N, U, Z	Need two helicopters at C (with one making two trips) Can go from RAF Valley to N then on to J
Group 4	A, F, G, L, W	Can go from Boulmer to G then on to F Two helicopters needed at L*
Group 5	B, G, H, S, V	Can go from Boulmer to G then on to H
Group 6	H, I, K, M, T	Can go from Boulmer to I then on to H
Group 7	D, I, U, X, Y	Can go from Portsmouth to X then on to Y where second helicopter is needed

*Students might consider allocating one helicopter to make both rescues, from base to incident to hospital then back to incident; the drawback is that people in difficulties would have to wait longer.

- **Let students do Task 2**. Each group will work on a different set of incidents. Distances should be rounded to the nearest 5 km, times to the nearest 5 minutes and cost to the nearest pound.
    - Discuss the cost-saving methods of sending one helicopter to two incidents. Are there any problems with this? (Answer: Rescue will be delayed for the second group.) If a helicopter returns to the incident for a second rescue, the time for the return trip should be included in the total rescue time.
    - What is the most expensive rescue? (Answer: Varies between groups, between about £3000 and £8000.)
- Task 3 (extension) relates to a real rescue carried out in October 2010. The locations can be found on data sheet 2.
- **Let students do Task 3 (extension)**. This could be set as homework.

Plenary

- Discuss the overall costs of the rescues. Could some incidents be avoided? Should those who are rescued be made to pay?
- How accurate were the students' figures? (Answer: All answers given below were based on maximum speed; in practice, this can never be achieved over the whole journey. Also, no searching time has been included; it is assumed those in danger were spotted immediately. So the real times, and therefore the real costs, would be significantly more.)
- What do students notice about the speed of Prince William's rescue? (Answer: His speed of 212.5 km/h is faster than the supposed maximum speed of the helicopter. Possible causes: inaccuracies in measurement; possible timing error; strong winds might have been blowing in the direction of the helicopter, thus increasing its speed.)

Outcomes

- Students will have completed calculations involving time, distance and speed.
- Students will have measured accurately on a map and applied a scale.
- Students will have planned shortest routes.

Improver **

Answers

Allow for some variation in the answers; this may arise from slight differences in the initial measurements taken from the map.

Task 1

1. Wattisham is the most appropriate base from which to send a helicopter.
2. The journey is about 145 km; 125 km to Littlestone, and then 20 km to hospital at Dover.
3. 145 km at 200 km/h would take about 45 minutes, plus 5 minutes for the rescue: total time = 50 minutes
4. 50 minutes at £2200 per hour = £1833
5. The most expensive single rescue is C, closely followed by Y and Q.
6. X is the cheapest.

   The cost of each rescue is given below.

		From	Distance (km)	Hospital	Distance (km)	Helicopter	Total distance (km)	Total time (min)	Cost (£)
A	4 people in missing sailboat	Lossiemouth	110	Thurso	10	Har3	120	55	1824
B	6 people in 2 small boats that collided	Lossiemouth	30	Lossiemouth	30	Har3	60	45	1493
C	16 on board broken-down merchant vessel	Lossiemouth	115	Aberdeen	25	Har3 two helicopters required. One needs to make two trips	140	One helicopter 75, second helicopter 165	7960
D	1 man taken ill on ship	Stornoway	225	Fort William	95	AW-139	320	70	3302
E	8 on board ship that caught fire	Boulmer	105	St. Andrews	25	Har3 2 required	130	60 × 2	3980
F	2 swimmers drifting out to sea with the tide	Boulmer	195	Ayr	10	Har3	205	70	2322
G	2 children stranded on a sandbank	Boulmer	75	St. Andrews	45	Har3	120	45	1493
H	2 adults in overturned rowing boat	Boulmer	140	Carlisle	50	Har3	190	65	2155
I	4 men in fishing boat battling against the tide	Boulmer	35	Sunderland	25	Har3	60	35	1161
J	5 exhausted swimmers trying to swim across Morecambe Bay	RAF Valley	130	Barrow-In-Furness	15	Har3A	145	70	2567

Improver **

K	2 adults and 3 children missing around the beach area	Leconfield	45	Scarborough	20	Har3	65	45	1493
L	12 men stranded on burning gas rig	Leconfield	50	Grimsby	30	Har3 two helicopters required	80	55 × 2	3648
M	5 adults on board sinking boat	Leconfield	105	King's Lynn	25	Har3	130	60	1990
N	1 man on board broken-down powerboat	RAF Valley	70	Aberystwyth	45	Har3A	115	40	1467
O	6 adults in fishing boat lost rudder control	Wattisham	90	Norwich	40	Har3A	130	70	2567
P	2 walkers slipped from cliff paths	Wattisham	55	Norwich	50	Har3A	105	40	1467
Q	24 crew stranded aboard a broken-down container ship	Wattisham	45	Ipswich	35	Har3A two helicopters required One needs to make two trips	80	one helicopter 70 second helicopter 140	7700
R	1 woman and 2 children in dinghy	Chivenor	50	Swansea	20	Har3	70	35	1161
S	2 surfers washed out to sea	Chivenor	50	Chivenor	50	Har3	100	40	1327
T	2 exhausted on board yacht	Chivenor	125	Penzance	25	Har3	150	50	1658
U	4 exhausted sailboarders	Brixham	80	Plymouth	35	AW-139	115	45	2123
V	12 on board boat run aground	Brixham	20	Torbay	20	AW-139	40	70	3302
W	1 child fallen from cliff	Brixham	65	Weymouth	15	AW-139	80	20	943
X	1 child overboard from ferry	Portsmouth	20	Portsmouth	15	AW-139	35	10	472
Y	16 adults and 9 children stranded on pleasure boat trip	Portsmouth	65	Brighton	15	AW-139 (13 rescued) and S-92 (12 rescued)	80	AW-139 80 S-92 75	7836
Z	1 man in sea trying to rescue his dog	Wattisham	125	Dover	20	Har3A	145	50	1833

Improver **

Task 2

1 Typical answers to this question can be found on the CD-Rom.
2 Students comment on how they decided to group rescues, where possible. They also work out the most distant rescue that a particular type of helicopter can carry out without refuelling.

Task 3

Students create a role-play script between rescue controller and pilot. They should use the available data to guide the pilot to the gas rig and back to Blackpool airport.

The gas rig is 85 km from the base, on a bearing of 044°. The average speed for the 24-minute journey was 212.5 km/h.

Blackpool Airport is 37.5 km from the rig, on a bearing of 101°. Reports elsewhere suggested this journey took 10 minutes, giving an average speed of 225 km/h.

Improver **

Tomorrow's world

Learning objectives
- **Representing Level 1/2**: identify and obtain information from tables and charts
- **Analysing Level 1/2**: apply a range of mathematics in an organised way
- **Interpreting Level 1/2**: interpret and communicate solutions to practical problems and draw conclusions

APP
Evidence for Using and applying mathematics Level 5, Numbers and the number system Level 4, Calculating Level 4, Handling data Level 3

PLTS
Develops Independent enquirers, Creative thinkers, Team workers, Effective participators

Every child matters outcomes
Make a positive contribution, Enjoy and achieve, Achieve economic well-being

Cross-curricular links
ICT, Science, History, English, Media studies

Underpinning maths
- Extracting information for and from tables
- Reading charts and diagrams
- Converting between measurements in the same system
- Calculating averages
- Displaying data graphically

Resources
- *Student book*, page 76–79
- Data sheet 1: Average download speeds
- Data sheet 2: Download times
- Data sheet 3: Teacher reference
- Calculators, graph paper
- Internet access

Context
All students should be familiar with different types of media storage, memory cards (such as those found in mobile phones), flash or pen drives and CD/DVD-Roms. They will know the term **broadband** as related to connecting to the internet. In this activity, students consider speeds and download capabilities of broadband and the way the future is shaping our use of the internet. They will also look at various types of media storage device, their uses and storage limitations. This activity also touches on the cost of software such as open-source – and therefore free – office software and students may explore whether it performs as well as most commercial products.

Lesson plan
This activity takes one to two lessons. Task 4 (extension) could be set as homework.

© HarperCollins*Publishers* 2010

Improver **

Starter

- Ask students how many of them download music, over the internet, from high-street stores or entertainment websites. Ask how many watch television through an internet television service. Ask students to indicate, by a show of hands, whether they have a memory card in their mobile phone, or a memory stick or pen drive. Ask students to explain the benefits of these storage devices.
- Explain that, until the last decade, these devices did not exist. Floppy disks were used, but only for storing text documents or small photographs. The first programmable computer, as such, was designed by Charles Babbage, in Victorian times, and was called a difference engine. (Interestingly, though, the first working model was not completed until the end of the twentieth century.) Before Babbage, there had been mechanical calculators but nothing that could be programmed. Early computers were used to perform calculations by cranking handles to turn internal cogs. Some people think that this gave rise to the term 'number crunching' for doing long mathematical calculations.
- Later electronic computers were extremely large, sometimes taking up huge dedicated rooms that had to be kept very clean and cool.

Main activity

- Discuss with students how technology at their school has changed. Ask them what they think the next decade will bring, in terms of technological developments.
- Read Task 1 with students. Explain that broadband speeds are measured, per second, in **bits**, **kilobits** or, increasingly commonly, **megabits** (10^9 bits) or even **terabits** (10^{12} bits). In brief, the bigger the number, the faster the connection. If necessary, explain the difference between **downloads** and **uploads**. Although download speeds may vary, upload speeds, for example, for uploading a video or pictures to a social networking site, don't change between most of the internet providers.
- *Note that, for the purpose of this activity, at least, bits are represented as b and bytes as B.*
- **Let students do Task 1**. Distribute data sheet 1 and graph paper. Make sure students choose a suitable scale for their bar charts. Suggest that they represent the advertised speed as the total height or top part of the bar; then they could shade the actual value below it. Remind students that there are 60 minutes in an hour and they shouldn't need to use a calculator to convert their answers to time in hours, just count in multiples of 60.
- Ask students to interrogate the information about internet speeds for May 2010, given on data sheet 1. Guide them to find the average highest and lowest speeds over the three time periods of the day for each supplier (these are given for your reference on data sheet 3). These figures apply to genuine internet service suppliers (ISPs) but have been anonymised. For question 2, they should find that the upload time was about 4 hours (actual time was close to 5 hours 15 minutes).
- Read Task 2 with students. Question 1 should be straightforward. Tell students that no internet service provider will tell you how much speed you lose, compared to their advertised speeds, because there are too many factors that affect it. The exchange to which a customer is connected has a very fast fibre-optic line running into it but, if old-style cable then connects the customer to the exchange, speeds will be much lower. The number of people online in the area, at any one time, will also affect the speed, as will the distance between the exchange and the house.
- **Let students do Task 2**. Help less able students to interpret the diagram.
- Read Task 3 with students and ask them to them work in pairs to use the internet. Alternatively, find the information they will need and have it available, printed out.

Improver **

- **Let students do Task 3**. Check they have found the information they needed. Help less able students to find their information, or give them the answers so they can complete the rest of the question. Remind them how to work out a percentage of an amount.
- Read Task 4 with students. Let them work in pairs or small groups to decide what they need to do, to 'future-proof' a computer, and to find the information from the internet or magazines.
- **Let students do Task 4**. Alternatively, this could be done as homework, especially if small groups are able to work together outside the classroom. Check that they have chosen a large external disk. Some may have included a built-in blu-ray player in their system. Encourage students to read reviews about open-source software, reminding them, if necessary, that it is free. Open-source operating systems are also available. Encourage students to research the types of file that can be read by open-source software. It will open almost any document.

Plenary

- Ask students for examples of how they could future-proof a computer system. What problems did they have trying to think ahead? Ask them how much disk space they allocated to music and videos.
- Write this information on the board and discuss similarities and differences in students' responses. Ask some students to justify their choices.

Outcomes

- Students will have understood practical problems and identified and obtained the necessary information.
- Students will have selected mathematics in an organised way to solve the problem.
- Students will have applied a range of mathematics to find the solution to their problem.
- Students will have interpreted the solutions to their calculations and drawn conclusions.

Answers

Task 1

1 a $\frac{3.3}{8} \times 100 = 41.25\%$, $\frac{6.5}{20} \times 100 = 32.5\%$, $\frac{8.7}{10} \times 100 = 87\%$, $\frac{15.7}{20} \times 100 = 78.5\%$

b Students should produce compound bar charts comparing maximum and minimum broadband speeds with advertised speeds. They should analyse the charts to see which suppliers do best in regard to claimed and actual speeds.

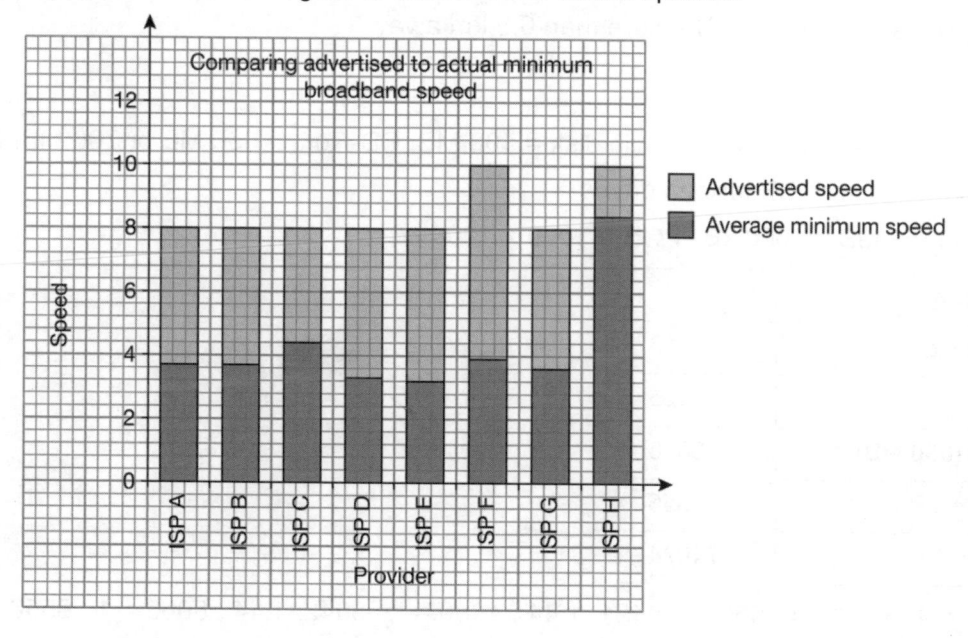

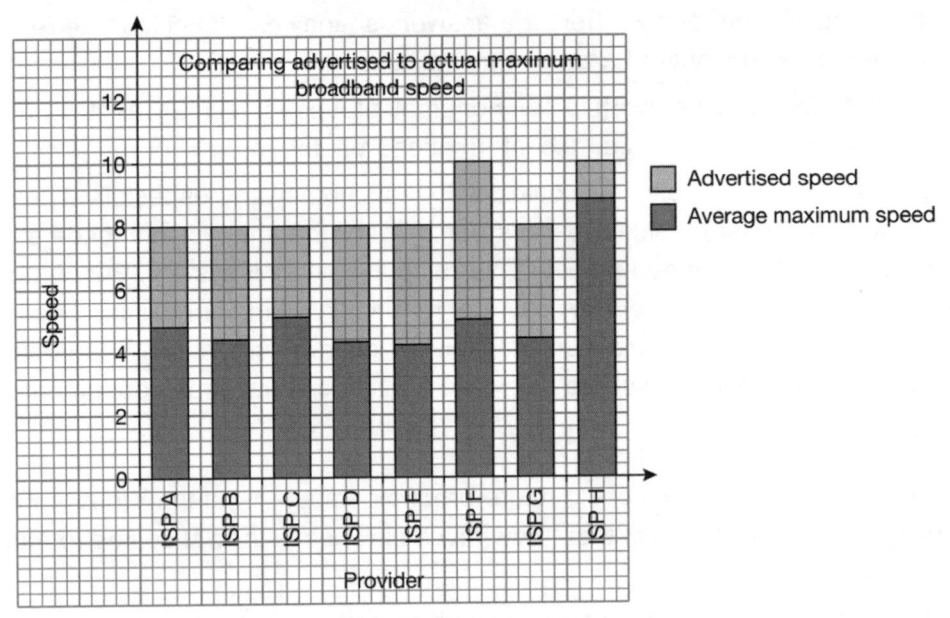

Improver **

Comparing advertised to actual maximum broadband speed

2 a $\frac{75}{30} \times 100 = 250$ min = 4 hours 10 min

b $\frac{200}{250} = 0.8$ megabytes per minute

The actual time was 5 hours 15 min: $5 \times 60 + 15 = 315$ minutes, $\frac{200}{315} = 0.63$ megabytes per minute

Task 2

1 a 5 Mbits: $5 \times 32 = 160$ seconds or 2 minutes 40 seconds
Dial-up: $10 \times 32 = 320$ minutes = 5 hours 20 minutes

b Dial-up because the download time is longer than the programme so it would keep freezing.

c $\frac{10\,000}{4} = 2500$ songs, $\frac{10\,000}{30} = 333$ 5-minute videos, $\frac{10\,000}{110} = 90$ 9-hour audio books, $\frac{10\,000}{200} = 50 \times 45$-minute TV shows, $\frac{10\,000}{600} = 16 \times 45$-minute HDTV shows, $\frac{10}{1.5} = 6 \times 2$-hour movies, $\frac{10}{4.5} =$ up to 2×2-hour HD movies, $\frac{10\,000}{60} = 166$ media player games.

2 a There is a linear relationship for distance from exchange to broadband speed for each type of connection, but the faster the connection the faster the speed drops off

b Under 10 Mbit/s **c** No more than 0.5 km away

Task 3

1 a For example, $3\frac{1}{2}$ floppy = 1.44 MB, zip disk = 100 MB, CD-Rom = 650 MB or 700 MB, DVD-Rom = 4.38 GB, 2 to 8 GB for pen drives

b Remembering 1 MB = 1000 kB, 1 GB = 1000 × 1000 kB

Media type	
Floppy disk	13
Zip drive	925
CD-Rom (650 MB)	6018
DVD-Rom	40555
8 GB pen drive	74074

c 1.44 : 100 = 1 : 69, 1.44 : 650 = 1 : 451, 1.44 : 4380 = 1 : 3042, 1.44 : 8000 = 1 : 5556

Improver **

2 a Students use the answer to their storage devices and divide by 4.7, 600 and 4 MB

	Photos	Film	Music
Floppy disk	0	0	0
Zip drive	21	0	25
CD-Rom (650 MB)	138	1	162
DVD-Rom	931	7	1095
8 GB pen drive	1702	13	2000

b Answers in megabytes

	Photos	Film	Music
Floppy disk	1.44	1.44	1.44
Zip drive	1.3	100	0
CD-Rom (650 MB)	1.4	50	2
DVD-Rom	4.3	180	0
8 GB pen drive	0.6	200	0

Note: Capacities of floppy disks are given for comparison only, as these devices are now largely obsolete and are incompatible with modern systems.

3 a

Media player	Cost	Cost per gigabyte	Difference
8 GB	£189.00	£23.63	–
32 GB	£249.00	£7.78	£15.85
64 GB	£329.00	£5.14	£2.64

b The difference between the 32 GB and 64 GB could give a difference of £2 per gigabyte between the 64 GB and 128 GB, £5.14 – £2 = £3.14 per gigabyte. So the price of a 128 GB model is likely to be 128 × £3.14 = £401.92

4 a 32 × 81% = 25.92 GB. Music 10.368 GB = 2692 tracks, photos = 6.48 GB = 1378 photos

b Space for podcasts = 9.072 GB, 9072 ÷ (45 minutes × 0.5 + 45 minutes × 4)
= 9072 ÷ 202.5 = 44.8 = 44 weeks

Task 4

- Students should find a computer with large hard disk, HDTV interface, blu-ray, large screen, and tabulate their results.

- Students should find 10 external hard disks and divide the cost by the size, in gigabytes, for each one and compare the data and choose a drive, based on their results.

- Students should calculate reasonable percentages of the space on their hard disk drive and allocate their choice of space for music, photos, videos, etc. They should find the number of each type of file that can be saved on their hard disk. They should remember that they need space for an operating system and computer programs.

- Students should have drawn a pie chart to show the maximum number of each type of file on their disk.

- Students should find up-to-date costs of software products. They should also refer to an open-office website to out find that their basic software is free. They should tabulate their results.

- Students should investigate the features and compatibility of commercial and open-source products, including help and support facilities. They should decide whether, after taking the purchase price into account, it is better to pay for commercial office software or to take the open-source route.

Improver **

Time management

Learning objectives
- **Representing Level 1/2**: identify information from different sources, including tables needed to solve the problem, and choose from a range of mathematics to find solutions
- **Analysing Level 1/2**: apply a range of mathematics to find solutions
- **Interpreting Level 1/2**: use results to produce various bar charts, explain what results show and draw conclusions

APP
Evidence for Using and applying mathematics Level 5, Numbers and the number system Level 4, Calculating Level 4, Handling data Level 3

PLTS
Independent enquirers, Creative thinkers, Reflective thinkers, Self-managers, Team workers, Effective participators

Every child matters outcomes
Be healthy, Enjoy and achieve, Make a positive contribution

Cross-curricular links
Geography, English, ICT, Citizenship, PSHE

Underpinning maths
- Extracting information from tables
- Extracting information from charts
- Reading maps and scales
- Rearranging formula
- Calculating percentages
- Producing questionnaires

Resources
- *Student book*, page 80–82
- Data sheet 1: Calendar for 2010 and 2011
- Data sheet 2: Activities timetable
- Coloured pencils, string, graph paper
- Scientific calculators Internet access

Useful websites
- www.direct.gov.uk/en/EducationAndLearning/14To19/Courseworkandexams/DG_10034950

Context
All students should be familiar with their own school timetable and the provision of school holidays and term times. They should have thought about time management and many will have part-time jobs and fit other activities into their lives. This topic is about looking at how they plan their time and reflecting on the time they spend on various activities.

Improver **

Lesson plan

This activity takes one or two lessons. It could be done in one lesson by concentrating on Tasks 1 and 3. Task 4 (extension) could be set as homework.

Starter

- Ask students to name different types of activity they do during a school week and how much time they spend on them. Ask how many students do more than 5 hours a week of sport. Find out how much time they spend a day on social networking sites and watching television. Write their answer on the board and ask them to estimate the average amount of time spent on each activity.
- Ask how many students have part-time jobs and how many hours they work a week. Ask if these students spend the same amount of time on the computer and watching television.

Main activity

- Read Task 1 with students. Discuss the table, which shows the days on which the school closes and the days on which Adam returns to school. Make sure that students realise that these dates should be included as school days. They need to find the total number of school days in the year (make sure they realise that they should not include weekends). Discuss what methods students will use to find the time Adam spends at school as a proportion of the whole school year.
- Distribute data sheet 1. Let students work in pairs if necessary. Remind students that dates do not fall on the same days every year. **Let students do Task 1**.
- Read Task 2 with students. Explain that weekend pay of time and a half means that Adam will be paid 1.5 times his normal rate of pay. Make sure that students know how to read a timetable, pointing out that dashes mean that the bus or train doesn't stop at that town or station.
- **Let students do Task 2**. Walk around the class and make sure students are allowing 10 minutes from the arrival and departure time of the bus in Scarborough, not the time from Muston. Make sure students realise that the proportions of time for the four categories (work, travel, sleep and other things) will be different for weekdays, Saturdays and Sundays. Remind students to check that their totals for each are 24 hours. Discuss what would be a reasonable amount of sleep (Answer: assume 8 hours a night). **Extend the task** by asking students to consider what sorts of things Adam might be doing when he is not working, travelling and sleeping and to calculate possible proportions of the day for these activities.
- Read Task 3 with students. Hold a class discussion about the types of activity they do outside school. Write a list on the board to remind students as they complete the task on their own. Discuss how students can estimate the amount of free time Adam has. Make sure students realise that they are now considering **out-of-school** time. Adam's school day ends at 1515. Discuss how much time Adam has available for his activities in the evening. Allowing time for Adam to get home for school and for an evening meal, students should conclude that he has about 4 hours each evening and about 13 hours on both Saturday and Sunday. Students can use these assumptions to estimate how much free time Adam has for watching TV and socialising. They might want to consider weekdays and the weekend separately, which would involve deciding, for example, whether Adam does his chores during the week or saves them all for the weekend. Discuss whether the proportions should be presented as fractions or percentages (Answer: percentages are easier to compare). Students should present their results graphically, perhaps in a pie chart.

Improver **

- **Let students do Task 3**. For question 2, some students might find data sheet 2, which is a blank timetable, helpful. Encourage students to be critical of their own use of time. **Extend the task** by pooling student's individual data and producing a stacked bar chart to show the results for the whole class. Students could compare their own times with the class averages.
- Look at Task 4 (extension) with students. Make sure that they all know what is required. Direct students to suitable websites to find how to plan a revision timetable. **Let students do Task 4**, either in class or as homework. Encourage them to keep their completed timetable in their planners.

Plenary

- Ask students for examples of activities on which they spend a lot of time. Were they surprised at just how much time they spend doing non-productive activities? How did their activities compare to those of other members of the class? Do they think that more people will spend more time using computers and less time on outside activities in the future?
- Ask, by a show of hands, how many students thought they had a good balance of activities before the lesson but don't think they have now.

Outcomes

- Students will have used maths to identify information needed to complete the tasks.
- Students will have carried out calculations and used appropriate checking procedures at each stage.
- Students will have interpreted the results of their calculations and drawn conclusions, giving explanations.

Answers

Task 1

1 a School days: September to October = 38 days, November to December = 35 days, January to February = 34 days, February to April = 25 days, April to April = 4 days, April to April = 4 days, May to May = 19 days, June to July = 36 days. Total = 195 days.

Adam spends 6.5 hours at school per day. Proportion of time spent at school during the year = (6.5 × 195) ÷ (24 × 365) = 14.5%

b $\frac{5}{6.5} \times 100 = 76.9\%$

c Students calculate the percentage of class time they spend on each subject and comment on their results.

Improver **

Task 2

1 a 5.25 hours × 3 × £3.64 = £57.33 and 8 × £3.64 × 1.5 = £43.68 giving a total of £101.01

b Weekdays, either the 0930 from Muston or 0926; the first will give him more time to walk to work and allows for delays. Saturday, 0836 will get him to work early but the next bus would get him in late.

2 Weekdays: work = 5.25 hours, $\frac{5.25}{24} = \frac{21}{96} = \frac{7}{32}$; travel = approximately 1 hour, $\frac{1}{24}$

Saturdays: work = 8 hours, $\frac{8}{24} = \frac{1}{3}$, travel = approximately 1.75 hours, $\frac{1.75}{24} = \frac{7}{96} \approx \frac{1}{14}$

Sleep = approximately 8 hours, $\frac{8}{24} = \frac{1}{3}$

Time for other things on weekdays approximately 24 − (5.25 + 1 + 8) = 9.75, $\frac{9.75}{24} = \frac{39}{96} = \frac{13}{32}$

Time for other things on Saturdays approximately 24 − (8 + 1.75 + 8) = 6.25, $\frac{6.25}{24} = \frac{25}{96} \approx \frac{1}{4}$

Time for other things on Sundays approximately 24 − 8 = 16, $\frac{16}{24} = \frac{2}{3}$

Some students might allow Adam more sleep at the weekend.

Extension: Students calculate the time Adam might spend having meals and on other activities such as sport and socialising.

Task 3

1 Time available on weekdays = 4 hours per day, 20 hours per week; time available at weekends = 13 hours per day, 26 hours per week; total = 46 hours
Sport = 7.5 hours, 7.5 ÷ 46 = 16%; paper round = 4 hours, 4 ÷ 46 = 9%; homework = 4 hours, 4 ÷ 46 = 9%; research or coursework = 2 hours, 2 ÷ 46 = 4%; downloading music and films = 5 hours, 5 ÷ 46 = 11%; chores = 3 hours, 3 ÷ 46 = 7%
Free time for watching TV and socialising = 46 − (7.5 + 4 + 4 + 2 + 5 + 3) = 20.5 hours, 20.5 ÷ 46 = 45% (round down to 44% to make total 100%).

Students should present their results in a chart or graph and comment on their results. They should conclude that Adam spends the largest proportion of his out-of-school time on sport. He spends more time downloading music and films than on homework, but more on homework and research or coursework combined than on downloading. His paper round and chores combined take the same amount of time as he spends on sport.

2 Students consider and comment on their own use of time.

Extension: Students compare their own use of time to the class averages.

Task 4 (extension)

1 a Students should use the school planner or the library or internet and write down effective ways to revise, for example, without music on, taking short breaks.

b Students should produce a grid showing time in evenings and at weekends for revision, prioritising key subjects or subjects in which they are weak and that need more time.

c Students should show, as fractions, the time per day or week they spend in school, in revising, on socialising and sleeping.

Improver **

GM foods

Learning objectives
- **Representing Level 1/2**: decide what information is needed and how to find it
- **Analysing Level 1/2**: work through calculations and check that answers make sense
- **Interpreting Level 1/2**: use results to produce graphs and charts, explain findings and draw conclusions

APP
Evidence for Using and applying mathematics Level 5, Numbers and the number system Level 6, Calculating Level 5, Handling data Level 6

PLTS
Develops Independent enquirers, Creative thinkers, Team workers, Effective participators

Every child matters outcomes
Make a positive contribution, Be healthy

Cross-curricular links
Science, Geography, History, English, Media studies, PSHE

Underpinning maths
- Calculating percentages
- Working with fractions
- Working with numbers of any size
- Producing a questionnaire
- Calculating averages
- Producing charts

Resources
- *Student book*, page 83–85
- Data sheet: GM foods
- Graph paper
- Coloured pencils
- Scientific calculators
- Internet access

Useful websites
- www.nerc.ac.uk/research/issues/geneticmodification/where.asp

Context
All students should have heard the term 'GM foods' although a few may not remember what the term 'genetically modified' means. This activity is about investigating the increase in GM crops over the last 10 years and finding out people's opinions on GM foods.

Improver **

Those who support the development of GM foods would say that the argument is simple – the number of people in the world is growing, with an estimated population of nine billion people predicted by 2050. The idea is not new. For 10 000 years, humankind has bred plants and animals to produce food more reliably and with less work.

However, the use of GM foods is surrounded by controversy. There is strong opposition from conservationist groups such as Greenpeace, who question both the safety and morality of 'tampering' with organisms' DNA and the motives of the multinational companies who are involved.

Lesson plan
This activity takes one or two lessons. If it is taught over two lessons, the survey in Task 4 (based on the questionnaire) could be set as homework, allowing for a larger number of questionnaires to be completed and to include a greater range of age groups.

Starter
- Ask students what they understand by the term **genetically modified**. Give an example, such as changing the DNA (the 'building blocks of life') of a plant so that it produces more fruit. Explain that the principle is not new; many plants have been developed as **hybrids**, to combine the best properties of two different strains. For example, if a stem of one strain of rose is cut and grafted onto another type of rose, the subsequent growth will have the properties of both plants. Farmers breed livestock and cattle from healthy animals that have desirable characteristics to produce improved offspring. Nature also does it this way.
- Opposition to genetic engineering comes from people who disapprove of the intrusive methods of combining DNA from dissimilar species.
- More information can be found on the website given above.

Main activity
- Ask students where they think our main food supplies come from. Explain that much of our food comes from other countries, not all of them within the EU. Countries outside the EU don't all have the same laws about labelling food to show where it has come from or how is has been produced.
- Read Task 1 with students. Remind students how to calculate a percentage. Use the male to female ratio in the class as an example, to find the percentage of the whole class that are males, dividing the number of males by the total number in the class, and multiplying by 100. Explain that a **hectare** is a metric measurement of area and that the **acre** is an imperial unit, which is still widely used by farmers and people selling land.
- Explain to students the terms **developing country** and **industrialised country**, which are also defined on the data sheet.
- **Let students do Task 1**. Remind them to check their calculations and to make sure the total of all percentages is 100%. Explain that figures for GM land use are high and stated in millions of hectares. Tell students that older books show areas in acres but modern books use the metric unit of hectares. (1 ha = 2.47 acres)
- Read Task 2 with students. Explain that many crops are now GM modified. Tell students they need to find the total for each crop to calculate the percentage that is the GM crop. Remind students that they must divide both the top and bottom fraction by the same number when cancelling. Explain the terms **numerator** and **denominator**.
- **Let students do Task 2**. Remind them how to use the EXP button on their calculator, with the negative number button if necessary, and make sure they can locate the buttons. Give an example of a number in standard form and emphasise that it should only have one number before the decimal point. (For example: 34.3 thousand is $34.3 \times 10^3 = 3.43 \times 10^4$)

Improver **

- Read Task 3 with students. Explain that in a **pilot survey** only a few people or a few questions are asked, to avoid wasting time asking hundreds of people to take part in a survey and then finding it hasn't answered the question they wanted to ask. Suggest that students use pilot questionnaires to gain an idea of the types of question they need to ask. Make sure that students understand what an open question is (for example, what did you have for breakfast?) and what a closed question is (for example, do you usually have anything for breakfast?). Encourage students to use appropriate response tick-boxes (for example, cereal, toast, just a drink, nothing).

- **Let students do Task 3.** Check that they have five suitable questions and let them work in pairs. Ask them to check each other's questions, commenting on whether each is open or closed and how it can be improved.

- Read Task 4 with students. Remind them to write down information they might want to ask in their questionnaire, bearing in mind the types of people they are going to ask to answer their questions. Explain what a **hypothesis** is and why a survey needs to be based on one. (For example, a statement to test a theory; it gives the survey a meaning.)

- **Let students do Task 4.** Move around the class and help students to find information on the internet. Check that their hypotheses can be proved or disproved. Make sure students have thought about how they will record people's responses. To avoid each student having to print 20 questionnaires, remind them to use tally charts or tables to record the responses. Remind them to check that their totals for each question are the same as the number of people they have asked, assuming that people were not allowed to choose more than one option for any question. They could conduct the survey for homework.

- Remind students that they shouldn't use a pie chart if they have a zero value for any part of their data, nor when there are too many categories. If working with more able students, show an example of a box plot on the board, using ages 14, 15, 16, 16, 17, 19, 23, 26, 27, 29, 38, median = 19, lower quartile = 16, upper quartile = 26.5.

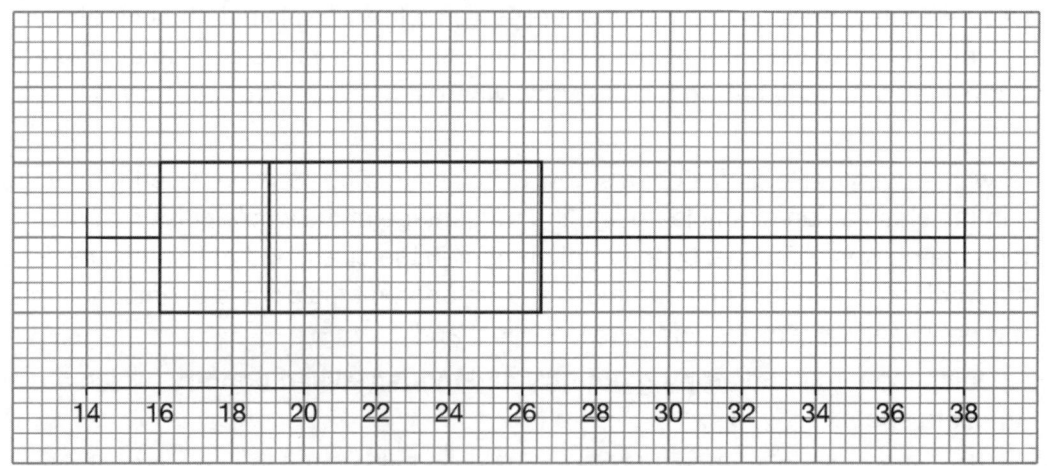

- **Let students complete Task 4.** Move around the class, helping students decide which type of chart is suitable for their results. Tell them that, for each question, they will need numerical data, such as totals, but do not need to produce a chart each time. Finally, remind students to look back at their hypotheses and see if they were correct. More able students could present their results as a slide presentation or a short documentary.

Improver **

Plenary
- Ask students for examples of open and closed questions. What do they think makes an effective and useful question? Ask what we call the type of information that comes from books. (Answer: Secondary information)
- Ask students to evaluate their surveys and ask what they would do differently if they were to do it again.

Outcomes
- Students will have used mathematics to identify a situation and the methods needed to find solutions.
- Students will have read information from charts and used appropriate checking procedures.
- Students will have carried out direct questioning.
- Students will have used a range of statistical methods to interpret the data and draw conclusions.

Answers

Task 1

1 a 100% − (46 + 16 + 15 + 6 + 6 + 3 + 2) = 100% − 94% = 6%

  b Industrialised: Canada + USA = 46 + 6 = 52%

  Developing: Paraguay + Brazil + Argentina + South Africa + China + India = 100 − 52 = 48%

2 a 2004 = 76.9 million, 2009 = 129.3 million hectares

  b In 2004, developing = 25.3 ÷ 76.9 × 100 = 32.9%; industrialised = 51.6 ÷ 76.9 × 100 = 67.1%

  In 2009, developing = 57.3 ÷ 129.3 = 44.3%; industrialised = 72 ÷ 129.3 = 55.7%

  c The percentage of land used for GM crops has increased in developing countries. If the percentage of land used for GM crops in Brazil has increased at a similar rate, it may be assumed that Brazil is a developing country.

  d 2004 to 2009 is 5 years, plus 5 years gives 2014.
  Growth rate for developing is 44.3% − 32.9% = 11.4% so 57.3 million + 11.4% = 63.8322 ≈ 63.8 million hectares.
  Industrial decrease is 55.7% − 67.1% = −11.4%, 88.6% of 72 million = 63.792 = 63.8 million hectares.
  Check using estimation or reverse calculation.

Improver **

Task 2

1 a

Crop	GM area	Conventional area	GM (%)
Maize	20	120	14.30
Soybean	55	35	61.11
Cotton	9	25	26.47
Canola	5	23	17.86

   b Total GM = 89, total conventional = 203, grand total = 292
      89 ÷ 292 × 100 = 30.5%

   c Maize = $\frac{20}{140} = \frac{1}{7}$, soybean = $\frac{55}{90} = \frac{11}{18} \approx \frac{3}{5}$, cotton = $\frac{9}{34} \approx \frac{1}{4}$, canola = $\frac{5}{28} \approx \frac{1}{6}$

2 a 8.81×10^7

   b $8.81 \times 10^7 \times 0.1 = 8.81 \times 10^6$ (8 810 000 km^2),
      $8.81 \times 10^7 \times 3.86 \times 10^{-3}$ = 340 066 square miles

   c 340 066 ÷ 84 300 = 4.033… so four times bigger than the British Isles.

Task 3

1 People are more concerned in 2010 than 2008, generally higher percentages.

2 No, because only 1000 took part in the survey, which is a very small percentage of the population.

Task 4

1 a Students should make notes on information such as types of GM food available.

   b For example, *Most people do not know they are eating GM foods.* Students should include about 10 questions including age (specific or grouped), gender.

2 Students should have completed data tables. Results will vary, depending on the question and the response expected.

3 a Check for correctly labelled charts, box plot of suitable data, calculation and use of the most appropriate average to make comparisons.

   b Check for explanation of all charts produced.

   c Check students refer back to the hypothesis and comments on findings.

Improver **

Flying the world

Learning objectives
- **Representing Level 1/2**: undertake problem-solving in an unfamiliar context and identify the necessary information to tackle the problem
- **Analysing Level 1/2**: apply relevant mathematics to find solutions to practical problems
- **Interpreting Level 1/2**: interpret results to multistage practical problems and then draw appropriate conclusions

APP
Evidence for Using and applying mathematics Level 5, Calculating Level 7, Shape, space and measure Level 6

PLTS
Develops Independent enquirers, Creative thinkers

Every child matters outcomes
Make a positive contribution

Cross-curricular links
Geography, English, Science

Underpinning maths
- Negative numbers
- Speed, distance, time
- Estimation
- Averages
- Measuring and drawing angles
- Bearings

Resources
- *Student Book* pages 86–89
- Data sheet: Flying the world
- Calculator
- Ruler, protractor

Context
All students should be familiar with a world map and should be able at least to locate the UK, even if they are unable to identify other countries around the world. All students should also be familiar with air travel, even if they have never taken a flight. This activity uses some of the mathematics involved in taking flights or working in the airline industry.

Lesson plan
This activity takes two lessons. The two extensions would make good homework exercises for each lesson. Task 5 would make a good whole-class activity.

Starter
- Ask students if they have any idea what time it is in Australia, right now.

Improver **

- Discuss with students why the time in Australia is different from what it is here. (Answer: The Earth takes 24 hours to rotate and, as it rotates, half of it faces the Sun, creating daylight, and the other half faces away from the Sun, so receives no light, creating night-time. Because Australia is on the other side of the Earth from the UK, when we have daylight Australia has night-time, and vice versa.)
- Ask students how we decide what time it is in different parts of the world. (Answer: Using standard time zones)
- Explain that different communities used to decide on their own local time. Then, long railway routes were built and it became very difficult to write timetables. That's when standard time zones were introduced.
- Ask students to guess approximately when they think that might have happened, railways being the clue. (Answer: The 1870s)

Main activity

- Ask students to look at the data sheet, which shows a world map. Explain that the vertical lines show different time zones.
- Ask students to discuss with a partner why some of the lines are not simple straight lines. (Answer: Some countries, such as Greenland, have decided to adopt a single time zone.) You could ask students to point to Greenland on the map.
- Ask students to put their fingers on the UK. Explain that Greenwich is the starting point for time zones. Starting from Greenwich, each time zone to the east is one hour ahead of the last, each time zone to the west is one hour behind the last. Check students know which way is east (to the right on the map) and which way is west (to the left on the map).
- **Let students start Task 1**, Give them a few minutes to do question 1. Make sure that they have marked −12 to +12 across the top of the map, before moving on.
- Suggest students work in pairs. Ask them to find Rome (in Italy) and Bangkok (in Thailand), then use the time zones on their maps to work out the time difference between these two cities. (Answer: +6 hours)
- Ask students, still in pairs, to find Rome (in Italy) again and Buenos Aires (in Argentina) and use the time zones on their map to work out the time difference between these two cities. (Answer: −4 hours)
- Now ask students to imagine they are all in Rome. One of them in each pair is going to Bangkok and the other to Buenos Aires. Ask them to decide which one of them is going where. Both leave at midday today, local time, in Rome. The one going to Bangkok arrives there at 04:30 tomorrow, local time in Bangkok; the one going to Buenos Aires arrives there at 21:30 tonight, local time in Buenos Aires. Ask students to guess who they think has the longer flight, in terms of its **duration**.
- Now challenge students to use the information they have been given about flight departures, arrival times and time-zone differences to work together and find out the actual durations of their flights, or their lengths in terms of time. Ask students to tell you whose flight takes longer. (Answer: Bangkok: 11 hours 30 minutes; Buenos Aires: 14 hours 30 minutes) Ask how many students guessed correctly before working out the answer.
- Discuss with students how they solved the problem. They should describe two alternative strategies:
    1. They started with the departure time and worked out the arrival time, and then the duration of the flight.
    2. They started with the departure time, worked out the duration of the flight and then found the arrival time.

Improver **

- **Let students complete Task 1.** You may decide to allow students to continue working in pairs as they complete question 2.
- For Task 2 (extension), encourage students to think about the best way to record key information. For example, you may suggest they use a table, as follows.

Who	Flight times	Time difference
Jonathan and Sam	Between 2 and 6 hours	—
Saskia and Zinnia	More than 7 hours	2 hours or less
Max and Zac	Between 6 and 8 hours	—

- **Let students do Task 2.**
- Look at Task 3 altogether. Ask students to look at the triangle. Explain that this triangle helps describe the relationships between distance, speed and time. Ask students to imagine they want to find speed, and to cover S with their finger. What do they see in the triangle? (Answer: Distance over time, or distance divided by time) Now ask students to imagine they want to find distance, and to cover D with their finger. What do they see in the triangle now? (Answer: Speed multiplied by time) Do the same for time, T.
- Now ask students to look at the table in question **1,** which shows distances between cities. Ask students to work in pairs to give an estimate of the average distance. (Answer: Students should give an answer between 14 000 and 16 000 km.)
- Ask students, still in pairs, to use the information in the table, and the map on data sheet 1, to estimate the distance between Cape Town and Auckland. (Answer: Students should recognise that this distance is similar to the distance between Lisbon and Hong Kong so could be estimated as 11 000 km.)
- Discuss with students what they understood by the terms 'estimate' and 'average'. (Answer: Estimate: do not calculate accurately, but use information to come up with a sensible approximate value. Average: middle or mean value)
- **Let students do Task 3.** Remind them to use the correct formula for each of their answers.
- **Extend** the task by asking students to refer again to the map on the data sheet. Ask them to choose two cities: one as a departure city and one as a destination or arrival city, and complete these tasks.

    1 Estimate the distance between the two cities.
    2 Use knowledge about the speed of aeroplanes to estimate the length, in hours, of the flight.
    3 If the flight leaves at midday local time in the country of departure, what time will it reach the destination city?

    They could work in pairs and check each other's answers.

- Ask students to return to the earlier context and imagine that the person in Buenos Aires now wants to see their friend in Bangkok. Although they take a direct flight, the aeroplane doesn't fly in a straight line. Ask students why this might be. Discuss the need to ensure aeroplanes follow a safe route, so they do not collide, they avoid bad weather, and they do not fly over unsafe or hostile areas of the world.
- Ask students to show the flight path on their map, on the data sheet: the flight leaves from Buenos Aires and flies approximately east, over Cape Town, then up to Bangkok.
- Ask students how this route may be communicated to a pilot. Discuss bearings with students and stress that these are always given as three figures.

Improver **

- Ask students to mark a north line at each of the three cities, Buenos Aires, Cape Town and Bangkok. Ask them to join each pair of cities with a straight line and then to use their protractors to measure the bearings from Buenos Aires to Cape Town (Answer: about 090°) and then Cape Town to Bangkok (Answer: 058°).
- Discuss with students what they need to remember when measuring angles. (Answer: Place the centre of the protractor exactly on the vertex of the angle and then lay the base-line of the protractor exactly along one side of the angle.)
- Ask students if the bearings are the same for the return journey. (Answer: No) Ask students to use their protractors to measure the bearings from Bangkok to Cape Town and then Cape Town to Buenos Aires. (Answer: 238° and 270°)
- **Let students do Task 4**. Remind them that bearings must be exact, so their measurements must be accurate.
- Look at Task 5 together. Read through the three-day roster and then the rules. Ask students, working in pairs, to make sure their roster doesn't break any of the rules. Discuss with students their strategies for checking the rules were not broken. Students should discuss how to work out the flight times to ensure rest periods are correct. (Answer: London to Dubai, flight time 7 hours, time difference +3 hours; Dubai to Addis Ababa, flight time 3 hours 15 minutes, time difference −1 hour; Addis Ababa to London, flight time 7 hours 30 minutes, the time difference is −2 hours) **Let students do Task 5**.

Plenary

- Discuss with students what they have learned from doing this task.
- Ask students to think where else schedules and rosters are required and what factors may need to be considered when compiling them. For example, you may discuss train timetables, how to ensure that trains connect appropriately and are in the correct place for the timetable to run again the next day. Alternatively, you may discuss factory rosters in which people work shifts, ensuring the correct number of people work at the correct times to ensure all the machinery and the process keeps working.

Outcomes

- Students will have extracted information from maps and tables and used the information to solve real-life problems.
- Students will have used estimation, averages and formulae to help them solve problems.
- Students will have drawn and measured angles and written them as bearings.

Answers

Task 1

1. Students should mark −12 to +12 for each time zone, at the top and bottom of the map.
2.

Departure city	Arrival city	a Time difference (hours)	b Length of flight (hours)
Paris	Los Angeles	−9 hours	11 hours 30 minutes
Tel Aviv	Lima	−7 hours	15 hours 20 minutes
Lisbon	Hong Kong	+8 hours	13 hours 15 minutes
Sao Paulo	Tokyo	+12 hours	24 hours
Auckland	Rome	−11 hours	24 hours 45 minutes

Task 2 (extension)

Jonathan and Sam: Banjul

Saskia and Zinnia: Cape Town

Max and Zac: Dubai

Task 3

1

Departure city	Arrival city	Distance (km)	Speed (km/h)
Paris	Los Angeles	9029	785.1
Tel Aviv	Lima	12 685	827.3
Lisbon	Hong Kong	11 044	833.5
Sao Paulo	Tokyo	18 560	773.3
Auckland	Rome	18 270	783.2

2 Students should estimate the average speed of an aeroplane to be about 778 km/h.

3 Students should estimate distances by identifying that Taipei to Madrid is a similar distance to Lisbon to Hong Kong; Brisbane to Reykjavik is a similar distance to Auckland to Rome, etc.

Students should use their estimated distances and the speed they estimated in question 2, to calculate length of flight (time) using the formula:

$$time = \frac{distance}{speed}$$

Approximate answers are as in the table below.

Departure city	Arrival city	Estimated distance (km)	Estimated length of flight (h)
Taipei	Madrid	11 000	14
Brisbane	Reykjavik	18 000	23
San Francisco	Brussels	9000	12
Buenos Aires	Shanghai	18 500	24
Santiago	Addis Ababa	12 500	16

Task 4

080 degrees; 115 degrees; 092 degrees
319 degrees; 289 degrees; 150 degrees

Task 5

1 Check students have chosen sensible flight times, and recorded them, taking account of time zones.

2 Check students have calculated distances making accurate use of the formula: speed = distance × time and they have summed distances to find the total distance travelled by cabin crew in the three days. They could also estimate distances, using the map.

3 Check students have measured bearings accurately.

Improver **

Your plaice or mine?

Learning objectives
- **Representing Level 1/2**: find required information from graphs and charts to solve the problem, using appropriate methods
- **Analysing Level 1/2**: work with scales on charts and diagrams and ensure calculations make sense
- **Interpreting Level 1/2**: use results to explain findings and draw conclusions

APP
Evidence for Using and applying mathematics Level 4, Numbers and the number system Level 4, Calculating Level 5, Handling data Level 3

PLTS
Develops Independent enquirers, Creative thinkers, Team workers, Effective participators

Every child matters outcomes
Make a positive contribution, Achieve economic well-being, Enjoy and achieve

Cross-curricular links
Science, Geography, English

Underpinning maths
- Interpreting graphs and charts
- Understanding fractions
- Calculating average (mean)
- Calculating a scale
- Producing charts

Resources
- *Student book*, pages 90–93
- Graph paper, tracing paper, coloured pencils and pens
- Rulers
- Calculators
- Internet access (optional for extension activity)

Useful websites
- www.shipais.com/index.php?map=uk

Context
All students should be familiar with reading information from charts and diagrams, although the context for this topic may be unfamiliar to them. In this activity, they investigate how patterns in deep-sea fishing are affected, not only by the stock levels of fish in the sea but also by the quotas imposed by the EU.

Lesson plan
This activity takes one to two lessons.

Improver **

Starter
- Ask students to name as many different types of fish as they can, that are found in the seas surrounding the UK. Ask what has happened to the UK fishing industry over the past decade. Ask students what other jobs they think fishermen could do. Expect limited answers and explain that although they are highly skilled in fishing, these people are likely to have few transferable skills.
- Explain what a **quota** is. (Answer: A fixed share or limit, in this case on the quantity, in tonnes, of fish that can be caught. There are different limits for different breeds of fish.) Tell students that UK deep-sea trawlers fish in the north, near Iceland.

Main activity
- Discuss deep-sea fishing in general and explain that the mesh size of a net used depends on the type of fish to be caught. The size of fish that can legally be caught is controlled. Generally, they must not be less that 30 cm long. If fish that are too small are caught, they are thrown back but usually die of shock. If small fish are not caught, they will grow much bigger.
- Read Task 1 with students. Make sure that students know which axis is which, and that the independent variable goes on the horizontal axis, the one that depends on it goes on the vertical axis. In this case, the years are along the bottom and the amounts of fish are up the side. Remind students to read the label on the axis to help them work out the value of the figures. In this case, the vertical axis is measured in thousands of tonnes.
- **Let students do Task 1**. Encourage them to write in full sentences when answering questions and to use numerical data when they describe the trend. As they have been asked to estimate, an exact value isn't required. Make sure students approximate their values for part **1c** to the nearest 10 and reduce their fraction to its simplest form.
- For question 2, remind students to read the label on the vertical axis, which again measures in thousands of tonnes. They should use the key to identify the types of fish. Explain that **gadoid** is the name for the family of fish to which cod, hake and other fish belong. Encourage students to describe the trend for each type of fish, as well as the overall trend revealed by the graph. Ensure students realise that whiting was not caught until 1980; help less able students to realise that they can tell this because there is no green line in the graph before this time.
- Read Task 2 and explain that when they use more than one graph students must always check the axes, to make sure they are comparing like with like, for example, both numbers (of people and fishing vessels), not a number with a percentage, as this could be misleading.
- **Let students do Task 2**. Move around the class, making sure they have read the information correctly from the graphs. Encourage students to use tracing paper to draw lines over the graph, or use a straight edge, such as a ruler, to read the measurements.
- Read Task 3 with students. Make sure that students know how to extract information from a table. **Let students do Task 3**. Check that students can obtain the correct values from the table in this task.
- Read Task 4 with students. Make sure they can interpret the map and the pie chart. **Let students do Task 4**.

Plenary
- Ask students to discuss if we should have fishing quotas or not. Ask them what could be the consequences if they did not exist. Ask for a show of hands of all those students that were surprised a cod could be 80 cm long.
- Discuss what makes a good chart or diagram and what can be misleading.

Improver **

Outcomes

- Students will have used maths to find information from graphs, charts and diagrams.
- Students will have used appropriate checking procedures.
- Students will have interpreted the solutions to their calculations and given conclusions in written form and graphical.

Answers

Task 1

1 a The trend for the graph shows that the cod quota was reduced dramatically in 2002 to 2003, was constant from 2003 to 2005 then saw a year-on-year decrease until 2007. Following the trend, the figure for 2008 would be approximately 18 000 tonnes.

b 48 000 – 20 000 = 28 000 tonnes

c Using $\frac{20\,000}{48\,000} \approx \frac{20\,000}{50\,000} = \frac{2}{5}$

2 a There has been an overall reduction in fishing catches. The catch size of Norway pout has fluctuated the most.

b It rose dramatically, haddock having the greatest increase, followed by Norway pout. The catches of cod didn't increase as much.

c Norway pout has provided the best yields.

d Catches of whiting were not recorded until the 1980s, since the line doesn't start until 1980.

3 a

Year	Stock	UK quota	Percentage of EU quota (%)
2002	43 000	20 000	47
2003	40 000	11 000	28
2004	37 500	10 000	27
2005	37 000	9000	24
2006	32 500	8000	25

b Remaining stock: 2002 = over-fished by 7000 tonnes; 2003 = 2500 tonnes remaining; 2004 = 10 000 tonnes remaining, 2005 = 9000 tonnes remaining, 2006 = 9000 tonnes remaining. The differences in stock levels and quota in 2002 revealed over-fishing by 7000 tonnes; 2003 showed a big positive margin of 2500 tonnes. The margin settles to 9000 tonnes per year. Stock levels seem to be declining, indicating that stock levels (which are estimates) were wrong or quotas for fishing were too high, leaving too few fish to breed and build up stocks.

Task 2

1 The numbers employed have declined at a greater rate than the number of fishing vessels.

2 The average number employed per vessel declined by about 15% over the period.

Improver **

Task 3

1. 1997: haddock = 82 000 tonnes, cod = 73 000 tonnes, plaice = 22 000 tonnes

   82 000 × 983 = €80 606 000, 73 000 × 1433 = €104 609 000, 22 000 × 1768 = €38 896 000. Total income = €224 111 000

2. For 2000: haddock = €1166 × 50 000 = €58 300 000; cod = €2073 × 40 000 = €82 920 000; plaice €2237 × 20 000 = €44 740 000; total = €185 960 000.

   For 2002: haddock = €1344 × 51 000 = €68 544 000; cod = €2269 × 30 000 = €68 070 000; plaice €2653 × 15 000 = €39 795 000; total = €176 409 000.

   The income decreased, year-on-year.

Task 4

The higher percentages for fish caught are for Northern North Sea and West of Scotland where the sea will be colder. Fishermen fish mainly where there are greater supplies of fish.

Improver **

Sleep

Learning objectives
- **Representing Level 1/2**: understand problems in familiar and unfamiliar situations, and collect and represent data, using ICT where appropriate
- **Analysing Level 1/2**: use probability to assess the likelihood of an outcome
- **Interpreting Level 1/2**: extract and interpret information from tables, diagrams, charts and graphs

APP
Evidence for Using and applying mathematics Level 5, Calculating Level 6, Handling data Level 6

PLTS
Develops Independent enquirers, Creative thinkers, Reflective learners, Effective participators

Every child matters outcomes
Be healthy, Enjoy and achieve, Make a positive contribution

Cross-curricular links
Science

Underpinning maths
- Selecting information from tables
- Percentages
- Constructing and interpreting graphs
- Constructing questionnaires and surveys

Resources
- *Student book*, pages 94–97
- Data sheet: Animal sleep requirements
- Calculators
- Graph paper
- Rulers
- Internet access (optional)

Context
Students may often feel tired, due to the stresses of adolescence and conflict of interests of various aspects of their lives. In this task, they will look at their sleep requirements and the reasons behind them, noting how people – and animals – do not all need the same amount of sleep.

Lesson plan
This activity will take two lessons. It could be done in one lesson by concentrating on Tasks 1 and 2. The surveys students are required to conduct in Task 5 and Task 6 may be used as homework. It is recommended that students do either Task 5 or Task 6.

Starter
- Ask students to calculate and write down how much sleep they got last night.
- Discuss these hours. Are they very varied? Do both sexes get similar amounts of sleep?

Improver **

Main activity

- Discuss the occurrence of dreams. Ask who regularly remembers their dreams and who rarely or never does. Is it true that everybody dreams? (Answer: Yes.) Why do some people remember dreams more than others? (Answer: It is probably related to the type of sleep they are having when they wake up.)

- Look at Task 1 with students. Many students will have heard of REM sleep. Ask what REM stands for. (Answer: Rapid eye movement.) Ask if they know when REM sleep occurs. (Answer: Throughout the night.)

- Explain that NREM (non-REM) sleep has different levels. It is very difficult to wake someone who is in the deepest level (level 4). It is usually when waking from REM sleep that people remember dreams.

- **Let students do Task 1**. Discuss the graph. Make sure students realise that they need to measure the horizontal scale.

- Look at Task 2 with students. The proportions of different types of sleep vary throughout the night; most stage 4 sleep occurs early on, and the proportion of REM sleep increases throughout the night. Getting too little sleep deprives you of both types of sleep, but not in the same proportions.

- Students with younger siblings can lead a discussion about how amounts of sleep relate to age, as younger children often go to bed earlier than older siblings. Establish from the class a consensus of how much sleep 10–13-year-olds get.

- Compare the class opinion with the figures shown in the bar chart in Task 2. Discuss the inaccuracies of such a chart; it suggests that 10–13-year-olds need 10.5 hours sleep, whereas 14–18-year-olds need 8.5 hours sleep. Do people suddenly need two hours less sleep when they reach their 14th birthday? (Answer: No. A line graph might be a better way of representing the information.) Students may notice that that age groups used for the graph are not consistent. For example, it is unclear whether a 3-year-old belongs in the '2–3 years' or the '3–5 years' age group; there is no group for people aged between 45 and 50. Stress that in real life they will come across graphs that do not follow the rules they have been taught; it is important always to read axis labels and scales carefully. **Let students do Task 2**. **Extend the task** by asking how students' answers contradict the graph in Task 1. Ask students for reasons.

- Discuss the trend in REM sleep. (Answer: The percentage and actual hours of REM sleep decrease with age; negative correlation.)

- Summarise, saying that the quantity of sleep changes throughout a human's life. Explain that students will now investigate what influences the sleep patterns of animals. Discuss any pets students have now or have had. Dogs sleep for a large part of the day; hamsters sleep virtually all day (because they are nocturnal). Ask students if they think the amount of sleep is dependent upon size.

- Look at Task 3 with students. Distribute the data sheet. **Let students do Task 3**. Transferring the information to a spreadsheet will speed up the process, particularly if they will be doing Task 4 (extension) as well. Make sure they are capable of doing this. Remind students to be consistent with units, as most weights are in kilograms but some are in grams or tonnes.

- Look at Task 4 with students. Task 3 showed no obvious correlation. Ask why this might be the case. (Answer: The weights are only approximations but, perhaps more importantly, the creatures come from a variety of different types of species. Ask how we could overcome this. (Answer: Draw separate scatter graphs for the different types of animal.)

Improver **

- **Let students do Task 4 (extension).** Ask for suggestions as to how they could use the spreadsheet to help. (Answer: By sorting on the 'Type' column, they can select the appropriate cells to add to the graph.) **Extend the task** by reminding students of the limited number of animals in each category and asking them to find information about other animals in each category and add their results to the graph.
- Task 5 and Task 6 offer a choice of surveys. Allocate one or other task, either choosing which students should do which, or allowing students to make the choice. They will need to design a data collection sheet (individually or collectively), whichever task they do.
- As a homework task, students should collect the necessary data for their surveys. If appropriate, set a target number of people, for example, 5 to 10, and then collate the data next lesson.
- During the second lesson, students should collate the data from the homework. Discuss possible problems or inaccuracies related to the survey. For example, some people might be unwilling to tell the truth about sleep patterns; some people might have been surveyed by more than one person and thus be included twice after collation of data.
- Students should draw appropriate charts. For the first survey, a bar chart similar to the one in Task 2 would be appropriate. A line graph might be more appropriate, but students are likely to have insufficient data without grouping. They will need to decide whether to plot the median or a mean 'hours of sleep' for each category.
- For the second survey, students could draw a scatter graph of hours of sleep against the lesson (by number) in which they feel most awake, and another of hours of sleep against the lesson in which they feel least awake.

Plenary
- Students' surveys should highlight some discussion points.
- Ask students whether they are getting the recommended amount of sleep.
- Ask if they think a later start and end to the school day would allow them to get more sleep. (See the comments in the answer section.)

Outcomes
- Students will have read tables and taken measurements.
- Students will have calculated one quantity as a percentage of another and found percentages of quantities.
- Students will have drawn and interpreted scatter graphs and bar charts and used a spreadsheet to construct graphs.
- Students will have designed a data collection sheet and collected data.
- Students will have chosen and drawn the most appropriate graph for a situation.

Improver **

Answers

Task 1

From 35% to 40%

Task 2

Age	Hours of sleep	% REM sleep	Amount of REM sleep
1–15 days	16	50	8 h
3–5 months	14	41	5 h 44 min
6–23 months	13	31	4 h 2 min
2–3 years	12.5	26	3 h 15 min
3–5 years	11.5	20	2 h 18 min
5–9 years	11	18	1 h 59 min
10–13 years	10.5	18	1 h 53 min
14–18 years	8.5	20	1 h 42 min
19–30 years	8	22	1 h 46 min
33–45 years	7	19	1 h 20 min
50–70 years	6.5	15	59 min
70–80 years	6	14	50 min

Extension

The graph in Task 1 shows 8 hours sleep, suggesting an adult, somewhere in the 19–45 age range, but the percentage of REM sleep indicates a child of under two years of age. This is probably because the graph overemphasises the amount of REM sleep required, to highlight how the quantity increases through the sleep period.

Task 3

The enormous variation in weights makes the scatter graph difficult to draw.

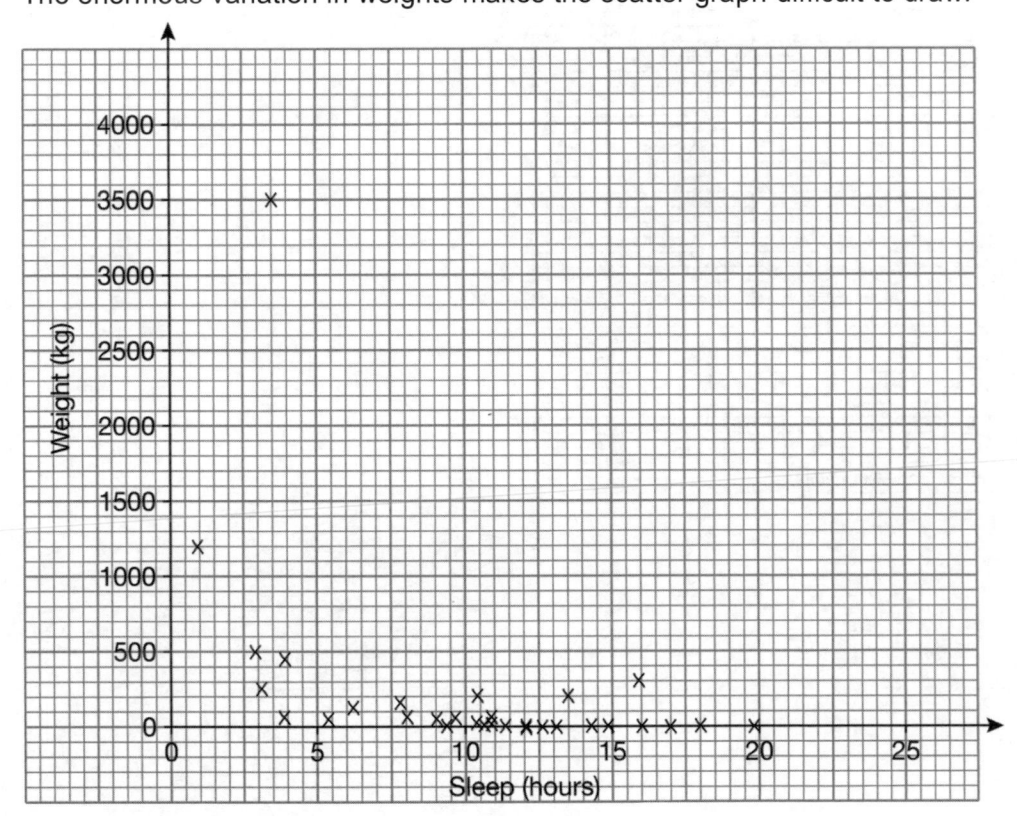

© HarperCollinsPublishers 2010

Improver **

Removing the two heaviest animals, the graph is easier to interpret:

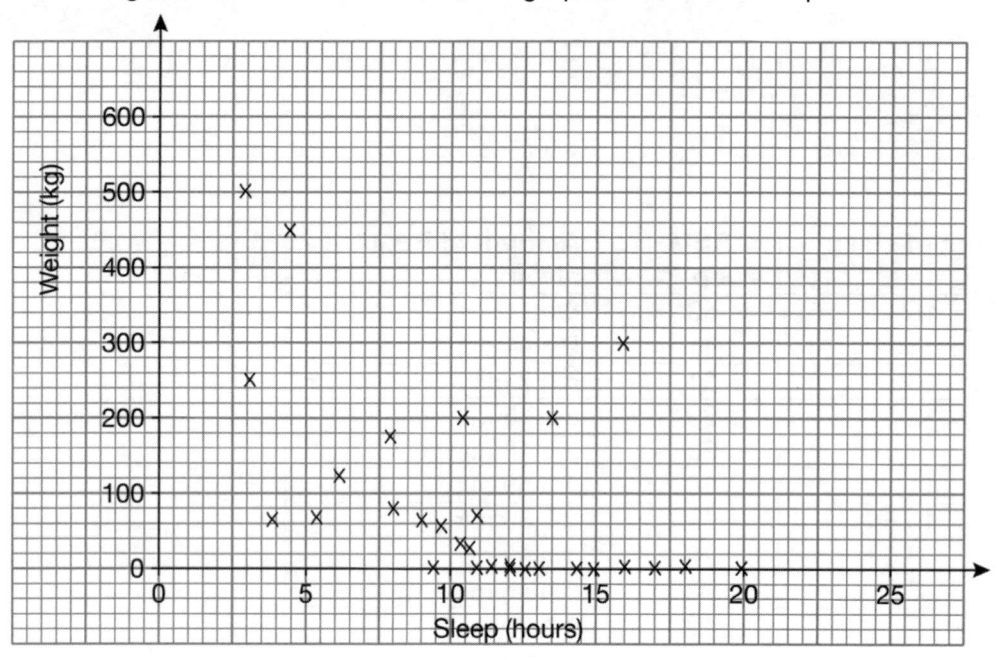

but shows little correlation.

Task 4

Cats

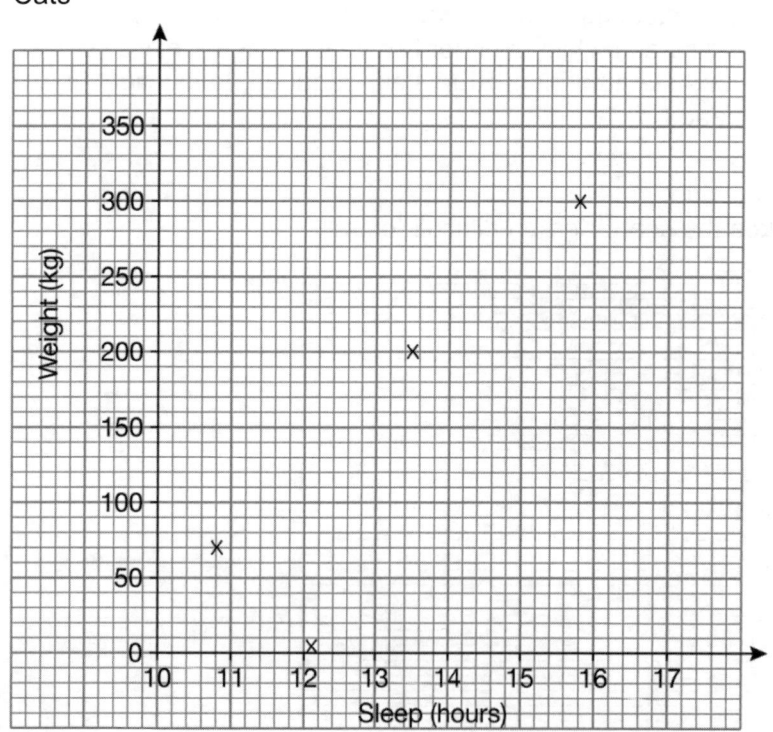

122 © HarperCollins*Publishers* 2010

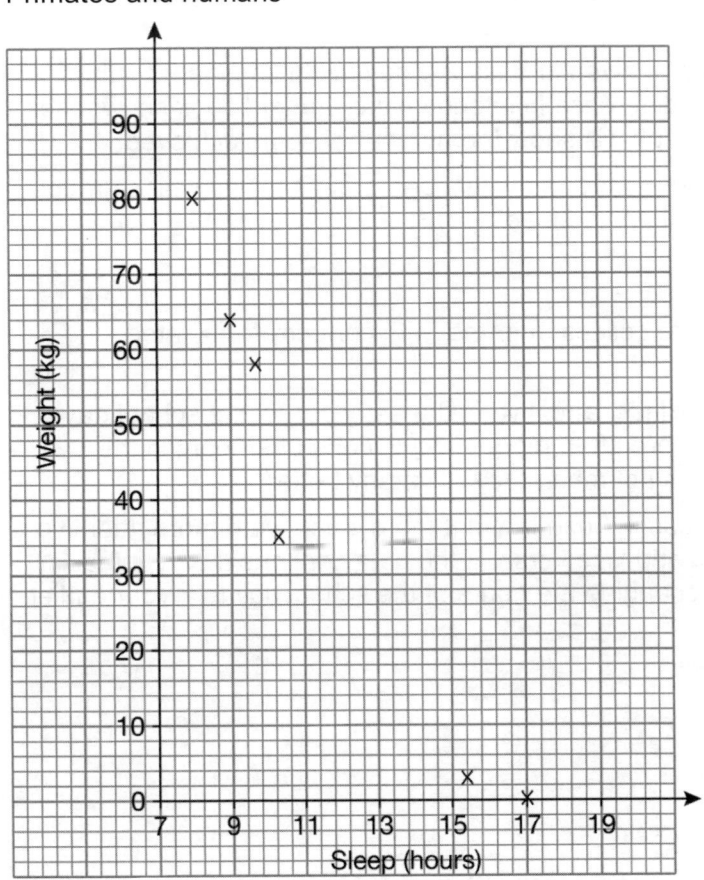

Improver **

Rodents

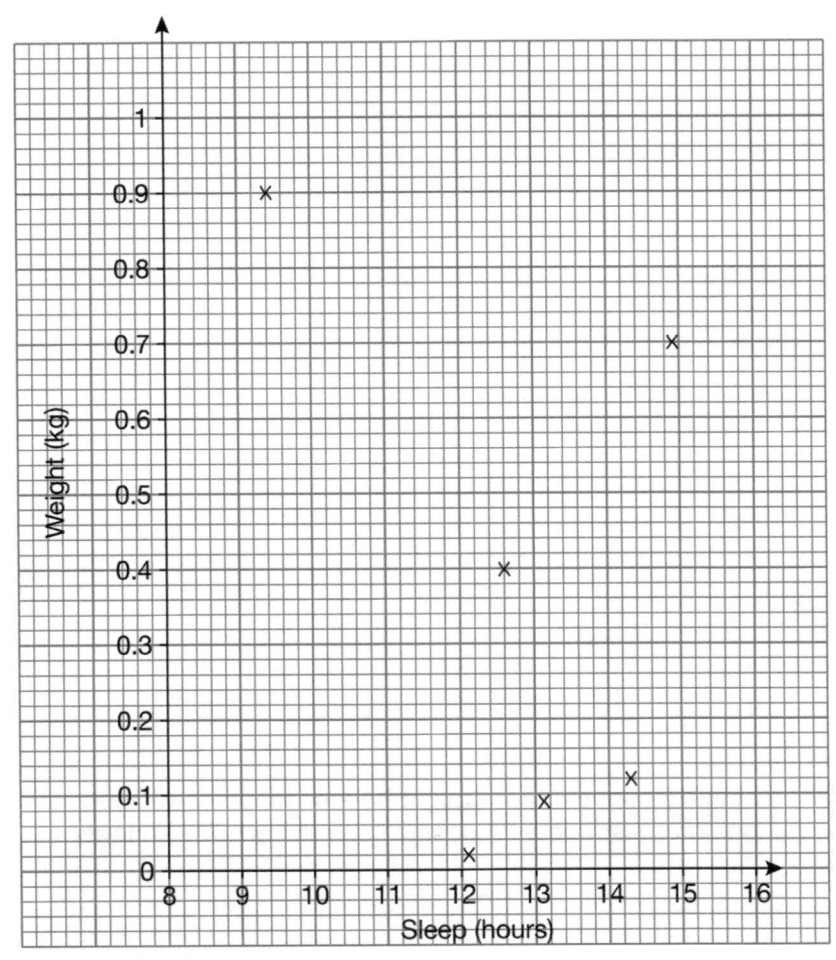

Improver **

Ruminant mammals

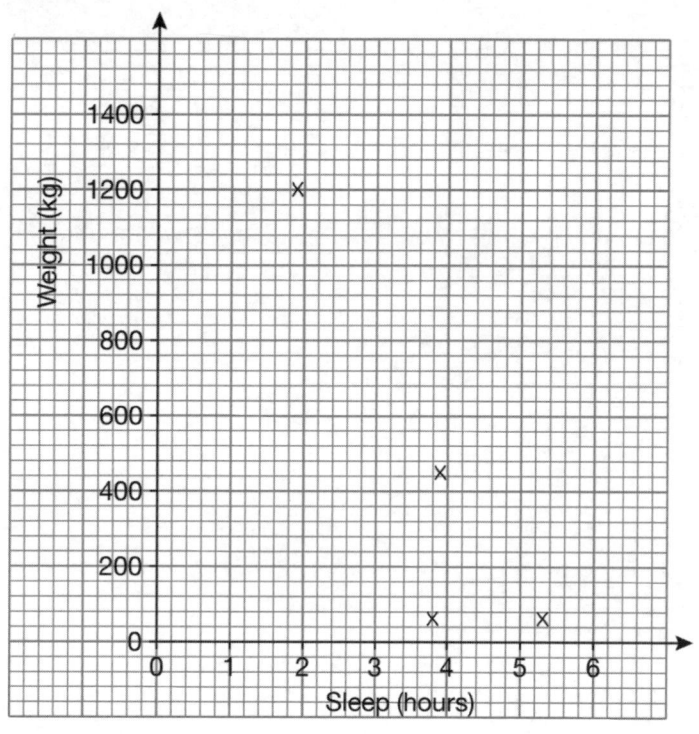

[Scatter graph with Weight (kg) on y-axis from 0 to 1400, and Sleep (hours) on x-axis from 0 to 6. Points plotted approximately at (2, 1200), (4, 400), (3, 20), (5, 20).]

The graphs are largely inconclusive.

The graphs for primates and ruminant mammals suggest there might be a negative correlation between weight and hours of sleep; the cats graph suggests a positive correlation. The rodents graph shows no correlation.

Task 5

1. Check that students create appropriate data collection forms, with correctly formulated questions.

2. Students can compare their graph to the one given in Task 2. They might comment on the small sample size of their survey, and the difference in intention; the *Student book* shows the number of hours needed, whereas their graph will show the number of hours achieved.

3. Students should examine the ranges of sleep reported within age groups to find which groups have the greatest variation in the number of hours sleep.

Task 6

1. Check that students create appropriate data collection forms, with correctly formulated questions.

2. There is a suggestion that adolescents are least attentive in the early part of the school day, and more awake later on. This is why they are often more difficult in the afternoon; in the morning they are more docile, but that does not mean they learn any better.

3. Students should analyse their findings to see if those that got more sleep were more attentive in the morning than those with less sleep, and vice versa. If the data confirms the hypothesis, do students think that there is a case for changing the hours of the school day to favour earlier or later lessons?

Selling online

Learning objectives
- **Representing Level 1/2**: undertake problem-solving in an unfamiliar context and recognise that business decisions often involve using mathematics
- **Analysing Level 1/2**: analyse all kinds of data, using appropriate mathematical approaches, to inform good business decisions
- **Interpreting Level 1/2**: interpret results to evaluate solutions to real-life problems and make recommendations

APP
Evidence for Using and applying mathematics Levels 6/7, Calculating Level 6, Handling data Levels 5/6

PLTS
Develops Independent enquirers, Effective participators

Every child matters outcomes
Achieve economic well-being

Cross-curricular links
ICT, Business, English

Underpinning maths
- Interpreting graphs
- Solving real-life problems
- Percentages
- Probability

Resources
- *Student Book* page 98–101
- Calculator
- Internet access (optional)

Context
All students should be familiar with buying and selling online, even if they have no experience of it. They also should be aware of advertisements being placed on websites. This activity is about the many aspects of mathematics involved in selling online.

Lesson plan
This activity takes two lessons. You may do it in one lesson by using Task 1, questions 1, 2 and 3 only, then considering only two of the online businesses (*Pooch Palace* and *Hats off*) in Tasks 2 and 3. Task 4 should be done in its entirety, then Task 5 (extension) could be set for homework. If you are planning this activity over two lessons, Task 6 would make a good small-group exercise.

Starter
- Tell students that selling online is big business. For example, the press reported that, in 2008, almost 4 million Britons spent over £100 million online on Christmas Day. Ask students if they are surprised by this.

Improver **

- Ask students what businesses they know of that sell goods or services online.
- Ask students to suggest the advantages for businesses that sell online. Students may consider reaching more buyers, being open 24 hours per day, seven days per week, and lower overheads.

Main activity

- Tell students that goods sold directly to the general public, whether through shops or online, are called **retail sales**.
- Ask students to discuss with a partner what percentage of retail sales they think are made online in the UK each year. Then collect some of the students' estimates.
- Now ask students to look at the graph for 2009–2010 under Task 1. Encourage them to use this graph to assess how good their estimates were.
- **Let students do Task 1**. Remind them to look carefully at the graphs when answering the questions. **Extend the task** by asking students if, on first glance at the graphs, they would think online sales rose more dramatically in 2008 or 2009–2010. Discuss how they would change the graphs to make comparison between them easier.
- Ask students how people pay for goods online. (Answer: Most online transactions are made with a debit or a credit card.)
- Explain that businesses pay a fee to guarantee the security of online card transactions and the receipt of their money. This fee can take two forms:
  – a monthly fee and then a payment for each sale, just like mobile phone contracts involve a monthly fee and a payment for each call
  – a percentage of every sale.
- Remind students how to use a percentage multiplier, by expressing the percentage as a decimal and then using it to calculate the percentage of a quantity.
- Use a quick-fire game to check students' understanding of percentage multipliers. Ask one student to give any percentage; then the next gives the multiplier and a new percentage. Work around the class so that everyone has a turn, ending up with the first student again.
- **Let students do Task 2**. Tell students to think carefully about the information they require to work out the cost of each deal.
- Tell students that a business that advertises in a magazine, newspaper or television channel has to pay a fee. The internet is no different: if you advertise on someone else's web page then you must pay.
- Run an internet search on 'clothes'. Point out the **sponsored links** on the right-hand side of the screen. Explain that these businesses pay to advertise there: each time someone clicks on a link to a business, that business pays the owner of the browser (such as Google) some money. This is called **pay-per-click**.
  Note: If you do not have internet access in the classroom, visit this web page beforehand and print copies for students to look at in the lesson.
- Read through the introduction to Task 3 together. **Then let students do Task 3**.
- Visit a national newspaper's online fashion pages. Ask students to identify who is advertising on that page.
  Note: If you do not have internet access in the classroom, visit such a web page beforehand and print copies for students to look at in the lesson.
- Ask students how the adverts differ. They should note the position and also the design.
- Let students read the introduction to Task 4, then discuss whether the experiment is well designed. For example, ask students why the web pages were shown in a random order.

(Answer: To be sure participants in the experiment didn't just remember the first or the last web page they had seen.)

- **Let students do Task 4**. Remind them that probability measures the likelihood of an event. Therefore, this task is all about working out the position and design of an online advert so that it is likely to be memorable.
- For Task 5 (extension), encourage students not only to critique the online adverts in Task 2, but also to suggest improvements. **Let students do Task 5**.
- Ask students to read through Task 6. Suggest they look back over the work they have done in all the previous tasks to help them decide on the content of their report. Then discuss the kinds of information they might include. Encourage students to think about using some calculations to support their recommendations.
- **Let students do Task 6**.

Plenary

- Ask students to discuss with a partner three things they now know about running an online business *that they didn't know before this lesson*. Discuss what they have learnt.
- Ask students if they can think of any other aspects of running an online business that may involve mathematics. They may talk about aspects of business that are common to online and offline businesses, such as accounts; they also may talk about measuring marketing success through the number of hits on a website, or the length of time spent on a web page.

Outcomes

- Students will have used a range of mathematical skills as they are applied in a real-life business scenario.
- Students will have been encouraged to analyse mathematical information to make good business decisions.

Answers

Task 1

1. 2008: begins in January; 2009–2010: begins in April
2. 2008: starts at 2.4 and goes up in increments of 0.2%; 2009–2010: starts at 0 and goes up in increments of 1%
3. Rising
4. a 3.8%   b   8%
5. Christmas shopping
6. Reason 1: December is a shorter Christmas shopping month.
   Reason 2: People may buy less online in December because they do not want to rely on the Christmas post.

Extension

Students should realise that the impression given at first glance is misleading. The vertical scales on the graph are not the same, which skews the figures.

2009–2010 shows greater growth. Students may give an explanation that in the 12 months of 2008 internet sales as a percentage of retail sales were at their lowest at 2.7% and at their highest at 3.8%, a rise of 1.1%; in the 12 months of 2009–2010 internet sales as a percentage of retail sales were at their lowest at 5.5% and at their highest at 8%, a rise of 2.5%.

Improver **

Task 2

1

	January internet sales	February internet sales	March internet sales	Total number of sales
Pooch Palace	87	96	72	255
Flying high	61	89	132	282
Hats off	204	329	124	657

2 a £116.40   b £123.96   c £228.96
3 a £0.80 or 80p   b £0.60 or 60p   c £0.34 or 34p
4 a £204   b £169.20   c £223.38
5 a Deal A   b Deal A   c Deal B

Task 3

1 Cost of advert = £0.09 × 5765 = £518.85; profit = (£20 − £12) × 53 = £424
No, they shouldn't continue.

2 Cost of advert = £0.11 × 4012 = £441.32; profit = (£15 − £4.50) × 94 = £987
Yes, they should continue.

3 Cost of advert = £0.15 × 10 924 = £1638.60; profit = (8.49 − 1.83) × 257 = £1711.62
Yes, they should continue.

Task 4

1 a $\frac{35}{132}$ b $\frac{50}{132} = \frac{25}{66}$ c $\frac{40}{132} = \frac{10}{33}$ d $\frac{6}{132} = \frac{1}{22}$ e $\frac{1}{132}$

2 a Top middle   b Across the bottom

3 a $\frac{15}{132} = \frac{5}{44}$ b $\frac{52}{132} = \frac{13}{33}$ c $\frac{65}{132}$

4 a Text and pictures of people using products   b Text only

Task 5 (extension)

The online advert for *Pooch Palace* is the worst, as it uses text only and no pictures. It may be improved by including a picture of a happy dog being shampooed and groomed. The online advert for *Flying high* may be improved by including pictures of happy people flying kites. The online advert for *Hats off* is the best, as it includes text and a happy person wearing a bobble hat.

Task 6

Students should:

- use Task 1 to make reference to graphs showing growth in online sales as a percentage of total retail sales year on year
- use Task 3 to recognise that Deal A is the better service for processing card payments initially; they may include some calculations to illustrate their point, for example, for 100 sales, 200 sales and 500 sales for the first three months:

Number of sales	Cost of Deal A	Cost of Deal B
100	£73	£50
200	£101	£100
500	£185	£250

- use Tasks 4 and 5 to make recommendations for monitoring pay-per-click and placing and designing the best possible online advert.

Improver **

Jewellery design

Learning objectives
- **Representing Level 1/2**: understand, use and calculate ratio and proportion, including problems involving scale
- **Analysing Level 1/2**: solve problems requiring calculation with common measures, including money, time and length; use a formula
- **Interpreting Level 1/2**: construct geometric diagrams; extract and interpret information from tables, diagrams, charts and graphs; interpret data and draw conclusions

APP
Evidence of Using and applying mathematics Level 5, Numbers and the number system Level 5, Calculating Level 6, Shape space and measure Level 6

PLTS
Develops Independent enquirers, Creative thinkers, Team workers, Self-managers, Effective participators

Every child matters outcomes
Enjoy and achieve, Make a positive contribution, Achieve economic well-being

Cross-curricular links
Art, Design and technology, Science, Business

Underpinning maths
- Accurate drawing
- Measuring lengths and angles
- Scales
- Reading tables
- Circumference of circles
- Calculating with money
- Calculating percentages

Resources
- *Student book*, pages 102–105
- Data sheet 1: Diamond designs
- Data sheet 2: Ring size chart
- Glass of water and straw (optional)
- Plain paper
- Calculators
- Rulers and protractors
- Internet access

Useful websites
- e.g. www.beadsunlimited.co.uk, but others are available

Improver **

Context
Most people use or wear jewellery of one sort or another, whether it is as simple as a plain ring, as flamboyant as what is worn by celebrities and in show business, or as exquisite as the Crown Jewels. This activity focuses on design, practicalities such as sizing rings, and making money from jewellery, both as a hobby and as a profession.

Lesson plan
This activity can be completed in one lesson, but would be better spread over two, to allow time for students' creativity. Task 4 (extension) may be used as a homework task.

Starter
- Do a quick survey of the class, asking them about their jewellery. Ask who wears rings, necklaces, earrings, and who has other body piercings. Ask where students buy their jewellery.
- Ask about the type of jewellery their parents wear, and whether it is significantly different from their own. Are there any family heirlooms? What sorts of stones do they recognise?

Main activity
- Discuss jewellery design. Ask students about symmetry in jewellery. Many pieces have symmetry in their design. Ask students to describe any of their own jewellery that has symmetry, perhaps making sketches on the board. Look for examples of line symmetry and rotational symmetry.
- Ask the students what they know about diamonds. (Answer: They may use words such as *hard*, *sharp*, *shiny*, *sparkling*, *bright*, *expensive*) Discuss the first two of these properties. Diamonds are extremely hard. When cut, they have well-defined edges. This combination means they can scratch glass surfaces very easily. Diamonds are the hardest naturally occurring material, and so are used industrially to make diamond-tipped tools used for cutting hard materials such as tiles.
- Ask students what makes a diamond so bright. As they think about it, students will realise that diamonds have no internal light source; their brightness results from light being reflected by its planes and surfaces. A skilfully cut diamond reflects most light from its internal back surfaces.
- Discuss how light appears to bend when it passes through transparent objects. Illustrate this with a straw in a glass of water. The straw appears to be bent or broken. If a diamond's facets are cut at the correct angles, light shines into the stone and bounces inside it before emerging.

Improver **

- Look at Task 1 with students. Read the information about cutting diamonds and then distribute data sheet 1, which takes students through the steps to draw a plan view of a cut diamond. Discuss the need for accuracy when cutting diamonds. Poorly cut diamonds will not sparkle. Many jewels are designed by first making large drawings and taking measurements. Therefore accuracy at the drawing and measuring stage is essential, as errors in the drawing will lead to errors in the jewel. **Let students do Task 1**.

- Look at Task 2 with students. Talk with students about buying rings. Without a jeweller's ring gauge, finding the correct size is not easy; the ring must fit over the knuckle, but not be loose. Ask if anyone knows how rings are categorised by size. They will probably be aware that shoe sizes are measured differently in England, Europe and the USA. The same is true of ring sizes. Distribute data sheet 2, which shows ring sizes as used in the three regions of the world.

- It might be useful here to remind students of the names of parts of the circle, and the relationship between circumference (C) and diameter (d). Ask students for the formula. (Answer: $C = \pi d$)

- **Let students do Task 2**. To **extend the task**, let students use string to find their own ring sizes. They will need to work in pairs to do this. Discuss how they would do it, talking about the sort of problems they might have.

- Discuss with students ideas for earning money. Extend the discussion to ask who gets paid for doing jobs at home. Some students may also work, outside school hours, to earn extra money. Discuss who works, where they work, what sort of work they do and their hourly rates of pay.

- Explain that some adults are self-employed. Some work from home. Suggest that students could do the same by making jewellery to earn some money. The advantages are that they can work from home and they can work as much or as little as they like. Of course, their income will depend on how much their materials cost, their productivity and their sales.

- Some students may already have made jewellery, either at home or in design and technology lessons. Discuss what they have made and the materials they used.

- Read Task 3 with students. This introduces the idea of start-up costs (in this case, of pliers). Point out that some items are sold individually; others in a pack by quantity, weight or length.

- Discuss students' ideas about profit. What influences their selling price? **Let students do Task 3**. Ensure that they realise that the items must be affordable, so people will buy them; however, their profit must eventually cover the initial outlay on the pliers. They must also take into account their time. There is little point in making 50p on a necklace if it takes an hour to make – 50p per hour is not a good hourly rate! They could try to estimate how long each item would take, and then rethink their pricing. To **extend the task**, ask students to design some jewellery and investigate the cost of making it. They could use internet searches to find ideas and prices.

- Look at Task 4 with students. Discuss what sort of work jewellers do: design, manufacture and sales were all mentioned in the *Student book*, at the start of this activity. Jewellers also undertake alterations and repairs. If necessary, discuss the steps students need to follow to calculate Charlie's annual profit (Answer: Calculate the cost of materials; calculate Charlie's total takings for the month; calculate Charlie's profit for the month; multiply this by 12 then subtract Charlie's overheads.)

- **Let students do Task 4**. Students could use a spreadsheet program to perform the calculations.

Improver **

Plenary
- Discuss what factors determine the cost of jewellery. Students should include the cost of materials, the cost of labour and a profit margin. The limiting factor is how much people are prepared to pay.
- Discuss how realistic the situation posed in Task 4 is. An individual, self-employed jeweller might not sell as many expensive items as a large, town-centre jeweller but overhead costs would be low and there would be no need to employ staff. The small-scale jeweller might maintain or increase sales by selling online and diversifying into necklaces, earrings and other low-cost items.
- Discuss the breakdown of Charlie's profit: slightly over half is labour costs, and the rest is made from the 30% added on to the price of materials.

Outcomes
- Students will have made accurate drawings and measurements and calculated diameters from circumferences.
- Students will have made calculations involving scales and more complex calculations with money.
- Students will have read tables.
- Students will have calculated percentages of quantities.

Answers

Task 1

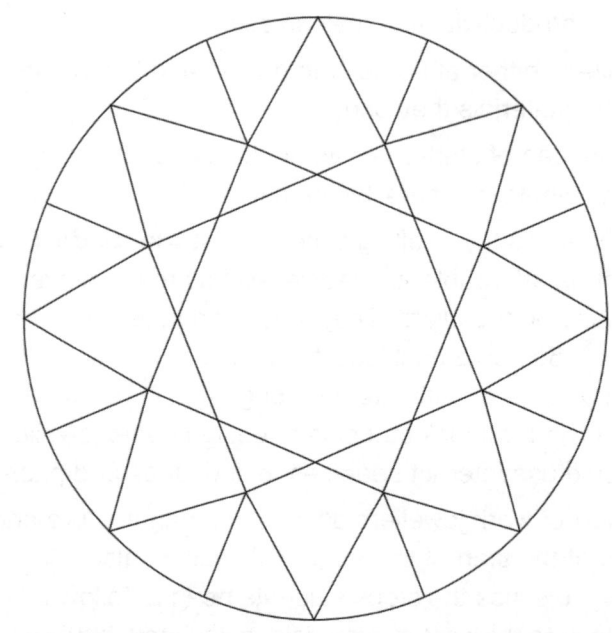

1
2 $a = 135°$, AB = 1.9 cm
3 $a = 135°$, AB = 1.9 mm

Task 2

1 Q$\frac{1}{2}$, R, R$\frac{1}{2}$ or S

2 a 10 in the USA

   b T, T$\frac{1}{2}$ or U in the UK.

3 I or I$\frac{1}{2}$

Improver **

Extension

Students will find it quite difficult to find their ring size in this way and are unlikely to be able to do it themselves, without a partner. They need to wrap a piece of string (or preferable fine cotton) round their finger, mark where the string overlaps and measure the distance between the marks. They will then need to divide by π to find the diameter. Looking at the ring sizes listed in data sheet 2, they will notice how small the differences are between one measure and the next.

Task 3

1 a £4.11   **b** £1.66   **c** £1.21   **d** £3.02

2 Students should show their estimates for the time it takes to make each item. They should show an hourly rate and selling prices, along with the percentage profit. A 50% profit would put the selling price of the items at £6.17, £2.49, £1.82 and £4.53 respectively. Selling one of each would give a profit of £5.01, or more than half of the cost of the pliers. However, it takes no account of the time factor involved. Assuming the bead necklaces take half an hour to make, then they might want to add on an extra £3 (equivalent to £6 an hour), whereas the earrings and the chain necklace would be quicker.

Suggested prices might be £7, £5.50, £4 and £5.50

Extension

Students will have other suggestions regarding selling prices.

Task 4

	Quantity	Unit cost (£)	Total cost (£)	Unit time (hours)	Total time (hours)
Resized rings	5	0	0	1.5	7.5
Sold rings:					
Silver, small diamond	7	114	798	2	14
Silver, medium diamond	3	218	654	2	6
Silver, large diamond	1	438	438	2	2
Gold, small diamond	2	138	276	2	4
Gold, medium diamond	7	242	1694	2	14
Gold, large diamond	4	462	1848	2	8
Rings made to customer's design:					
Gold	1	21	21	8	8
Silver with three small diamonds	1	328	328	8	8
Gold with large diamond	1	453	453	8	8
Total cost			**6510**		**79.5**

Total cost of materials is £6510, materials + 30% = £8463

Labour = 79.5 hours @ £30 per hour = £2385

Total takings for the month = £8463 + £2385 = £10 848

Profit for the month = £10 848 − £6510 = £4338

Annual profit = £4388 × 12 − £11 000 = £41 056

Improver **

Buying your first car

Learning objectives
- **Representing Level 1/2**: find information from different sources, including tables, needed to solve the problem and use appropriate methods to solve it
- **Analysing Level 1/2**: work through the calculations for averages and calculate percentages
- **Interpreting Level 1/2**: use results to produce various bar charts, explain findings and draw conclusions

APP
Evidence for Using and applying mathematics Level 3/4, Numbers and the number system Level 4/5, Calculating Level 5, Algebra Level 4, Handling data Level 3

PLTS
Develops Independent enquirers, Creative thinkers, Reflective learners, Team workers, Effective participators

Every child matters outcomes
Make a positive contribution, Achieve economic well-being

Cross-curricular links
English, Media studies, Business studies, ICT

Underpinning maths
- Extracting information from tables and charts
- Calculating averages
- Using formulae
- Working with percentages
- Producing charts and tables

Resources
- *Student Book* pages 106–109
- Data sheet: Buying your first car
- Coloured pencils, graph paper
- Calculators
- Internet access, newspapers and magazines

Useful websites
- www.autotrader.co.uk
- www.parkers.co.uk

Context
All students should be familiar with a range of different makes and models of car and appreciate the difference in running costs of a larger car compared to those of a smaller car. In this activity, students investigate costs associated with buying a suitable first car and the rate at which cars depreciate.

Improver **

Lesson plan
This activity takes two lessons. Less able students who do not have time to complete Task 5 (extension) could be asked to do it as homework.

Starter
- Ask students to list as many makes and model of car as they can, in one minute. Ask if any of the cars they have listed would be suitable 'first cars'. Write examples on the board. Say that insurance for new drivers is very expensive, and would be the biggest cost in running their first car. Explain that having a car with a bigger engine size usually means you pay more for insurance. Give, as an example, a typical amount of £1200 for car insurance for an 18-year-old, although women usually get cheaper insurance than men do.

- List the costs associated with running a car. Explain that it is a legal requirement that every car that is three or more years old is tested annually for road-worthiness, by an approved garage. This is called the MOT test, relating back to when it was introduced by the then Ministry of Transport. Explain that before a car can be driven on the road it has to be insured, display a valid road-tax disc and, if necessary, have passed the MOT. Mention that cars also require regular servicing and maintenance (changing the oil, filters, brake pads, tyres, etc.).

- Explain that another term used in connection with a car is **mpg**, which is the number of miles the car will travel, in typical conditions, on one gallon of fuel. Although fuel is more commonly sold in litres, the mpg rate is still commonly stated. Discuss the conversion between gallons and litres (1 gallon ≈ 4.55 litres) and ask students to suggest how they might change an mpg figure to give the distance the car would travel on one litre of fuel.

Main activity
- Discuss what cars students might consider buying. Encourage them to think of models with small engines (typically 1.0 litre), low value and good fuel economy. (Examples might include Citroen Saxo, Peugeot 106.)

- Read Task 1 with students. Remind them that they are being asked what car they would like, not what they can afford, but to keep it sensible, no dream cars.

- Having put them into suitable groups, depending on their abilities, **let students start Task 1**. Give them three minutes to list five cars. Offer advice as necessary and remind students to think about running costs (fuel, MOT, breakdown recovery). Encourage students to discuss costs that group members may already know about, for example, how much an older brother or sister pays for insurance.

- Interrupt group discussions and write on the board some up-to-date examples of costs, before students reach question **4** of the task. Include typical figures, such as MOT £55, insurance £1200, breakdown recovery £140, fuel £1638 (based on 12 000 miles at 40 mpg at £1.20 per litre), servicing £150, maintenance £300. **Let students complete Task 1**. Discuss whether students' assumptions were very different from the real-life figures.

- Read Task 2 with students. They could work in pairs for this task. If internet access is available, suggest suitable websites to interrogate car prices. Alternatively, distribute local or national papers (car sections only). Allow students a suitable amount of time (for example, 30 minutes) for their research and remind them only to select suitable cars.
Note: If no resources are available, or time is at a premium, distribute the data sheet.

- Remind students how to calculate the mean, median, mode and range. Write definitions on the board for students to copy into their books.

Improver **

- **Let students do Task 2**. Distribute graph paper, make sure students choose a suitable scale for their graph and reassure them that there is no need for pin-point accuracy when plotting mileages. If computers with spreadsheet software are available, suggest more capable students draw a custom-type chart for price and mileage on the same graph.

- Read Task 3 with students. Look at the table describing calculation of road tax. Explain that carbon dioxide (CO_2) emissions are the amount of carbon dioxide released into the air, in grams, for every kilometre travelled. Practise extracting information from the table, such as the road tax for six months for tax band F (£68.75) or the emissions rate for band J (186–200 g/km).

- Tell students that, in real life, information is often embedded in text, not laid out like it is in text books. Help them to extract information from the statements in the *Student book* (36 000 miles, sale price £2970, insurance £1195, 46 mpg). Explain the term mpg again (miles travelled per gallon of fuel, 1 gallon ≈ 4.55 litres). Show them how to use the table again to find the CO_2 emissions for a car in tax band G (151–165 g/km).

- **Let students do Task 3**. Make sure they correctly look up the road tax for band G (£150 for the year), add in the MOT cost of £55 and the price of the car (£2970). Check that they multiply the number of gallons by 4.55 in question 2. Remind them that question 4 is asking for a grand total so they need to include all their previous answers.

- Read Task 4 with students. If appropriate, explain your reasons for choosing your own car (for example, price, seating capacity, as a second car). Discuss Smart cars. Explain that most of them attract zero road tax but some fall into the £35 band. They are exempt from the London congestion charge and do about 75 to 99 mpg depending on whether it runs on petrol or diesel. Explain that cars that run on diesel usually give better mpg rates.

- Explain that the value of a new car falls by thousands of pounds as soon as it leaves the showroom, but garages offer a warranty in case anything goes wrong with the car. This means that, within a fixed period, certain repairs will be free. Say that another problem is that car insurance is related to the value of the car.

- Explain that, in this context, **finance** means borrowing the money to buy a car, usually from a bank or through a finance company. Interest is charged, often at high rates, and regular payments are made until the loan is repaid in full.

- **Let students do Task 4**. Make sure they understand the problem, taking 40% off the initial price, then taking 10% off the resultant value each subsequent year, to find the value after five years. Let more able students calculate 80% of £9995 and ask them to explain why this does not give the same drop in value. (Answer: Because they should take 10% off a reducing balance each time.) Remind students there are 12 months in a year. (5 × 12 = 60 months)

- Read Task 5 with students. Make sure they know what they have to do.

- **Let students do Task 5**, either in class or as homework.

Plenary

- Ask students what they should look for when buying a first car.
- Ask for examples of suitable makes and models of car. Ask students if they were surprised by the costs associated with running a car.
- Choose suitable students and ask them to explain what their bar charts from Task 2 show. Ask how mileage and age affect the price of a car. Find out the most common colour of car from the students' research.
- Ask how many students think they will be able to afford a car when they are 18 years old.

Improver **

Outcomes

- Students will have used mathematics to identify information supplied in a table or in newspapers to find a solution.
- Students will have carried out calculations and used appropriate checking procedures.
- Students will have interpreted the solutions to their calculations, used graphs and drawn conclusions.

Answers

Task 1

1. Check suitability of cars chosen.
2. Expect justifications such as good mpg, cheap first car, plenty around for spare parts, small engine size, cheap and easy to modify.
3. Using the figure of £1200 (given previously) for insurance, students may suggest: car £2000, insurance £1200, fuel £1500, breakdown cover £140, road tax £150, MOT £55, total = £5045
4. Based on the figures suggested: car £3000, insurance £1200, breakdown £140, MOT £55, fuel £1638, maintenance £300, road tax £150, total = £6483. They may have a cheaper or more expensive car.

Task 2

1. Students' tables should include information based on information they have found, or on the data sheet.
2. These answer are for values on the data sheet. Others may vary.

	Price (£)	Mileage
mean	1201	77 858
mode	500	N/A
median	1092	81 100
maximum	2995	120 000
minimum	500	10 000
range	2495	110 000

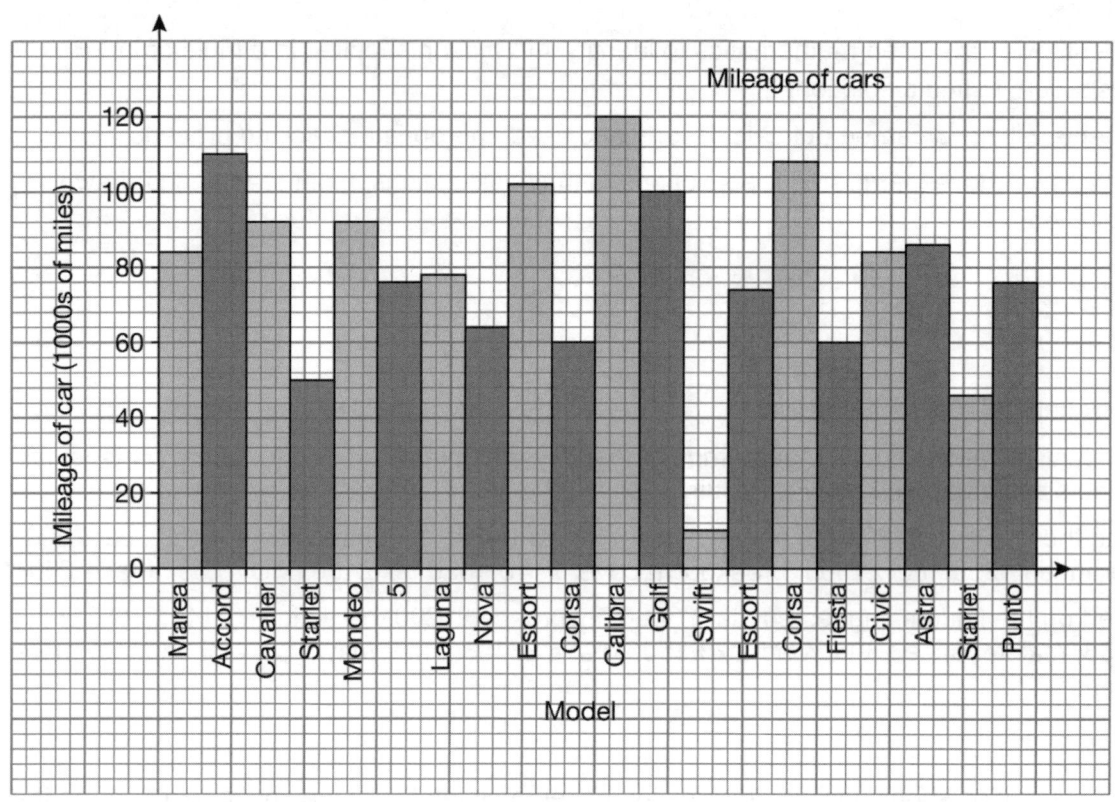

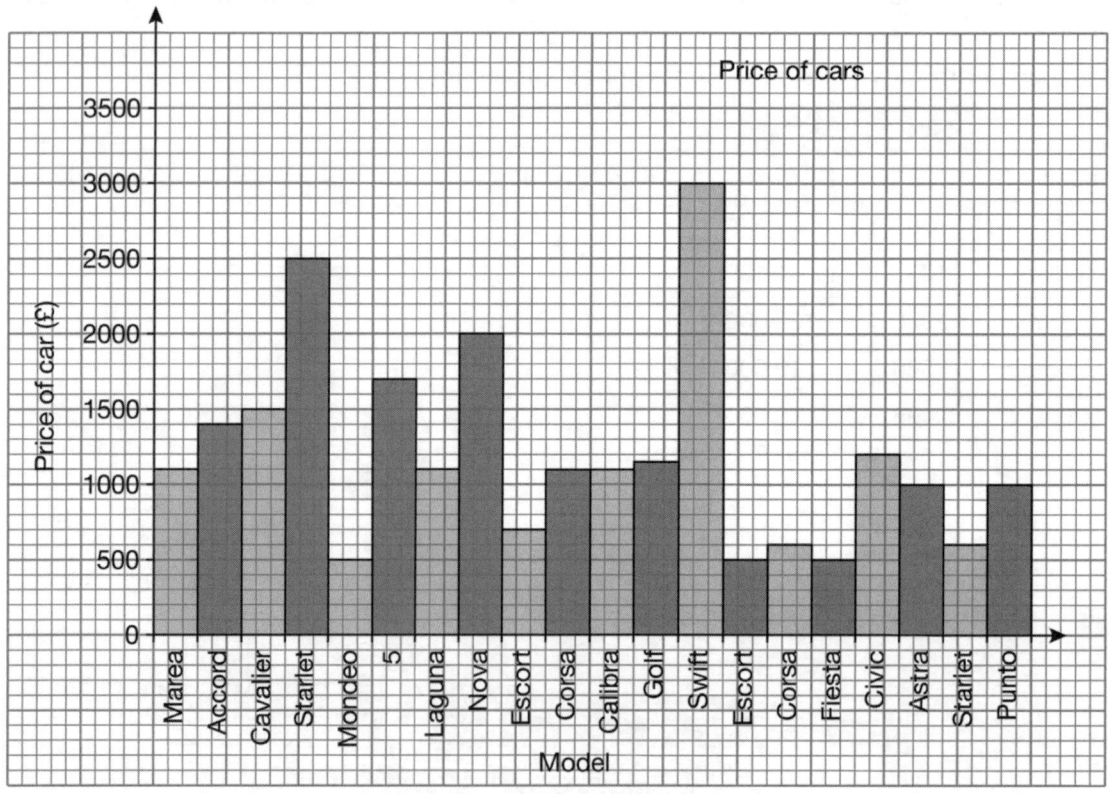

Improver **

3

Mileage of cars

Bar chart showing Mileage of car (1000s of miles) against Model:
- Marea: 85
- Accord: 110
- Cavalier: 92
- Starlet: 50
- Mondeo: 92
- 5: 76
- Laguna: 78
- Nova: 64
- Escort: 102
- Corsa: 60
- Calibra: 120
- Golf: 100
- Swift: 10
- Escort: 74
- Corsa: 108
- Fiesta: 60
- Civic: 84
- Astra: 86
- Starlet: 46
- Punto: 76

Price of cars

Bar chart showing Price of car (£) against Model:
- Marea: 1100
- Accord: 1400
- Cavalier: 1500
- Starlet: 2500
- Mondeo: 500
- 5: 1700
- Laguna: 1100
- Nova: 2000
- Escort: 700
- Corsa: 1100
- Calibra: 1100
- Golf: 1150
- Swift: 3000
- Escort: 500
- Corsa: 600
- Fiesta: 500
- Civic: 1200
- Astra: 1000
- Starlet: 600
- Punto: 1000

Improver **

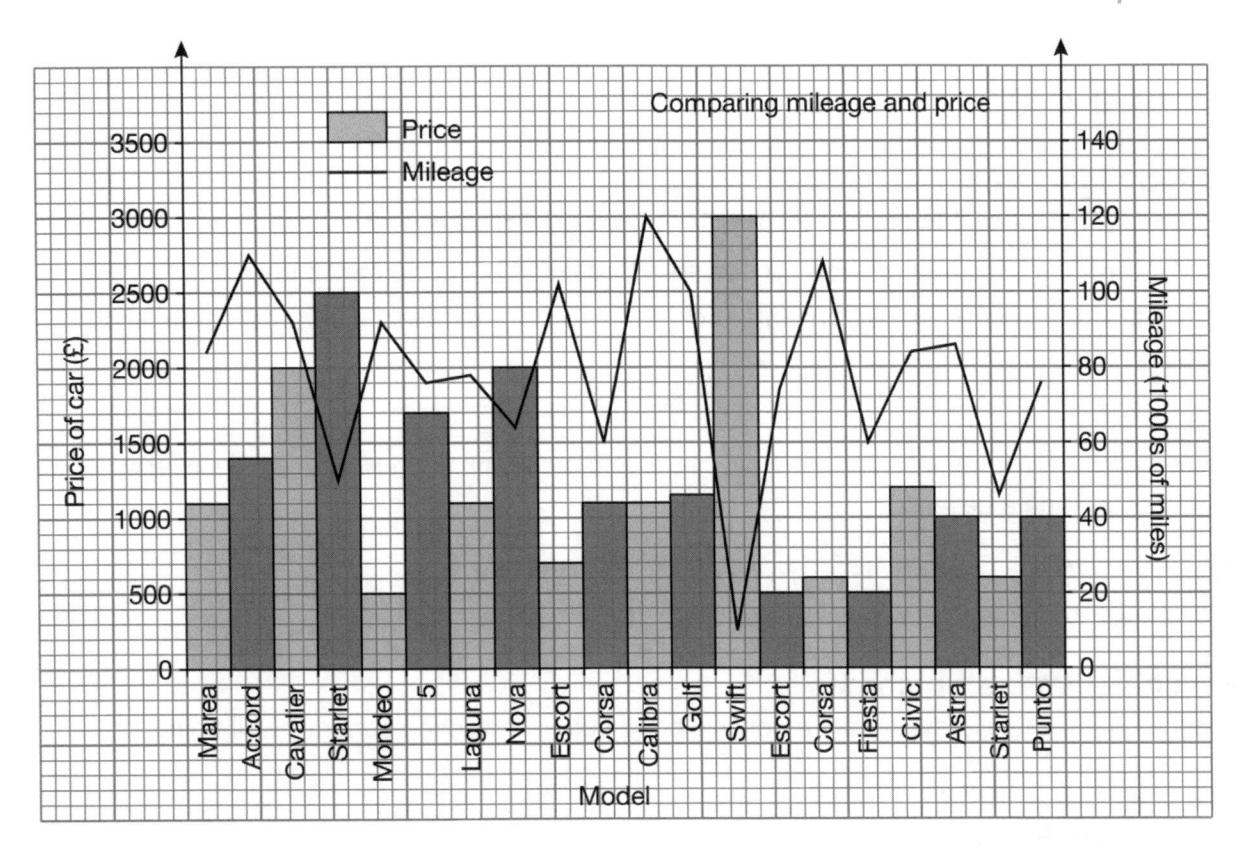

Comments: Students will notice that the more expensive the car the lower the mileage, highlighting that the car is newer than those with a higher mileage and lower price.

Task 3

1. Price of car £2970, insurance £1195, road tax £150, total = £4315
2. 12 000 ÷ 46 = 260.869… × 4.55 = 1186.956… × £1.20 = £1424.35 (£1424.347…)
3. a A 10-gallon tank costs £54.60 to fill.
   b A 17-gallon tank will cost £92.82
4. £1424.35 + £250 + £150 + £4315 = £6139.35

Task 4

1. End of year 1 = £5997, end of year 2 = £5397.30, end of year 3 = £4857.57, end of year 4 = £4371.81, end of year 5 = £3934.63
2. £9995 + 9% = £10 894.55 ÷ 60 = £181.58 per month
3. £9995 − 40% − 10% − 10% = £4857.57 by end of year 3. Finance, £181.58 × 36 month = £6536.88 paid off loan amount, £9995 − £6536.88 = £3458.12 outstanding. Profit on car of £4857.57 − £3458.12 = £1399.45. Yes, he could pay off the finance.
4. Car is worth £5997, finance paid = £181.58 × 12 = £2178.96, £9995 − £2178.96 = £7816.04. No, he couldn't sell the car and pay off the finance.

Task 5 (extension)

1. Students should find the price of a car, road tax costs, add breakdown, repair costs. (They may not be able to obtain an insurance quotation due to age limitations.)
2. Students should find the cost of the same model by using a price-guide website that lists prices for second-hand cars. Could vary the question by deciding to sell after 1, 1.5 or 2 years.

Improver **

Fish and chips

Learning objectives
- **Representing Level 1/2**: find the information necessary to solve a problem
- **Analysing Level 1/2**: use mathematics to solve problems involving metric units
- **Interpreting Level 1/2**: extract and interpret information from tables, diagrams, charts and graphs

APP
Using and applying mathematics Level 5, Numbers and the number system Level 6, Calculating Level 6, Handling data Level 5

PLTS
Develops Independent enquirers, Team workers, Effective participators

Every child matters outcomes
Be healthy, Enjoy and achieve, Make a positive contribution, Achieve economic well-being

Cross-curricular links
Food technology, Science, English

Underpinning maths
- Writing numbers in standard form
- Reading and interpreting graphs
- Calculating percentage increases and decreases
- Using compound measures

Resources
- *Student book*, page 110–113
- Calculators
- Data sheet: Fish and chips

Useful websites
- www.food.gov.uk
- www.eatwell.gov.uk/healthydiet/nutritionessentials/fishandshellfish
- www.potato.org.uk

Context
Most students will have bought and eaten takeaways, including fish and chips. They may be aware that fried food is unhealthy. They may also be aware that occasionally, health stories relating to the quality of food being produced becomes big news. The tasks include investigating the economics of selling fish and chips, and touches on the environmental issue of over-fishing.

Students compare the fat and calorie content of fish and chips to that of other takeaways, and discover that they might not always be getting what they think.

Lesson plan
This activity will take one lesson. Task 4 (extension) or Task 5 could be set as homework.

Improver **

Starter
- In pairs, students discuss their favourite foods. Ask each pair to report back.

Main activity
- Collate students' responses to make a list of their favourite meals. Discuss which types of food are produced at home, which are takeaways and which are eaten in fast-food outlets.
- Carry out a quick class survey of who has had a takeaway meal during the last week.
- Narrow the survey to fish and chips. Ask who has eaten fish and chips during the last month, and who has eaten fish and chips during the last week. Compare these figures to the national statistic: over half the UK adult population visits a fish and chip shop at least once a month, and 15% of the UK adult population eat fish and chips once or twice a week.
- Discuss with students the difficulties with reading numbers with lots of zeros and how it can be easy to misread them or get the number wrong when keying them into a calculator.
- Ask students if they know of any other ways of representing very large numbers and introduce the idea of standard form. Demonstrate writing numbers in the form $a \times 10^n$ where $1 \le a < 10$ and n is a whole number.
- Distribute the data sheet, which contains various sorts of data about fish and chips.
- **Let students do Task 1**.
- Ask students to compare the fat content of fish and chips to that of the burger and medium fries. According to the figures provided, fish and chips have less than half the fat of the latter.
- Ask students which fish they usually eat. Discuss with them the issue of over-fishing and the associated problem of dwindling supplies.
- **Let students do Task 2**.
- Discuss the cost of fish and chips locally. Explain that prices vary considerably around the country and ask for reasons for such variations. (Answer: Cost of fish and potatoes locally, which in the case of fish might be linked to distance from a fishing port or fish market; competition from other fast-food or takeaway outlets.)
- Discuss the principle of supply and demand: things that are in short supply can be more expensive than things that are more commonly available. This applies to buying and selling on internet auctions, where rare items will cost more. **Let students do Task 3**.
- Discuss Task 4 (extension). Ask students if they have ever thought about what happens to the oil after it has been used to fry fish and chips. Discuss how many times a fish and chip shop uses the oil before changing it. There is more information about the benefits of eating fish on the website given above.
- **Let students do Task 4 (extension)**. Make sure that students read the text before answering the questions.
- Look at Task 5 with students. Read through the article. **Let students do Task 5**, in small groups or as homework.

Plenary
- Discuss the newspaper article with students. How do they feel about it? Would they even know the difference between cod and haddock?
- Discuss which takeaways or fast foods students think are the 'healthiest'.
- Have they ever had a doner kebab? Do they know what is in it? (Answer: Usually lamb, but they may contain other types of meat and very high quantities of fat.)
- Remind students that adding too much salt, and also tomato ketchup (many brands contain a lot of sugar) will make fish and chips a more unhealthy option.

Improver **

Outcomes

- Students will have used mathematics to gain insight into a socially relevant phenomenon.
- Students will have used standard form to deal with large numbers.
- Students will have calculated percentages.
- Students will have used mathematics to look at the economics of running a business.
- Students will have developed ideas to help them become more aware as consumers.

Answers

Task 1

1. 8500 or 8.5×10^3 in the UK, 11 000 or 1.1×10^4 in the UK and Ireland
2. 35 000 or 3.5×10^4
3. 277 000 000 or 2.77×10^8 portions of chips, 300 000 000 or 3×10^8 portions of fish and chips
4. 20.724 g or 2.0724×10^1
5. 66 000 000 000 g = 6.6×10^{10} g, or 66 000 000 kg = 6.6×10^7 kg (It would be sensible to round it to 7×10^7 kg.)
6. 48 g or 4.8×10^1 g

Task 2

1. Cod
2. Herring
3. Between 200 000 tonnes and 250 000 tonnes
4. Haddock
5. 79.4%

Task 3

1. Haddock is cheaper.
2. There are greater stocks, so more are likely to be caught. It may be less popular with customers.
3. 92p for a cod, 74p for a haddock
4. About 95p
5. Roughly 163%
6. The owner has costs of heating and lighting, cooking oil, cooking (electricity) costs, staffing costs, business rates and premises to maintain, possibly advertising and many others.

Task 4 (extension)

1 About £400.

2 Some of the advantages and disadvantages include:

Advantages

Biodiesel is better for the environment as it gives off less harmful fumes.

It comes from renewable sources, unlike petro-diesel, which comes from oil supplies that are dwindling.

Most diesel cars need little or no modification to run on biodiesel.

Set-aside land in the UK could grow crops to produce biodiesel.

Disadvantages

Used cooking oil will not produce enough biodiesel to replace all petro-diesel.

Biodiesel can be made from crops such as rapeseed, but the cost varies enormously according to the crop harvest, and is unlikely to match the cost of petro-diesel.

Task 5

1 **a** They can save up to 57% of the wholesale price of the fish.

   b 250 portions of 400 g = 100 kg of fish.
   100 kg fish costs 100 × £11.75 = £1175
   Fish and chop shop owners can save up to 57% of £1175 ≈ £670

2 **a** The fine, if a shop owner is caught passing off cheap varieties as cod or haddock, is £6000. They would only need to get away with the deception for 9 days to make as much money as they would be fined. Their reputation would be harmed but they might take the risk, to increase profits.

   b Students should discuss the impact on human health of exposure to bacterial contamination and industrial waste. They could use internet searches to collect evidence.

Advanced ***

The Milky Way

Learning objectives
- **Representing Level 2**: identify information needed from a table and choose from a range of mathematics to solve problems
- **Analysing Level 2**: apply mathematics in an organised way to find solutions, and use appropriate checking procedures
- **Interpreting Level 2**: explain what results show, draw conclusions and explain findings pictorially, as appropriate

APP
Evidence for Using and applying mathematics Level 4, Numbers and the number system Level 4, Calculating Level 4, Algebra Level 5, Handling data Level 3

PLTS
Independent enquirers, Creative thinkers, Team workers, Reflective learners

Every child matters outcomes
Enjoy and achieve, Make a positive contribution

Cross-curricular links
Science, ICT, History, English

Underpinning maths
- Using standard form
- Extracting information from tables
- Rearranging and using formulae
- Calculating volumes
- Calculating with time

Resources
- *Student book*, page 114–117
- Data sheet 1: Planetary data
- Data sheet 2: Teacher reference
- Scientific calculators, rulers
- A3 paper (or larger if available)
- Compasses, string and pins or pegs (optional, to draw ellipse)
- Internet access

Context
All students should be familiar with the terms **galaxy** and the **Milky Way** and with the idea of **planets** orbiting the **Sun**. They should realise that the planets are a long way away; they may be unfamiliar with the actual distances and the time it takes, even for light, to travel these distances. In this activity, they will find the distances from the Earth to other planets in our galaxy. They will also compare the speeds of light and sound.

Advanced ***

Lesson plan
This activity takes two lessons. It could be done in one lesson by focusing on Tasks 1 and 4. Task 5 (extension) could be done as homework.

Starter
- Ask students to name as many planets as they can in our solar system. Then ask if they know their order from the Sun. Ask if they know which planet we are from the Sun and if they have heard of the television programme 'Third rock from the Sun'. Why have they called it this? (Answer: Earth is the third planet from the Sun) Ask students if there is a difference between the speed at which light and sound travel. (Answer: Yes, light travels much faster.)
- List the planets on the board, in order of distance from the Sun.

   Mercury **V**enus **E**arth **M**ars **A**steroids **J**upiter **S**aturn **U**ranus **N**eptune **P**luto

   Ask students to think of a mnemonic to remember them. A suggestion is:

   My **V**ery **E**nergetic **M**aiden **A**unt **J**ust **S**wam **U**nder **N**orth **P**ier

   Remind students that asteroids are not planets but there is a large group of them that circle the Sun in an orbital motion.
- Explain that distances in science are always measured in metres. The distances between planets are so big we use standard form. Give the example on the board that the distance from the Sun to the Earth is about 150 000 000 km × 1000 (to change to metres) and is therefore 1.5×10^{11} metres in standard form. Ask students to convert the distances from the Sun given on data sheet 1 into metres in standard form, perhaps asking individual students to convert one distance each. Address any difficulties students have with standard form ($a \times 10^n$, where $1 \leq a \leq 10$ and n is an integer).

Main activity
- Discuss with students how vast the universe must be and suggest that there could be several thousand billion (10^{12}) stars. Each star is a sun and may have its own planets in orbit, just like our Sun. Explain that a light year is the distance light travels in a year, and is not just a term made up and used in science fiction. Light travels 3×10^8 m in one second. Explain that, if they were to work out the number of seconds in a year, then multiply by 3×10^8, they would find the distance light travels in a year.
- Read Task 1 with students. Give students an example of using the formula for the volume of a sphere ($V = \frac{4}{3}\pi r^3$), so the volume of a football of diameter 0.3 m is 0.014 m³. Volumes of planets will be very, very large.
- **Let students do Task 1.** Check students' volumes before they try to calculate the density. Answers are given on data sheet 2, for your reference. Explain to students the term **composition**, and that some planets are actually composed of, or made up of gases and do not have any land or solid matter. Tell students to compare the size of each planet with that of the Earth, expressing it as a decimal number.
- Read Task 2 with students. Explain that, because of the distance to the stars and the time it takes the light to get to us, the real positions of the stars have changed by the time we see them. Tell students the stars don't really move across the sky. We are rotating, so we move under them.
- **Let students do Task 2.** Remind them how to rearrange the formula if needed. Remind students that the distance from Earth to the Sun is approximately 1.5×10^{11} metres.

Advanced ✱✱✱

- Read Task 3 with students. Explain that they will need to represent the orbits of the planets as circles. They must use a common scale for all the orbits. Ask students which measurement from data sheet 1 they need to use. (Answer: Distance from the Sun) These distances are given in millions of kilometres. Suggest that students treat the numbers as if they were centimetres, and divide by 300 (using A3 paper) to find the lengths to use.

- **Let students do Task 3**. Check that they use the correct values from data sheet 1, and that they have the correct answers before they start to draw their circular orbits. Supervise students as they use compasses. Make sure they use a single point to represent the Sun and that all circles are drawn from this point. Help students who are less dextrous to draw the smaller orbits of the planets. Students could use different colours to show the different orbits.

- Explain that visible light, which we can see, is part of the **electromagnetic spectrum**. Other parts of the electromagnetic spectrum include radio waves, used for transmitting information such as radio broadcasts. Radio waves are also used to activate remote locking systems, controlled by car key fobs. **Extend this part of the activity** by encouraging interested students to do an internet search to find out more.

- Read Task 5 with students, reminding them that, on bonfire night, after they see the fireworks explode, there is a small delay before they hear the noise. This is because sound travels much more slowly through air than light does. If you want to go into more detail you can tell them sound travels at different speeds depending on the medium through which it is travelling. When you are under water everything sounds different because sound travels faster through water than through air.

- **Let students do Task 4**. For question 1, make sure they change kilometres to metres before finding the time. Explain what the negative power on their calculator screen means. For question 2b, they must convert metres to kilometres, then kilometres to miles.

- Students could work in pairs or small groups to do question 3. Do not give too much help for this question. Let students try to work out that the distance between the Earth and Pluto needs to be divided by the speed of light. Do not comment yet on whether Robbie will crash to an untimely mechanical death at the bottom of the cliff. Students should divide 250 m by 0.5, or use an alternative appropriate method, to get an answer of 500 seconds.

- Hold a class discussion on students' answers to question 3, but expect most of the class to think the probe will survive because they have not remembered the time it took for the initial picture to get to the screen on Earth.

- Discuss Task 5 (extension) with students. Ask how long a space journey they think would be reasonable (for example, a year? several years?) Discuss how they can work out which planets it would be possible to reach in this time in the NASA space shuttle. Do they think space travel to all the planets would be possible at the speed of light? How could they work this out? **Let students do Task 5 (extension)**. Remind them that Earth is the third planet from the Sun and that they could use their drawing of the orbits to help them with this task.

Plenary

- Ask students if they think space travel to distant planets or other solar systems is possible. Find out how many students feel comfortable about using standard form. Ask if they think it is better than using ordinary numbers when the numbers are so big.

- Ask the class if anyone can work out approximately how far away lightning would be if they counted eight seconds before hearing the bang. (Answer: 5 seconds to a mile, or 3 seconds to a kilometre, so less than two miles away.)

Advanced ***

Outcomes

- Students will have used maths to find information from a table.
- Students will have constructed diagrams to show information clearly.
- Students will have interpreted the solutions to their calculations and given conclusions in numerical form.

Answers

Task 1

1. Venus, $1.5 \times 10^{11} - 1.08 \times 10^{11} = 4.2 \times 10^{10}$ m or $150 - 108 = 42$ million km

   Pluto, $5.91 \times 10^{12} - 1.5 \times 10^{11} = 5.76 \times 10^{12}$ m or $5910 - 150 = 5760$ million km

2. a See data sheet 2
   b See data sheet 2
   c Mercury and Venus, because they have similar densities.
   d Earth = 1, Mercury = 33 ÷ 598 = 0.1, Venus = 0.8, Mars = 0.1, Jupiter = 317.7, Saturn = 95.2, Uranus = 14.5, Neptune = 17.2, Pluto = 0.0

Task 2

1. $3 \times 10^8 \times 2.58 \div 2 = 3.87 \times 10^8$ m = 387 000 km
2. $1.5 \times 10^{11} \div 3 \times 10^8 = 500$ seconds, $500 \div 60 = 8.33\ldots = 8$ minutes 20 seconds

Task 3

1. a If using A3 paper, divide radius of each orbit (distance from Sun) by 300 to give radius (in cm) to be drawn. All circles have same centre point.

   Circle diameters of: M = 2 mm, V = 4 mm, E = 5 mm, M = 8 mm, J = 2.6 cm, S = 4.8 cm, U = 9.6 cm, N = 15 cm and P = 19.7 cm (Students may not be able to draw the smaller circles with great accuracy.)

   b Max = Earth + Saturn (opposite ends of their orbits) = 150 + 1430 = 1580 million km

   Min = Saturn − Earth (closest in their orbits) = 1430 − 150 = 1280 million km

Task 4

1. a 300 000 000 ÷ 330 ≈ 1 million times faster
   b 1.6 km = 1600 m, $1600 \div 3 \times 10^8 = 5.3 \times 10^{-6}$ seconds or 0.000 005 3 s

2. a 1600 ÷ 330 = 4.8484 = 5 seconds
   b 330 × 17 = 5610 m
   5620 ÷ 1000 = 5.6 km
   5.6 ÷ 1.6 = 3.5 miles away

3. a Time = distance ÷ speed = $7.8 \times 10^{10} \div 3 \times 10^8 = 260$ seconds
   b 250 m at 0.5 m/s will take 500 seconds, time for image to get back to Earth = 260 (not including thinking and reaction time), return signal to STOP of 260 seconds, time = 2 × 260 = 520 seconds. Robbie will have driven over the cliff 20 seconds before he got the command.
   c Sensible comments, many will have forgotten the time for the images to get to Earth.

Advanced ***

Task 5 (extension)

The table shows how long it would take to reach each planet from Earth using the NASA space shuttle.

Planet	Distance from Earth (m) Maximum	Minimum	Time to travel to planet (in days) Maximum	Minimum
Mercury	2.08×10^{11}	9.20×10^{10}	3.09×10^{2}	1.37×10^{2}
Venus	2.58×10^{11}	4.20×10^{10}	3.83×10^{2}	6.2×10^{1}
Earth				
Mars	3.78×10^{11}	7.80×10^{10}	5.61×10^{2}	1.16×10^{2}
Jupiter	9.28×10^{11}	6.28×10^{11}	1.38×10^{3}	9.32×10^{2}
Saturn	1.58×10^{12}	1.28×10^{12}	2.34×10^{3}	1.90×10^{3}
Uranus	3.02×10^{12}	2.72×10^{12}	4.48×10^{3}	4.04×10^{3}
Neptune	4.65×10^{12}	4.35×10^{12}	6.90×10^{3}	6.45×10^{3}
Pluto	6.06×10^{12}	5.76×10^{12}	8.99×10^{3}	8.55×10^{3}

Depending on how long they decide is reasonable for a space journey, students may conclude that travel to Mercury, Venus, Mars and possibly Jupiter is possible in the NASA space shuttle.

The ability to travel at the speed of light would make greater distances much more possible. For example, the minimum distance from Earth to Pluto would take only $5.76 \times 10^{12} \div 3 \times 10^{8}$ = 19 200 seconds = approximately 5.3 hours, in comparison to 8.44×10^{3} days = 23 years!

Advanced ***

On your bike

Learning objectives
- **Representing Level 2**: recognise that mathematics can be used to solve real-life problems and identify the mathematical methods required to solve such problems
- **Analysing Level 2**: apply appropriate mathematics to find solutions
- **Interpreting Level 2**: interpret and communicate solutions to multistage practical problems and draw conclusions using mathematical justifications

APP
Evidence for Using and applying mathematics Level 8, Algebra Level 8

PLTS
Develops Creative thinkers, Effective participators

Every child matters outcomes
Make a positive contribution

Cross-curricular links
History, Design and technology, Science

Underpinning maths
- Ratio
- Rearranging formulae
- Setting up and solving equations
- Real-life problems
- Real-life graphs
- Finding the equation of a line from its graph

Resources
- *Student book*, pages 118–123
- Data sheet 1: Frame sizes
- Data sheet 2: On your bike
- Calculators
- Bicycle catalogues (optional)
- Internet access (optional)

Context
- Students are likely to have ridden bicycles, even if they have never paid attention to the gears, size of wheels or the tyre pressure.
- This activity gives students the opportunity to explore the mathematics that is relevant to choosing, riding and maintaining bicycles.

Lesson plan
This activity takes two lessons. Task 6 would make a good homework exercise, and could be done in pairs or small groups with students presenting their work to the rest of the class during the next lesson.

Advanced ***

Starter

- Explain to students that this activity is all about the mathematics of bicycles. Ask students what mathematics they think may be involved in choosing, maintaining or riding a bicycle. Make a list to return to at the end of the lesson.
- Tell students that when you choose a bicycle you should consider the frame size. Ask students to look at data sheet 1.
- Point out that it would be difficult for a shop assistant working in a cycle shop to memorise all these different frame measures for different customer heights. Ask students how they might use mathematics to make it easier. Suggest that they might find the ratio of the middle height and middle frame size for each entry in the table.
- Remind students that to compare the ratios they need to be in the same format, either $1 : n$ or $n : 1$. Work with students to find the first ratio $150 : 47.5 = 3.16 : 1$.
- Let students find the other ratios of rider height : frame size.
- Ask students to imagine they were working in a cycle shop. What would they do to help each customer choose the appropriate bicycle frame size? Students should say that they would measure the customer's height and divide by 3.2.

Main activity

- Tell students that ratios have always been important when thinking about bicycles, e.g. ratios of wheel size or gear ratios.
- **Let students do Task 1**, questions 1 and 2. Discuss the new names they have invented for the penny-farthing, based on their findings.
- Look at Task 1, question 3 with students. Discuss how to work out the distance a bicycle moves forward for one turn of the pedals on a penny-farthing, using only the wheel diameter. (Answer: Students should already know that the circumference of a circle is πd.)
- For Task 2 (extension) encourage students to use the equations they set up in Task 1, question 3 to help them. **Let students do Task 2**.
- To lead into Task 3, ask students about pedalling a bicycle up a really steep hill. Tell them it can be made easier by choosing the right gear. Explain that gears are simply cogs with different numbers of teeth that enable us to move our bicycles forward different distances for each turn of the pedals. This means that if they choose a low gear when going uphill, then a rear gear wheel with an increased number of teeth is selected. In practice, this means the back wheel goes more slowly but allows us to turn the pedals more easily.
- As an example, suggest that they set their gears so the chain is around a front gear wheel with 52 teeth and a rear gear wheel with 26 teeth. Ask students to find the gear ratio of the front gear wheel to the rear gear wheel, giving the answer in the form $n : 1$. Students should answer $2 : 1$. Tell students that this means that the rear wheel turns twice for one revolution of the pedals. Ask students how far the bicycle would move with one turn of the pedals, if the wheels are 26 inches in diameter. (Answer: $2 \times \pi \times 26$)
- **Let students do Task 3**. You may need to remind them about imperial measures, in particular, 12 inches = 1 foot, 3 feet = 1 yard, 1760 yards = 1 mile. They should work out for themselves that there are 63 360 inches in 1 mile.
- **Let students do Task 4 (extension)**. Encourage them to match the bicycles to the correct activity only after they have done all their mathematical calculations to inform their decisions.
- Distribute data sheet 2. Ask students to discuss with a partner what they notice about the graphs and the axes.

Advanced ***

- Ask students to share their observations. Students may make reference to the units for tyre pressure. This unit is **pounds per square inch** (psi) and is the amount of force that is exerted on an area of one square inch. Students should also notice that the axis does not begin at zero.

- Read the introduction to Task 5 with students. Ask them to look at the linear graph for tyre width 37 mm on data sheet 2. Then ask students to discuss with the person next to them the method they would use to find the equation for this line, where x is the load on the wheel and y is the tyre pressure.

- Discuss with students their methods. They should make reference to $y = mx + c$ where m is the gradient and c is the y-intercept. However, they should also note that because the y-axis does not begin at zero they cannot use the y-intercept. Therefore, discuss with the students identifying two points on the line, and using them to work out the gradient, m. Then substitute the x-values and y-values into the equation $y = mx + c$ to work out c.

- Ask students to identify two points on the line for tyre width 37 mm, e.g. (100, 61) and (60, 44).

- Remind students how to calculate the gradient $\frac{\text{change in } y}{\text{change in } x}$, e.g. $\frac{61-44}{100-60} = 0.43$.

- Now ask students to substitute their gradients and the x-values and y-values for one of their points into $y = mx + c$, e.g. $61 = (0.43 \times 100) + c$, so $c = 18$. Suggest students substitute the x and y values for the other point into the equation $y = 0.43x + 18$ to check the value of c.

- Now ask students to read 'How to use data sheet 2'. Then work with the person next to them to use their equation and calculate tyre pressure for the tyre on each bicycle wheel with a total load of 96 kg and tyre width 37 mm. (Answer: Rear wheel: $0.65 \times 96 = 62.4$ kg, minimum tyre pressure $= 0.43 \times 62.4 + 18 = 45$ psi; front wheel: $0.35 \times 96 = 33.6$ kg, minimum tyre pressure $= 0.43 \times 33.6 + 18 = 32$ psi)

- **Let students do Task 5**. Remind them to take account of the total weight load. This should include the bicycle itself, as well as the rider and any luggage.

- Encourage students to look back over the work they have done in this activity. Discuss with them the parts of the bicycle they have considered and the mathematics they have used to learn more about them.

- **Let students do Task 6**. It would be a good paired or small-group activity. It may help students to have some bicycle specifications to refer to. These can be obtained from catalogues published by bicycle retailers or printed from the internet.

Plenary

- Return to the class list from the Starter to the lesson, itemising the mathematics students thought may be involved in choosing, maintaining or riding a bicycle.
- Ask students if, having undertaken this activity, there is anything they could add to this list.
- Ask students if they can think of any other information about bicycles where mathematics may be required to analyse performance. Students may give examples such as braking distances in different weathers; comparisons between types of bicycles (e.g. recumbent bicycles, unicycles and tricycles); statistics on numbers of people who use bicycles in different countries.

Outcomes

o Students will have used mathematics to gain insight into the history, selection, maintenance and workings of a bicycle.

o Students will have used ratio and equations of lines to understand the mathematics of physics, in particular gear ratios and pressure.

Advanced ***

Answers

Task 1

1. large wheel diameter: small wheel diameter range from 42 : 20 to 60 : 14, that is from 2.1 : 1 to 4.3 : 1

   Penny-diameter: farthing diameter = 30.81 : 20 = 1.54 : 1

   Therefore, the ratio between the wheels of the penny-farthing bicycle is never representative of the ratio between the coins it is named after.

2. a 25 pence or £5 diameter : half-penny diameter = 38.61 : 17.14 = 2.25 : 1

   25 pence or £5 diameter: 5p = 38.61 : 18 = 2.15 : 1

   b Students may give the bicycle nicknames to reflect this finding, such as the twenty-five-half, or the five-five.

3. a $s = \pi d$ b $s = p\pi d$ c $p = \dfrac{s}{\pi d}$

Task 2 (extension)

1. 54 inches
2. 51 inches
3. 44 times

Task 3

1. Highest gear = 42 : 12 = 3.5 : 1; Lowest gear = 22 : 30 = 0.73 : 1
2. Distance in the highest gear = 285.9 inches; Distance in the lowest gear = 59.6 inches
3. Speed ranges from 3.4 miles per hour to 16.2 miles per hour

Task 4 (extension)

Bicycle A: Highest gear = 26 : 32 ≈ 0.81 : 1; Lowest gear = 56 : 10 = 5.6 : 1; Speed ranges for bicycle of wheel diameter 28 inches = 4.0 miles per hour to 28.0 miles per hour. Activity 2.

Bicycle B: Highest gear = 24 : 38 = 0.63 : 1; Lowest gear = 30 : 14 = 2.14 : 1; Speed ranges for bicycle of wheel diameter 22 inches = 2.5 miles per hour to 8.4 miles per hour. Activity 3.

Bicycle C: Highest gear = 20 : 28 = 0.71 : 1; Lowest gear = 46 : 15 = 3.07 : 1; Speed ranges for bicycle of wheel diameter 26 inches = 3.3 miles per hour to 14.2 miles per hour. Activity 1.

Task 5

1. For tyre width 37 mm: $y = 0.43x + 18$; For tyre width 32 mm: $y = 0.6x + 18$; For tyre width 28 mm: $y = 0.65x + 31$; For tyre width 25 mm: $y = 0.85x + 35$; For tyre width 22 mm: $y = 1.08x + 42$; For tyre width 20 mm: $y = 1.21x + 56$

2. a Bicycle A: rear wheel load = 60.45 kg, tyre pressure = 129 psi; front wheel load = 32.55 kg, tyre pressure = 95 psi

   b Bicycle B: rear wheel load = 57.85 kg, tyre pressure = 53 psi; front wheel load = 31.15 kg, tyre pressure = 37 psi

   c Bicycle C: rear wheel load = 61.75 kg, tyre pressure = 87 psi; front wheel load = 33.25 kg; tyre pressure = 63 psi

Task 6

Students should at least make reference in their training manuals to heights of customers and recommended bicycle frame size (as discussed in the Starter to this lesson); gear ratios, wheel diameters in relation to speed; and tyre width and corresponding tyre pressures.

Advanced ***

Water usage

Learning objectives
- **Representing Level 2**: find information to solve the problem, using appropriate tables and the internet
- **Analysing Level 2**: work through the calculations and check that answers make sense
- **Interpreting Level 2**: use results to produce graphs, drawings and numerical lists to explain findings and draw conclusions

APP
Evidence for Using and applying mathematics Level 7, Numbers and the number system Level 3, Algebra Level 5, Shape, space and measures Level 6, Handling data Level 8

PLTS
Independent enquirers, Self-managers, Team workers, Creative thinkers

Every child matters outcomes
Make a positive contribution, Achieve economic well-being, Enjoy and achieve

Cross-curricular links
Science, Construction and the built environment, English

Underpinning maths
- Converting units in different systems
- Extracting information from diagrams
- Calculating averages
- Constructing cumulative frequency graphs
- Producing box plots
- Calculating volumes of composite shapes
- Carry out effective research

Resources
- *Student Book*, pages 124–126
- Calculators, graph paper
- Internet access

Context
All students should be familiar with bathroom fittings. They will be familiar with internet searches and with looking for best prices on goods. Some may be familiar with methods for heating water, such as combi boilers or hot-water cylinder systems.

Lesson plan
This activity takes one lesson. Task 3 (extension) can be set as homework, perhaps over a week.

Advanced ***

Starter
- Explain that there are different methods of supplying hot water to the taps and showers in a house. One of the main methods is through a combi boiler, by which water is heated only when it is needed. The other requires a hot-water tank, which is heated either electrically or from a gas or solid fuel boiler. The tank is insulated to keep the water hot. Explain that as water flows out of the tank and is used, it is refilled automatically by the cold-water mains feed.
- Ask students if they know whether they have a hot-water tank, where it is and how big it is. Ask them to estimate its size and its capacity. Ask students if they have a bath, shower or combination of the two at home.

Main activity
- Read Task 1 with students. Remind them that use of the ≤ or ≥ signs ensures that no value can go into two ranges. Explain that the diagram simply shows the pump between the tank and the shower.
- Remind students how to draw a cumulative frequency curve. Demonstrate, on the board, and make sure they know how to derive the information for a box plot from the graph. Remind students to use the middle values when calculating an estimate of the mean from the data in the table.
- **Let students do Task 1**. Make sure they have correctly added the number of pumps. Distribute graph paper. Facilitate learning and give feedback and praise for good work.
- Read through Task 2 with students. Talk about water temperatures and ask students for examples of two facts. Use appropriate questions to elicit that water freezes at 0° C (Celsius) and boils at 100° C. Explain that most people prefer to take a shower at a temperature of about 45–50° C. In a dual-feed shower, hot and cold water are mixed before they come out of the shower head. Remind students that the volume of a cube with sides of 10 cm is 10 × 10 × 10 cm^3 = 1000 cm^3 which is 1 litre. Draw an analogy with a car engine, which may be described, for example, as a 1.0 litre engine or 1000cc. Direct students to look at the table, which shows flow rates in litres per second. Write the formula for the volume of a cylinder and the volume of a sphere on the board. Discuss with students the round part on top of the cylinder and ensure they recognise it as approximately half a sphere.
- **Let students do Task 2**. Walk round the class and make sure students are correctly converting time in seconds to minutes and seconds. Make sure they have found the volume of a sphere then halved the value and added it to the volume of the cylinder. Remind students how to find the radius of the cylinder as half the diameter of the base. Students need to multiply litres per second by 60 to convert to litres per minute.
- Read Task 3 (extension) with students. Discuss uses of water in and round the home. For example, if younger siblings have a paddling pool and students know the volume of water it contains, how could they find the time it would take to fill it if they know the mains water flow rate from the tap? **Let students do Task 3 (extension)** as homework.

Plenary
- Discuss with students what they have learnt about water usage in the home. Are they surprised by how much water a shower can use? Discuss why it is important that we reduce the amount of water we use.

Outcomes
o Students will have used maths to identify the information needed to complete the task.
o Students will have used a range of mathematics to find solutions.
o Students will have interpreted the solutions to their calculations and drawn conclusions.

Advanced ***

Answers

Task 1

1 a

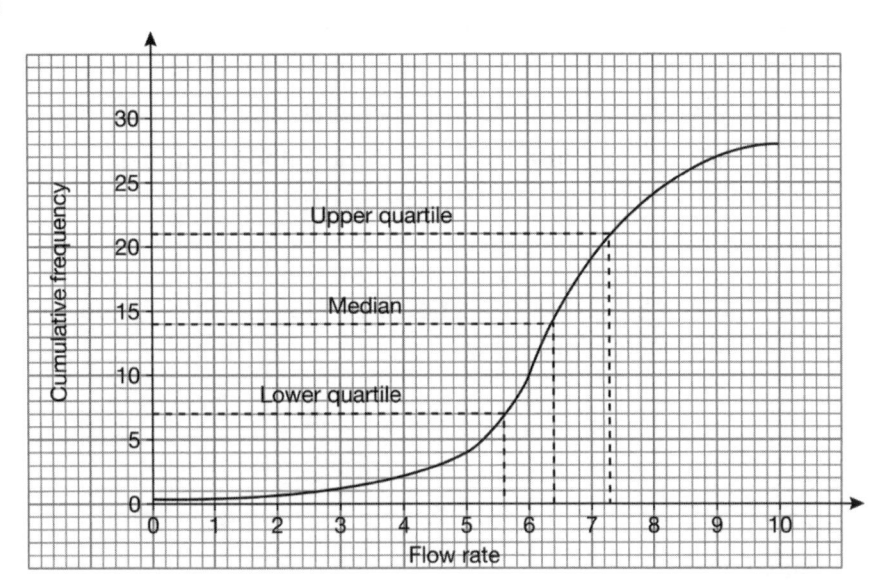

b

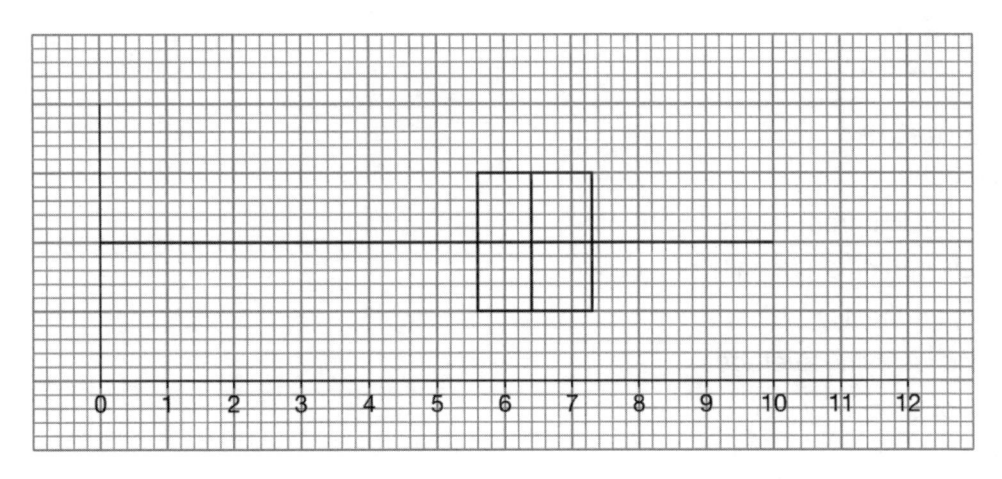

c Median flow rate is 6.4 litres/min

2 a Estimated mean = 6.23 litres/min

b The mean and median are very similar with a difference of 0.17 litre/min

Task 2

1 a 520 − 120 seconds = 400 ÷ 60 minutes = 6 minutes 40 seconds

b 6 minutes 40 seconds = $6\frac{2}{3}$ minutes; $6\frac{2}{3}$ minutes × 6.23 litres/min = 41.5 litres

2 a volume = $\pi r^2 h + (\frac{4}{3}\pi r^3) \div 2$ = 137 444.68 + 32 724.92 = 170 169.6 cm^3 ÷ 1000 = 170 litres

b 170 ÷ 6.23 = 27 minutes

c No, because the flow rate into the tank is greater than the flow rate out of the tank. (This assumes that water is flowing out only to the shower.)

3 0.1 × 60 = 6 litres/minute compared to 6.23, approximately the same flow rate.

Task 3 (extension)

Students should present the results of their investigations in an engaging manner.

Advanced ***

Crash investigation

Learning objectives
- **Representing Level 2**: understand non-routine problems and identify the mathematical methods needed to solve them
- **Analysing Level 2**: apply a range of mathematics to find solutions
- **Interpreting Level 2**: interpret and communicate solutions to multistage practical problems in an unfamiliar context and situation

APP
Evidence for Using and applying mathematics Level 7, Numbers and the number system Level 7, Calculating Level 5, Algebra Level 5, Handling data Level 5

PLTS
Independent enquirers, Effective participators

Every child matters outcomes
Make a positive contribution, Stay safe

Cross-curricular links
Science, English, Media studies

Underpinning maths
- Interpreting graphs
- Extracting information from tables
- Converting between different units of measures
- Understanding probability
- Calculating and justifying average
- Using direct proportionality
- Using formula
- Displaying data graphically

Resources
- *Student book*, pages 127–129
- Data sheet: Fatalities on UK roads
- Scientific calculators, graph paper
- Internet access (optional)

Context
All students should be familiar with road hazards, road accidents and national speed limits on the roads around built-up areas. Some students will be familiar with the range of speed limits across UK roads. All students should be familiar with miles per hour as a measure of speed.

Lesson plan
This activity takes one lesson. Most of the tasks could be done by students working in groups. Task 3 question 3 could be set for homework.

Advanced ***

Starter
- Ask students what the speed limits are around town, on single carriageways, on country roads and on motorways. Ask if they think reducing the speed in built-up areas to 20 mph is reasonable or if they think a decrease of 10 mph doesn't make much difference.
- Explain that on the continent in Europe and Ireland speed limits are given in kilometres per hour (km/h). In science lessons, they may work in metres per second (m/s) and will need to know how to convert between units.

Main activity
- Discuss the different types of accident that happen on our roads. Include cars and motorbikes hitting pedestrians, low-speed accidents, high-speed accidents involving just one vehicle and multi-car pile-ups on motorways. Explain that, as the number of vehicles on the roads has increased, you would expect the probability of anyone being involved in an accident to have increased, but this has not been the case.
- Discuss with students the measures the Government has introduced to reduce the incidence of accidents. Include the compulsory wearing of seatbelts, drink–driving laws, reduced speed limits and, more recently, speed cameras.
- Read Task 1 with students. Remind them that if they have to explain an answer they should use the data provided; questions in maths rarely rely on their opinion.
- **Let students do Task 1**. Tell them to read carefully what they are being asked to do, in question 2. Discuss what method they need to use to compare the figures. (Answer: percentages)
- Remind students to convert miles per hour to kilometres per hour before reading the information in the cumulative frequency diagram. Ask students how many kilometres there are in a mile. (Answer: 1.6 km.)
- Discuss the use of speed cameras on the roads. Explain that there are three ways in which speed cameras can detect a speeding motorist. Gatso and mobile cameras use a radar or laser beam, directed at the passing vehicle. The beam bounces back to the camera, giving the exact speed of the vehicle. Less common Truvelo and DS2 systems use loops in the road that trigger a speed camera if a vehicle is moving too fast. The third method is the one used by average speed cameras. Explain generally about these but do not, at first, say how they actually work. Ask the students to explain how they think an average speed camera works on, for example, a motorway. (Answer: They take two photographs, at two points a fixed distance apart, then find the time it takes the vehicle to travel between these two points and use this information to calculate the average speed.)
- Read Task 2 with students. Andy has clearly broken the speed limit but, based on averages, why might he think he should not get a speeding ticket? Remind students how to calculate the mode, mean and median. Write definitions on the board, if necessary.
- **Let students do Task 2**. If necessary, stress that it is the *average* speed over the *whole* distance for which the speed restrictions are in place, not 'snapshot' values of the speed as they pass each camera. Someone who slows down to go past the cameras, but speeds up between them, is unlikely to get away with speeding.
- Read Task 3 with students. Introduce the idea of proportionality, giving as an example the basic formula, $F = ma$, which means that the force, F, is proportional to the acceleration, a. In simple terms, the faster you run, the more it hurts if you collide with a lamppost. The acceleration increases at the same rate as the force with which you hit the post. Explain that m, the mass, is constant; you don't get lighter or heavier while you are running. Show students the

Advanced ***

notation for writing 'force is proportional to the acceleration', $F \propto a$. If the mass is constant, then $F = ka$ where k = mass. It is usual to use k for the **constant of proportionality**.

- **Let students do Task 3**. Remind them that when they have generated a formula with a constant, k, they need to find the value of the constant. Then they can use their value for k to find the answer to question 2. Check that students have the correct value for k before they start question 2. When they rearrange the formula, check that they have $v = \sqrt{\dfrac{D}{k}}$. Each car, taking into consideration its weight, tread on the tyres and road conditions, will give a different value for the constant, k. Explain to students that they will not have taken the driver's thinking distance into account in their calculations. Discuss suitable methods for displaying the stopping distances from stationary to 100 mph (e.g. a line graph).

Plenary

- Ask students for examples of speed limits and where they are found. Ask students if they think it is ever acceptable to exceed speed limits. Ask if they agree with reducing speed in built-up areas and let them explain their reasons.

Outcomes

o   Students will have used maths to identify a situation and identified the methods needed to find solutions.
o   Students will have given opinions based on factual information.
o   Students will have investigated a range of maths to solve a problem.
o   Students will have interpreted the solutions to their calculations and drawn conclusions.

Answers

Task 1

1   There has been a downward trend. 'All road users' has dropped from just over 7000 to 3000 casualties while 'pedestrians' has fallen less, from about 3000 to just over 500.

   Additional: The total number of deaths in road accidents fell by 7% to 2946 in 2007 from 3172 in 2006. However, the number of fatalities has remained fairly constant over the last 10 years.

2   a   The table below shows that, in all years, the greatest risk of fatality was for motorcyclists, with the percentage risk being highest in 2006 (60.6%) and lowest in 2005 (57.9%). Of the types of transport listed, the safest was the car, with only 1.4% risk of fatality in 2006 and only 1.3% risk in 2007. Overall, the numbers of fatalities **per billion kilometres** stayed the same over the four-year period and the relative risks from the different forms of transport were also similar over the period. There was no discernible trend. Students' answers should include some or all of this summary, including numerical analysis. Discuss why the rounded percentages do not always total exactly 100%.

	2004		2005		2006		2007	
Type of transport	Number of fatalities	% of total	Number of fatalities	% of total	Number of fatalities	% of total	Number of fatalities	% of total
Motorcycle	105	60.1	97	57.9	107	60.6	97	58.0
Pedestrian	35	20.0	35	20.9	36	20.4	36	21.5
Bicycle	32	18.3	33	19.7	31	17.6	32	19.1
Car	2.6	1.5	2.6	1.6	2.4	1.4	2.2	1.3
Totals	174.6	99.9	167.6	100.1	176.4	100	167.2	100.9

Advanced ***

b The second table in the task shows total fatalities in 2007 for the same modes of transport as in the first table. The table appears to show that the bicycle was the safest form of transport, with only 157 fatalities (6.5%), while car travellers were subject to 1257 fatalities (51.6%). These figures appear to contradict those in the first table, especially since car travel accounts for over half of all fatalities in 2007. The solution is that, as shown in the first table, the number of fatalities relates to the greater distances involved in car travel. From this point of view, cars are relatively safe and bicycles, which are used mainly for short journeys, are less safe (19.1% of all listed fatalities per billion kilometres).

3 a For this data, the higher the collision speed the greater the change of fatal accidents.

Students need to convert speed. 30 mph × 1.6 = 48 km/h, 40 mph × 1.6 = 64 km/h, 60 mph × 1.6 = 96 km/h

48 km/h: an answer of about 0.35; 64 km/h: an answer of about 0.8; 96 km/h: an answer of 1.0.

b The cumulative frequency diagram shows that a relatively small increase in speed leads to a much greater increase in incidence of fatal accidents. If the limit is reduced from 30 mph to 20 mph it results in the probability decreasing from about 0.4 to 0.1.

Task 2

Using the speeds Andy noticed as he drove, his mode speed was 50 mph, the median 50 mph and the mean 50.7 mph. Two of these averages do not exceed the speed limit; the mean does, but only slightly. His actual average speed over the 9 miles was $9 \div \frac{9.5}{60} = 56.8$ mph (remember, time is in hours), so Andy should get a speeding ticket.

Task 3

1 a $D \propto v^2 \Rightarrow D = kv^2$

b $D = 33.33$ ft, $v = 30$ mph, $33.33 = k \times 30^2$, $33.33 \div 900 = k$, $k = 0.037$

2 Speed, $v = \sqrt{\frac{D}{k}} = \sqrt{\frac{50}{0.037}} = 36.8$ mph

3

Stopping distances

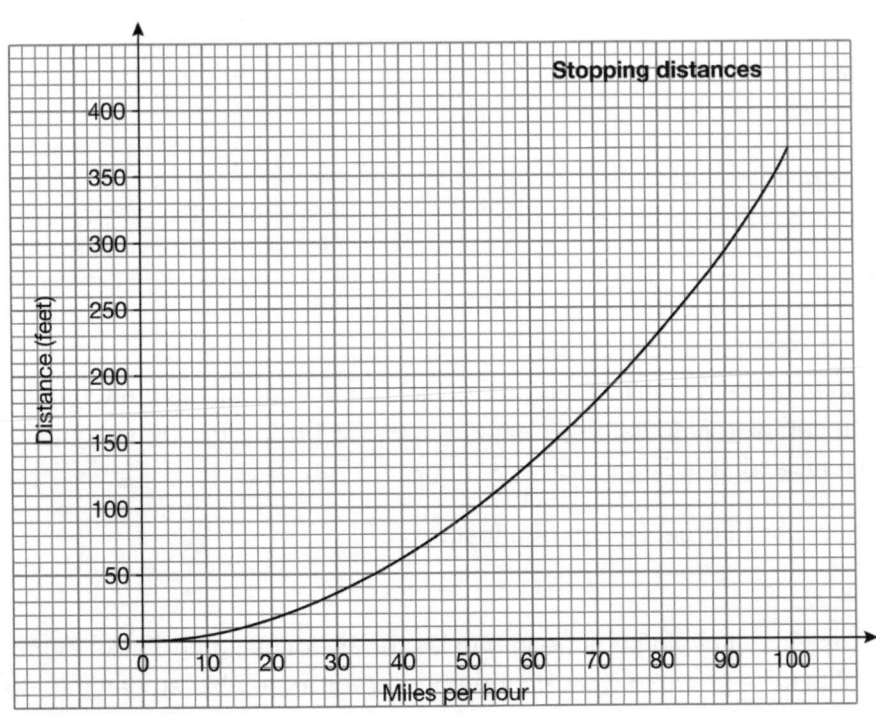

Students should notice that stopping distances do not increase linearly. The stopping distance more than doubles from 70 mph to 100 mph.

Advanced ***

Glastonbury Festival

Learning objectives
- **Representing Level 2**: use metric and imperial conversions and draw graphs to find solutions
- **Analysing Level 2**: find areas of trapeziums and pentagons; calculate moving averages
- **Interpreting Level 2**: interpret data to spot trends and extrapolate

APP
Evidence of Using and applying mathematics Level 6, Numbers and the number system Level 7, Calculating Level 8, Shape, space and measure Level 7, Handling data Level 6

PLTS
Develops Independent enquirers, Reflective learners, Team workers, Effective participators

Every child matters outcomes
Stay safe, Be healthy, Enjoy and achieve, Make a positive contribution, Achieve economic well-being

Cross-curricular links,
Music, Economics, Media studies, ICT, Design and technology

Underpinning maths
- Calculating percentage change
- Reverse percentages
- Calculating areas of rectangles and triangles
- Trigonometry
- Converting between metric and imperial units
- Estimating
- Calculating moving averages
- Extrapolation from graphs

Resources
- *Student book*, pages 130–133
- Calculators
- Internet access (optional)

Context
Many students will have an interest in festivals, and a significant number will have attended one. Some may also have been camping in tents. Their experiences will be useful when estimating camping space around a tent, and standing space at a stage.

The task touches on the successful organisation of a festival.

Lesson plan
This activity will take two lessons. It could be done in one lesson by focusing on Tasks 2 and 5. Task 3 (extension) is suitable for a group to work on together, or for more able students to do as homework.

Advanced ***

Starter
- Discuss festivals with students. Ask these questions.
- Who has been to a festival?
- Where was it held? When?
- What was the weather like?
- Did they camp?
- What facilities were provided (food retailers, drink, toilets, first aid)?
- What were these facilities like (clean or dirty, expensive, large queues)?
- How safe was it? (security presence)

Main activity
- Explain that students are going to investigate different elements of the Glastonbury Festival.
- Discuss why a ticket costs nearly £200. What are the costs to the organisers? (Answer: Paying the performers, policing, medical staff, staging, lighting, sound equipment, electricity, fencing, toilet hire, amongst many others.)
- Discuss the problem of an event that may have reached its maximum capacity. Explain that the site cannot hold an audience greater than 150 000. The facilities and entertainment need to 'improve' year on year, so the costs go up and therefore so does the price of tickets.
- Look at Task 1 with the students. Discuss whether the regular large increases in ticket prices can be justified. (Answer: In the early years the festival audience was growing, reaching 12 000 in 1971, 18 000 in 1981, 105 000 in 2000, and 150 000 by 2003. This was achieved by attracting more and bigger bands, so the ticket price had to increase. However, this was balanced by greatly increased revenue from the larger audience. In a commercial sense, the ticket price can be justified by the way all the tickets sell within hours, or less than an hour, of going on sale.). **Let students do Task 1**.
- Look at Task 2 with the students. Ask any students who have camped at festivals how closely together tents are pitched. Guy ropes can be a hazard! Did they have difficulty in locating their own tents? (Some festival-goers attach flags to their tents to make them easier to find.) Try to reach an agreement as to a minimum distance between tents. Discuss how to find how much land area an average two-person tent will need. (Answer: Treat each tent as a rectangle, allow an addition half-metre on each side, and find the average of these areas.) **Let students do Task 2**.
- Discuss what students have discovered from Task 2. They may have found that the tents have more space than their agreed minimum, but less than the *Event Safety Guide*. Bear in mind that some tents will be smaller (one-person tents) and others might be larger (family or four-person tents).
- Discuss any very large events students have experienced. Ask students to describe the size of audience and the amount of space that was available. Whereabouts is there least space? (Answer: At the front, because people tend to move forward to the stage.)
- Ask how they could estimate the average amount of space needed per person standing at such an event. (Answer: Compare to the number of people who can stand comfortably in the school hall, or part of it. Take a class or year group to the hall, and see how much space they take up when standing comfortably.) **Let students do Task 3 (extension).** Less able students may benefit from working in groups. Alternatively, this task could be set as homework.

Advanced ***

- Look at Task 4 with the students. Ask what comes to mind when they think about the Glastonbury Festival. If necessary, ask about the weather. What are the issues with weather at such an event? (Answer: If it's wet, it's very muddy, as thousands of people are walking over fields; if it's sunny, there is a danger of sunburn, heatstroke and dehydration.)
- Ask students to suggest what people attending the festival should take to Glastonbury, to be prepared. (Answer: Waterproof clothing, wellies, sun cream, hat, bottled water) **Let students do Task 4**.
- Refer students back to the table of admission costs in Task 1. Ask how they might use this information to predict the cost in future years. (Answer: Looking at average annual increases, or plotting a graph and extrapolating.)
- Discuss tent design and how it is changing. Suggest that a possible trend might be towards tipi tents, which have a larger floor area but also accommodate more people. Suggest that a different style of tent might lead to an increase or decrease in the number of tents the site can hold. **Let students do Task 5**. Point out that if they tackle the first part by considering annual percentage increases, they will have to make a decision about the years when there was no festival. Discuss the methods they suggest. Students may need support with the second part, about tent sizes, but encourage students to think about proportions and ratios. Trigonometry is needed to find the area of the pentagon.

Plenary

- Task 5 shows how difficult it is to make predictions. Ask what other factors will affect the ticket price. (Answer: Wages and employment levels will influence people's ability and willingness to pay. If wage rises are low and unemployment rises, fewer people might be prepared to pay a higher ticket price. Possible crowd disturbances one year could put people off attending in future years.)
- What assumptions have been made in the calculations for Task 5? (Answer: That prices will continue to rise by a constant factor, and what that factor is. That tent sizes will be as predicted; the calculations assumed two people in every two-person tent, but only five in a six-person tent. It did not allow for different-sized tents, but assumed all tents will be of the same size.)
- Ask how reliable the predictions are. (Answer: The tent prediction suggests that numbers could remain roughly static with different tent designs; the cost prediction is so wide to be of little use. The lower limit is probably closer to reality, as it is based on more recent years, even if it is based on a smaller sample.

Outcomes

- Students will have calculated percentage change, repeated percentage increase and reverse percentages.
- Students will have calculated areas of rectangles, triangles, trapeziums and pentagons.
- Students will have used knowledge of angles in regular pentagons and used trigonometry to calculate sides of right-angled triangles, in estimating realistic amounts of space required.
- Students will have calculated moving averages and plotted them on graphs.
- Students will have interpreted graphs, calculating means.
- Students will have used ratio and proportion.

Answers

Task 1

1 **a** 50%   **b** 23%   **c** 36%   **d** 13%

Advanced ***

2 Percentage increases are lower in more recent years than in the early years. Figures in italics indicate an increase over two years, after a festival-free year.

Year	1979	*1981*	1982	1983	1984	1985	1986	1987	*1989*
Increase	>25%	*<10%*	<10%	>25%	<10%	10–25%	<10%	10–25%	*>25%*

Year	1990	*1992*	1993	1994	1995	*1997*	1998	1999	2000
Increase	>25%	*25%*	10–25%	<10%	10–25%	*10–25%*	<10%	<10%	<10%

Year	*2002*	2003	2004	2005	2006	2007	2008	2009
Increase	*10–25%*	<10%	<10%	10–25%	<10%	<10%	<10%	10–25%

3 £185

Task 2

1 Treating each tent as a rectangle, and allowing 0.5 m on each side, the areas are: A: 7.32 m², B: 7.92 m², C: 10.89 m², D: 11.28 m². The mean of these is 9.35 m².

The *Event Safety Guide* allows 10 000 ÷ 430 = 23.26 m² per tent.

The space available at Glastonbury allows 285 × 4047 ÷ 85 000 = 13.6 m²

Tents at Glastonbury have more space than students' likely estimates, but less than recommended by the *Event Safety Guide*.

2 Inaccuracies are present because you have used the mean of four two-person tents. There will be larger and smaller tents than this. Some will be pitched closer together (particularly when friends travel together and take more than one tent), others will be further apart.

Task 3 (extension)

1 A reasonable estimate might be from 0.7 m² to 1 m² per person. The Ricoh Arena in Coventry has an area of 6000 m² and can hold 8000 people, allowing 0.75 m² per person.

2 To allow sufficient room, it would probably be best to allow a minimum of 1 m² per person, or 90 000 m² altogether.

3 A roughly triangular shape is needed. This is comparable, on a much larger scale, to the situation in a classroom, when people at the front of the classroom but at the left and right edges find it harder to see the board.

Task 4

1 78.28, 77.76, 77.56, 69 mm

2

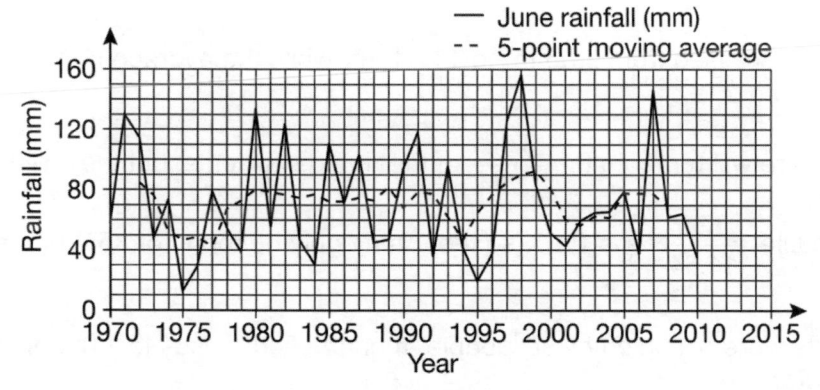

3 The annual figures vary significantly. A moving average helps to identify trends as extremely dry or wet months are levelled out.

Advanced ***

4 There is no real overall trend. There is a little evidence (1998, 2007) to suggest that there is more chance of a very wet June, but, in the years between, the month was relatively dry. It is possible that the weather is becoming a little more extreme (either wetter or drier), but further evidence is needed.

Task 5

1 The mean percentage increase between 1979 and 2009 is 12.5%. (The equation $a^{30} = \dfrac{175-5}{5} = 34$ gives an answer of a = 1.1247, or a 12.5% increase.)

A 12.5% annual increase from 2009 to 2030 is 175×1.125^{21} = £2076, whereas a 13% increase suggests a 2030 price of £2279.

A graph highlights the difficulty in making long-range predictions. It shows an exponential curve, but is not smooth enough to make sensible predictions.

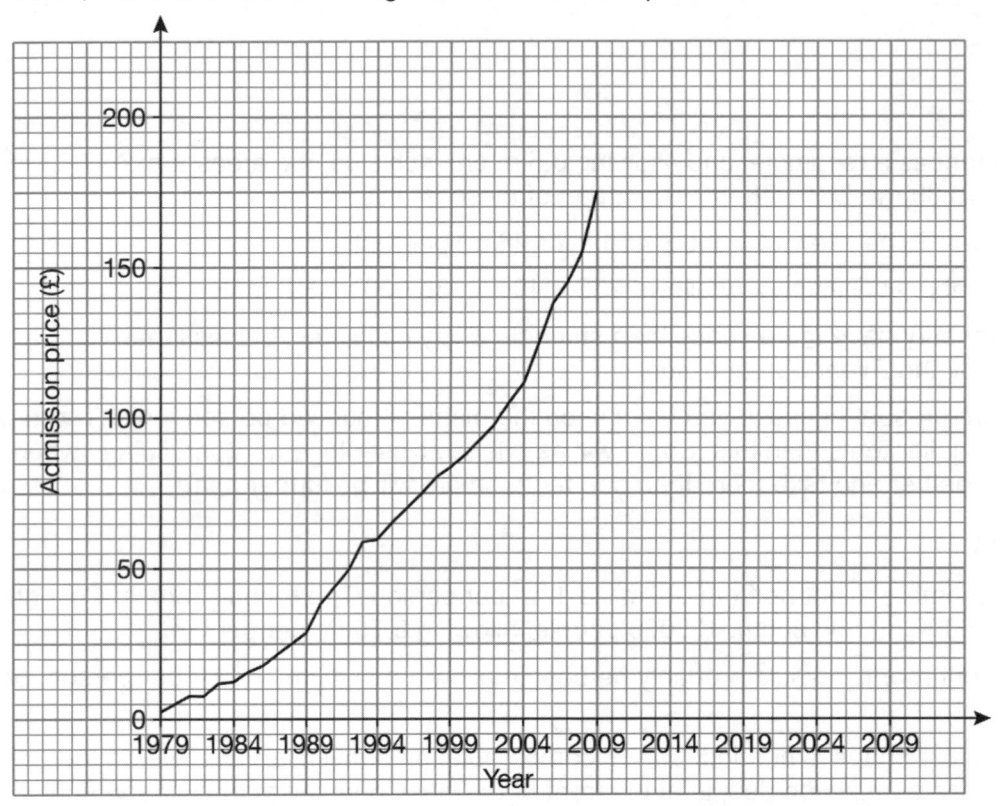

More significant is that the percentage increases are lower in more recent years than in the early years. For the ten years up to 2009, the average percentage increase was 7.8%, which would produce a 2030 figure of £847. A prediction of between £847 and £2279 is rather vague, but it is difficult to be more specific.

2 11.64 m²

3 a The average tent size has increased from 3.96 m² to 11.64 m², while the average number of people in a tent has risen from 2 to 5.

  b Based on these figures, there will be room for $\dfrac{3.96}{11.64}$ of the number of tents, but they will hold $\dfrac{5}{2}$ times as many people. $\dfrac{3.96}{11.64} \times \dfrac{5}{2} = 0.85$, so there may only be room for 85% of the current campers.

  However, if all the tipi tents were occupied by six people, then the figure rises to 1.02, or a 2% increase in the campers.

Advanced ***

Leaving smaller footprints

Learning objectives
- **Representing Level 2**: find information needed to solve the problem and use appropriate methods to solve it
- **Analysing Level 2**: work through the calculations and check answers make sense
- **Interpreting Level 2**: use results to produce graphs and charts, explain findings and draw conclusions

APP
Evidence for Using and applying mathematics Level 6, Calculating Level 7, Algebra Level 7, Handling data Level 6

PLTS
Develops Independent enquirers, Creative thinkers, Team workers, Effective participators

Every child matters outcomes
Make a positive contribution, Achieve economic well-being

Cross-curricular links
Science, Geography, English, Media studies

Underpinning maths
- Calculating averages
- Using formulae
- Using exponential growth
- Producing charts

Resources
- *Student book*, page 134–137
- Data sheet: Map of Europe
- Scientific calculators, compasses and protractors
- Coloured pencils
- Internet access (optional for Task 5 extension activity)

Useful websites
- footprint.wwf.org.uk
- www.carbonfootprint.com/calculator.aspx (for a more advanced calculator)
- www.nature.org/initiatives/climatechange/calculator (for a more advanced calculator)

Context
All students should be familiar with the idea of renewable and non-renewable energy sources. In this activity, students investigate how electricity is generated and the depletion of natural resources, working towards thinking about ways to reduce their carbon footprint.

Lesson plan
This activity takes one or two lessons. Students who do not have time to complete the work on their carbon footprint could complete Task 4 and then do Task 5 (extension) as homework.

Advanced ***

Starter

- Ask students to name as many renewable and non-renewable energy sources as they can. List them on the board. Make clear what renewable and non-renewable sources of energy are. (Answer: Renewable – wind, solar, geothermal, tidal/wave power, hydroelectric (HEP) and biomass; non-renewable – coal, oil, gas, nuclear.)
- Explain that the amount of coal used worldwide is measured in billions of tonnes per year. Write an example of 450 billion on the board and ask students to change it into standard form. (Answer: 450 000 000 000 = 4.5×10^{11})

Main activity

- Discuss with students how transferring energy from one form to another is never 100% efficient. Give the example of an electric filament lightbulb, in which most of the energy is transferred into wasted heat, not light. Explain that low-energy bulbs are more efficient and generate less heat. Ask students how, if they use bulbs of different wattages around the house, they could work out the average efficiency.
- Read Task 1 with students. Remind them that the use of the instruction **compare** implies that they need to find averages. Briefly review the three forms of average: **mode**, **mean** and **median**. You could ask for volunteers to explain each one.
- **Let students do Task 1**. Encourage them to try to work out each average and justify which one is more appropriate than any other. If necessary, you could write on the board definitions of mode, mean and median. Remind students about the importance of checking their own calculations before you check their answers for the averages.
- Remind students that there is too much information to make a pie chart; they should have drawn a bar chart with a suitable scale, labelled axes and an appropriate title.
- Look at Task 2 with students. Explain that the world coal reserves are located all around the world. The numbers are very large so they can use standard form rather than numbers with lots of digits. Remind students how to convert a number into standard form and how to use the EXP button on their calculators. Make sure every student knows where the power button is on their calculator. If necessary, pair able students with those unfamiliar with standard form or compound growth.
- **Let students do Task 2**. Remind students of BIDMAS/BODMAS when working out the formula and to find the value of the expression in brackets. (Answer: 1.025) Check students have rounded appropriately, when writing the answer down, but encourage them to use the answer on the calculator for question 2 part b. Encourage students to try doubling 2.5% growth (5%), doubling again (10%), and so on. Discuss what happens to their answers. At the end of the task, tell students that the actual number of years of supplies of coal remaining in 2020 will be lower, because 14 years' worth of coal has been used up from 2006 to 2020. So 14 years needs to be taken off their answer. Also, with an annual 2.5% increase, the actual amount of coal used each year is 102.5% of the previous year's figure; the yearly 2.5% increase is on the new amount, not the original figure of 7.075 billion tonnes.
- Read Task 3 with the students. Refer to the map and explain that only the countries that are coloured in are to be included. They should ignore countries shaded grey. Distribute the data sheet, or use atlases or prepared world maps (perhaps from the internet). Encourage students to work together, in pairs.
- **Let students do Task 3**. Remind them to check the total number of countries they have on the map with the total in their table. Check all students have the correct number of countries under each heading before they start to produce a pie chart. Remind students to label sections as they go along, use colours if available.

Advanced ***

- Put students into suitable groups of four, depending on their ability. Read through Task 4 with them and explain that they have to compare the two pie charts. These only show percentages. Students need to consider whether the overall amount of electricity generated may have increased from 1971 to 2004.
- **Let students do Task 4**. Move among groups and encourage discussions leading to production of statements. For example ask:
  - 'By how much has the use of gas increased?'
  - 'What might the section for 'other' include?'

  If there is not enough time for the online carbon footprint calculator part of the task, set it as homework. Recommend students to use one of the online calculators listed above. Ask students to write a list of ways in which they can save energy at home, for example, turning televisions and other appliances off rather than putting them on standby, turning off the computer at night, unplugging mobile phone chargers.
- **Let students do Task 5 (extension)**. Distribute coloured pencils for posters when students are ready. Alternatively, to link the topic to media studies, ask students to make a 5-minute documentary about carbon emissions, to encourage people to reduce their carbon footprint.

Plenary

- Ask students for examples of how they could reduce the amount of energy they use. Include how they travel to school, how often they buy new clothes, where they get their food from, if they have their food delivered.
- Ask students if a pie chart always gives them the information they need, or whether it only shows what the person that produced it wants them to know.
- Ask, 'Is the world reducing its carbon emissions?'

Outcomes

- Students will have used mathematics to analyse a situation and identified the methods needed to find solutions.
- Students will have used appropriate checking procedures.
- Students will have interpreted the solutions to their calculations and drawn conclusions.

Advanced ***

Answers

Task 1

1. As they have been asked to compare, students should bring in the three averages: mode = 90, mean = 51.7, median = 41.5. The mode, at 90, indicates hydroelectric and tidal power, but as these are also two of the highest values this average does not represent the data effectively. The mean should give a more realistic figure. The median could also be used, or a combination of the mean and median. The most suitable display for this discrete data would be a bar chart.

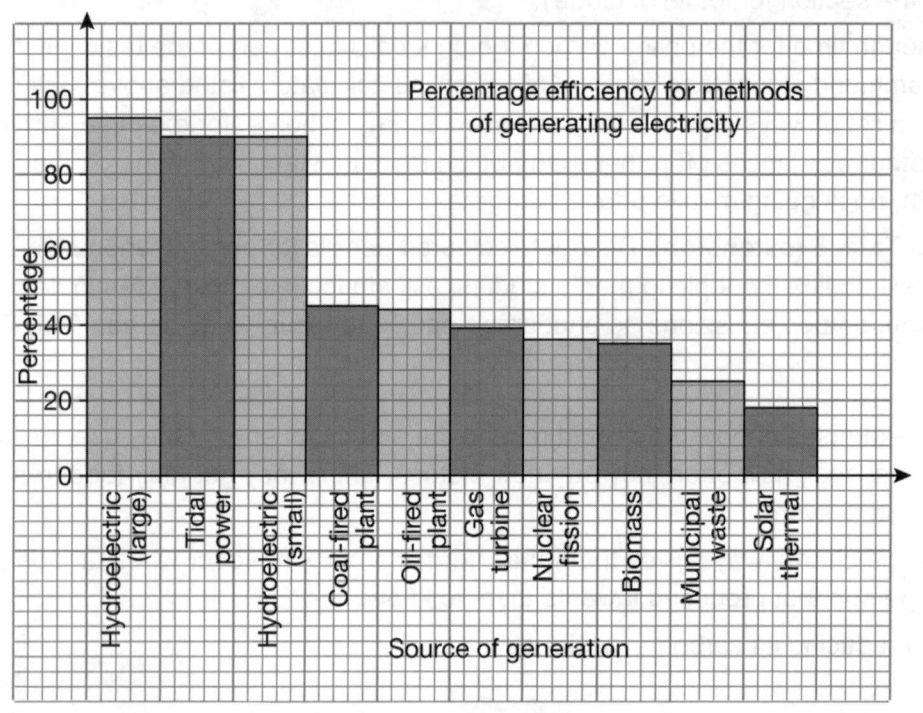

2. Hydroelectric and tidal power have exceptionally high efficiencies. Coal-fired plants produce above-average efficiency, when compared to the median, but below-average efficiency, compared to the mean. The efficiency of coal is good, compared to the average and to other sources of generation other than hydroelectric and tidal power.

3. a Efficiency = 40 ÷ 100 = 0.4

   b 0.4 represents 40%, this is 5% less than the value given in the table.

Task 2

1. $9 \times 10^{11} \div 7.075 \times 10^9 = 127.208\ldots$ so 127 years

2. a $N = 7.075 \times 10^9 \times (1.025)^{14} = 9\,996\,789\,783$ or 10 billion

   b Using 9 billion tonnes and the full answer on the calculator, $9 \times 10^{11} \div$ Answer = 90.02 years

   If rounded, this gives $9 \times 10^{11} \div 1 \times 10^{10} = 90$ years

   c The 2020 rate is higher than the current rate, more coalfields may be discovered. There may be more or less coal in the reserves than expected; there may be fewer years of coal supply because of compound annual growth of 2.5%; by 2020, 14 years of coal will have already been used up.

   d Coal supplies will run out sooner.

Advanced ***

Task 3

1 a

Energy production	Countries	Total
< 1%	None	0
< 5%	Belgium, Czech Republic, Hungary, Lithuania, Poland	5
< 10%	Bulgaria, Cyprus, Estonia, Greece, Ireland, Netherlands, Slovakia, UK	8
< 20%	France, Germany, Italy, Turkey	4
< 30%	Croatia, Denmark, Finland, Romania, Slovenia, Spain	6
< 40%	Latvia, Portugal	2
> 40%	Austria, Iceland, Norway, Sweden	4
	Total	29

b

Suitable title for pie chart

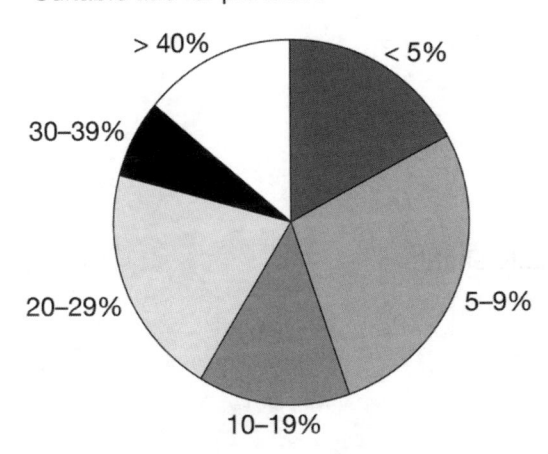

Energy production	Angles for pie chart
< 5%	62°
< 10%	99°
< 20%	50°
< 30%	74°
< 40%	25°
> 40%	50°
Total	360.0°

2 Students should refer to their own pie charts and the original data they collected in their tables, not information from previous tasks.

Task 4

1 Examples of suitable statements include: The proportion of coal used has decreased negligibly; the proportion of oil used has decreased by more than 3 times; the proportion of nuclear has gone up by more than 7 times.

2 Students should produce their own carbon footprints.

Task 5 (extension)

Check students produce a colourful poster with key points from the tasks.

Advanced ***

Can we hold back the sea?

Learning objectives
- **Representing Level 2**: find information needed for the task, from bar charts of monthly rainfall and rates of coastal erosion
- **Analysing Level 2**: apply a range of mathematics to produce suitable graphs, including a method to find the amount of land eroded
- **Interpreting Level 2**: interpret results and draw mathematical conclusions for the amount of land lost and reclaimed, both in the UK and abroad

APP
Evidence for Using and applying mathematics Level 8, Calculating Level 7, Algebra Level 7, Handling data Level 6

PLTS
Independent enquirers, Creative thinkers, Effective participators

Every child matters outcomes
Enjoy and achieve

Cross-curricular links
Geography, Geology, Media studies, ICT, English, Citizenship

Underpinning maths
- Using standard form
- Interpreting graphs
- Extracting information for tables
- Using the trapezium rule
- Displaying data graphically
- Calculating averages
- Calculating scales

Resources
- *Student book,* pages 138–141
- Data sheet 1: Table of coastal erosion figures
- Data sheet 2: Map of Holland
- Scientific calculators
- Graph paper and tracing paper
- Internet access

Useful websites
- www.youtube.com/watch?v=b8UDxFw-RoA&feature=related
- www.thepalm.ae
- www.gpsvisualizer.com/geocode and www.gpsvisualizer.com/elevation
- www.timesonline.co.uk/tol/news/environment/article6938356.ece

Advanced ***

Context
All students should be familiar with coastal erosion and the effect it is having on property and local communities near the coast. Students will know about the floods of 2007 and the devastation caused to the UK. In this activity, they will look at the rate of erosion of the UK coastline and additional reasons why land is being lost at such a high rate.

Lesson plan
This activity takes two lessons. It could be done in one lesson by focusing on Tasks 1 and 2. Task 5 (extension) could be set as homework.

Starter
Ask students about causes of coastal erosion. (Answer: Sea waves, currents and rain.) Explain that erosion caused by the sea is a huge problem; houses can be swept into the sea as the coastline is washed away. Tell students that the composition of the land (the basic material that makes it up) affects the rate at which the land is eroded.

Give as an example the white cliffs of Dover. Explain that they are constantly being eroded. If they weren't, they would not stay white but would be covered in vegetation. Only small amounts fall off, however, because they are made of chalk.

As another example, tell students about the four-star hotel in Scarborough, called Holbeck Hall, where a form of erosion called soil creep occurred. A build-up of water in the boulder-clay rock under the foundations of the hotel caused the land to slip into the sea.

Main activity
- Discuss with students how certain parts of the UK's coastline are being eroded faster than others because of the different compositions of the soil. Because of this, it would be difficult to predict the time when the UK vanishes into the sea.
- Read Task 1 with students. Explain that it requires them to think about the relationship between area and perimeter. Ask students whether or not they think that the area of a shape will be the same, no matter what shape it is, as long as the perimeter doesn't change. You could demonstrate, with a piece of string, how a fixed length can be rearranges into shapes of different area. Discuss shapes with a perimeter of, say, 36 cm. These could include a square of side 9 cm (area 81 cm^2), a rectangle 6 cm by 12 cm (area 72 cm^2) and a rectangle 3 cm by 15 cm (area 45 cm^2).
- **Let students do Task 1.** Make sure they convert 88 cm to metres.
- Read Task 2 with students. Remind them how to produce a scatter graph and explain the word **correlation**. Discuss what factors other than the height of the cliff might affect the erosion rates (for example, current).
- Discuss how to plot the graph for question 2. Make sure students realise that the location points are at 50 m intervals. Since all the distances are in metres, the same scale can be used on both axes. The points should be joined with a smooth curve to give a realistic approximation of the coastlines. Check students understand that in order to plot the position of the coastline in 1960 they need to add the total erosion at each point to the distance to the coastline in 2010.
- Discuss with students how to find the area under a curve. Explain that the area can be split into trapeziums; point out that the tops of some of the trapeziums will be slightly above the curve and some slightly below; these tend to balance each other out, so the total area should be a good estimate. Ask students if they recall how to find the area of a trapezium. Read through the explanation of the trapezium rule with students.

Advanced ***

Ask how the trapezium rule can be used to find the amount of land lost between 1960 and 2010. (Answer: Find the area under both curves, then subtract the 2010 area from the 1960 area.) **Let students do Task 2**. If spreadsheet software is available, students could use it to calculate the area under the curves.

- **Extend the task** by asking students to use the average erosion figures to predict the amount of land likely to be lost in the next 10 years. Students need to find the predicted erosion at each location point by multiplying the average erosion per year by 10 and subtracting their answers from the 2010 distances. If they wish, they can then plot these on their graph to get the predicted coastline for 2020. They can find the amount of land predicted to be lost by subtracting the area under the 2020 curve from the area under the 2010 curve (found in question 3).

- The stretch of coastline monitored in Task 2 is only 1 kilometre long. Discuss the practicalities of using the method described for longer stretches where there may be buildings. It may not be possible to establish a straight baseline with posts at regular intervals. Ask how this problem could be overcome. (Answer: Posts can be positioned at more convenient locations and map references used to determine their positions for the calculations.)

- Read Task 3 with students. Ask them to describe what the first bar chart shows. Point out that the rainfall has been normalised. This means that an average, for the period from 1971 to 2000, is taken to be 100%. Tell them that bars that extend down from the 100% line are not negative values, but show rainfall that was less than the average for 1971 to 2000.

- **Let students do Task 3**. Check that they have read the correct values from the bar charts. For question 2, tell students to use 2.54 cm per inch (25.4 mm is equivalent to 1 inch) and remind them how to calculate the mode, mean and median.

- Read Task 4 with students. Distribute graph paper, tracing paper and data sheet 2, which gives a map of Holland. Ask students to find out the real size of an area represented by a square of side 1 cm or 1 mm on the graph paper. They should use the scale to determine the actual size. Suggest that, for greater accuracy, students work with bigger squares, such as of side 2 cm, which they can subdivide into millimetres rather than working with a scale for a smaller square. **Let students do Task 4**.

- Read Task 5 (extension) with students. Discuss the list of bullet points and suggest students choose two to focus on. Explain that some densely populated parts of the UK, such as coastal regions and London, are prone to flooding, both tidal and by rivers. Some parts of the country are only a few metres above the level of high tide. As well as investigating various towns and cities, students may enjoy finding out how far their own homes are above sea level. They can do this by using the first gpsvisualizer.com link (in the list above) to find the longitude and latitude (enter 'UK' followed by their postcode) and copying and pasting these measures into the box at the bottom of the second website to find the altitude.

- Explain that Dubai is using coastal erosion barriers to shelter an area of sea in which to build a multi-billion dollar project. It is intended to provide homes and a holiday resort for the rich and famous. Students can use the internet to find information about the Palm Island project. A video of the construction work can be found at the YouTube link listed above. Encourage students to include images and videos in their presentations and say that the best ones will be shown to the class.

- **Let students do Task 5 (extension)** for homework.

Plenary

- Ask students if they were surprised at how fast certain parts of the UK are falling into the sea. Ask students what the contributing factors were to the 2007 flooding.

Advanced ***

- Explain that the problem in some areas would not have been so severe if drainage systems had been kept clean and maintained. Tell students that many parts of the country are having drainage systems put in place at the side of roads and river banks are being raised to take a higher volume of water.
- Discuss the altitudes of students' houses and compare these to areas around Hull, or another city close to the sea.

Outcomes

o Students will have used maths to identify a situation and obtained the information needed to find solutions.
o Students will have used a range of maths to find a solution.
o Students will have interpreted the results of their calculations and graphs.
o Students will have drawn conclusions from their results and provided mathematical justification.

Answers

Task 1

a $5 \times 5 = 25$ cm^2, $6 \times 4 = 24$ cm^2, $7 \times 3 = 21$ cm^2, $8 \times 2 = 16$ cm^2, $9 \times 1 = 9$ cm^2, a different shape gives different areas with the same perimeter.

b $0.88 \times (11\,073 \times 1600) = 15\,590\,784$ m^2,
$94\,600 \times 1600 \times 1600 = 2.421\,76 \times 10^{11}$ m^2

$2.421\,76 \times 10^{11} \div 15\,590\,784 = 15\,533$ years

This is a huge number of years but, as can be seen from the rectangle exercise, the length of coastline is not the only factor affecting the area eroded. As the size of the UK decreases, the length of the coastline will also decrease.

Task 2

1 There is no correlation between the height of the cliff in 1960 and the total erosion over the last 50 years.

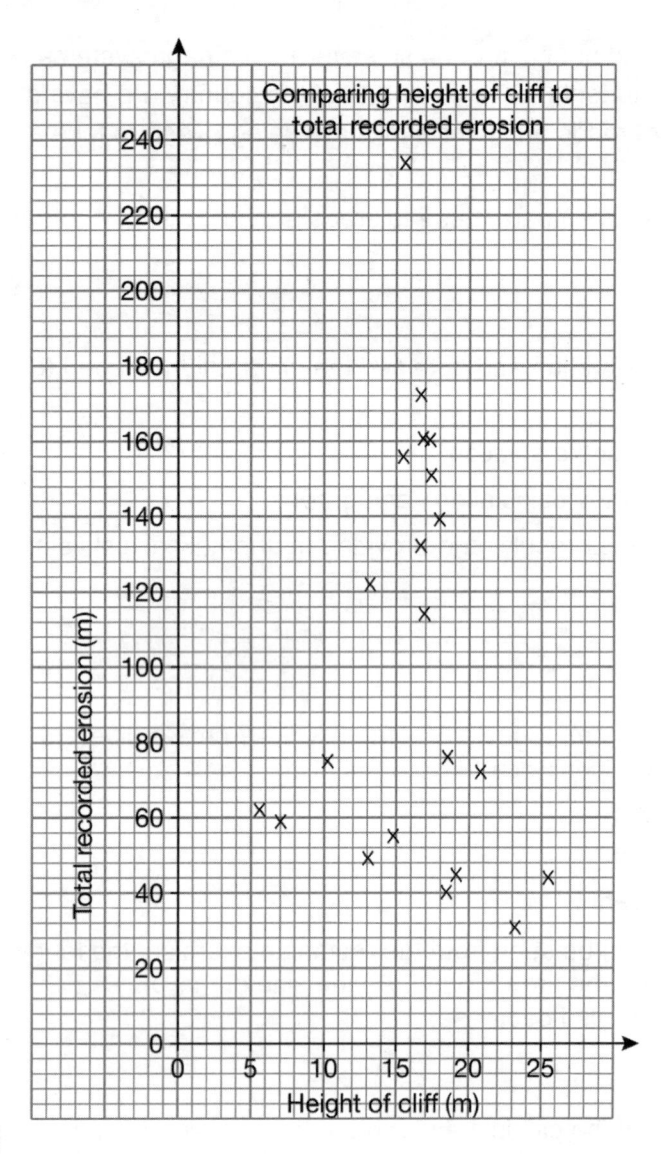

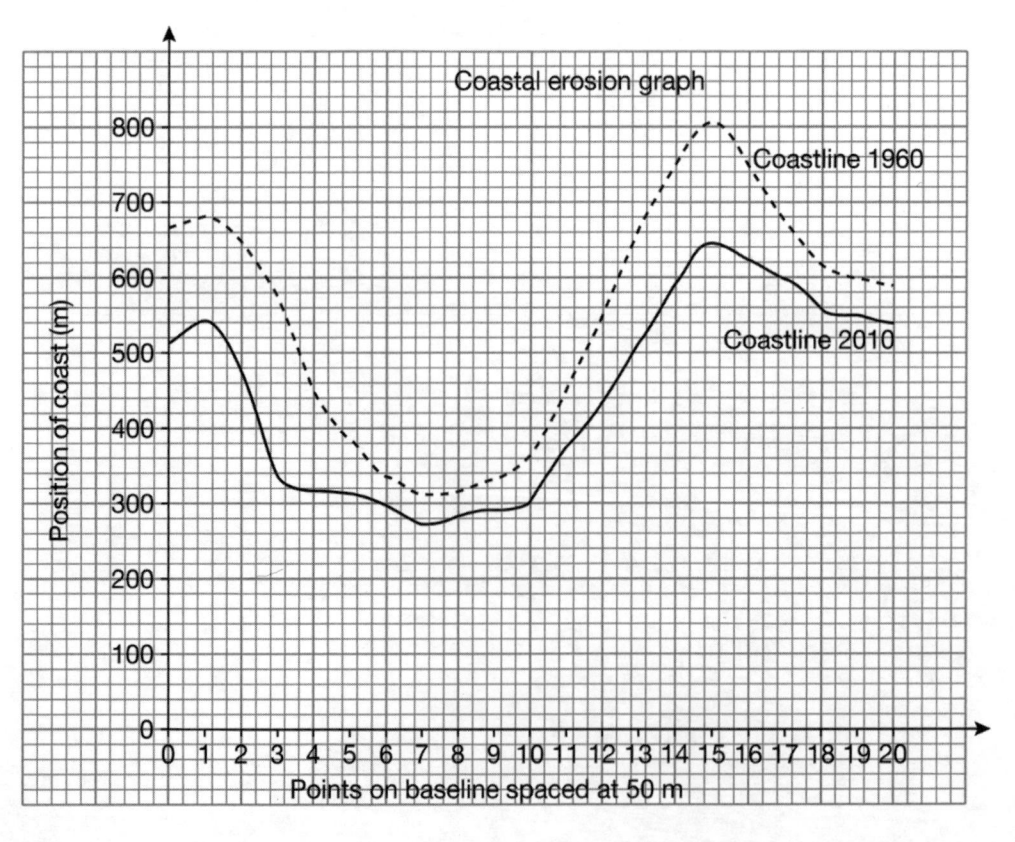

Advanced ***

Comparing height of cliff to total recorded erosion

2

Coastal erosion graph

Advanced ***

3 Area in 2010 = $50(\frac{509}{2} + 541 + 474 + 337 + 318 + 311 + 294 + 270 + 281 + 285 + 300 + 373$

$+ 434 + 512 + 589 + 642 + 621 + 595 + 558 + 550 + \frac{539}{2})$

= 440 450 m²

Area in 1960 = $50(\frac{665}{2} + 680 + 647 + 571 + 450 + 383 + 338 + 310 + 312 + 330 + 362 + 449$

$+ 548 + 663 + 749 + 803 + 743 + 670 + 617 + 599 + \frac{594}{2})$

= 542 675 m²   Land lost = 542 675 − 440 450 = 102 225 m² or 0.1 km²

Extension

Location point	Distance to coastline in 2010 (m)	Average erosion per year (m)	Predicted additional land lost by 2020	Predicated distance to coastline in 2020 (m)
0	509	3.12	31.2	477.8
1	541	2.78	27.8	513.2
2	474	3.46	34.6	439.4
3	337	4.68	46.8	290.2
4	318	2.64	26.4	291.6
5	311	1.44	14.4	296.6
6	294	0.88	8.8	285.2
7	270	0.80	8.0	262
8	281	0.62	6.2	274.8
9	285	0.90	9.0	276
10	300	1.24	12.4	287.6
11	373	1.52	15.2	357.8
12	434	2.28	22.8	411.2
13	512	3.02	30.2	481.8
14	589	3.20	32.0	557
15	642	3.22	32.2	609.8
16	621	2.44	24.4	596.6
17	595	1.50	15.0	580
18	558	1.18	11.8	546.2
19	550	0.98	9.8	540.2
20	539	1.10	11.0	528

Area in 2020 = $50(\frac{477.8}{2} + 513.2 + 439.4 + 290.2 + 291.6 + 296.6 + 285.2 + 262 + 274.8 +$

$276 + 287.6 + 357.8 + 411.2 + 481.8 + 557 + 609.8 + 596.6 + 580 + 546.2 +$

$540.2 + \frac{528}{2})$

= 420 005 m²   Predicted land lost = 440 450 − 420 005 = 20 445 m² or 0.02 km²

© HarperCollins*Publishers* 2010

Advanced ***

Task 3

1 We have had drier autumns and winters than expected, with a regular pattern of rainfall during February–March usually under the expected amounts, based on 1971–2002 figures. However, 2007 showed a very wet February. Overall there were months above and below the percentage norm for each year.

Total for 2004 ≈ 1300, 1300 ÷ 12 = 108.3%, total for 2005 ≈ 1175, 1175 ÷ 12 = 97.9%, total for 2006 ≈ 1240, 1240 ÷ 12 = 103.3%, total for 2007 ≈ 1065, 1065 ÷ 8 = 133.1%

The average UK rainfall is represented by the 100% level on the graph. This is actually the average rainfall for the period 1971–2001. The period January to August 2007 had rainfall over 30% above normal, so the year could be expected to be wetter than average.

2

Months	Inches	Millimetres
January	2.8	71.12
February	2.8	71.12
March	1.4	35.56
April	0.2	5.08
May	5.8	147.32
June	5.5	139.7
July	4.5	114.3
August	1.3	33.02
September	1.5	38.1
October	3.6	91.44
November	1.9	48.26
December	1.4	35.56

Students finds the average rainfall, e.g. mean = 69.2 mm, modes are 35.56 and 71.1 mm, median = 59.69, range = 142.24

3 Students should comment that a mean of 69 mm is 2.7 inches and so May, June and July were well above average. Several consecutive months of greater than average rainfall could lead to soil-slip making coastlines more susceptible to being washed away at high tides. The first bar chart suggests that three consecutive months of such heavy rainfall is unusual.

Task 4

 a Students should trace the outline of Holland onto graph paper and count the squares, then use the scale to find the area of a square and thus find the total area of Holland.

 b Students should shade in the area that has been reclaimed and count the squares of reclaimed land, then use the scale calculated in question 1a to find the area of land reclaimed.

 c Students should divide their answer for the amount of land reclaimed by the area of Holland and comment on how close they are to 70%.

Task 5 (extension)

Students should produce a presentation of their findings, perhaps including images or short movies. They may have found the height above sea level of various cities, sea-level predictions and details of coastal erosion defences. They may have found figures on the construction, amount of land claimed, tide heights and costs of the project in Dubai. They may have compared these with the construction and costs of coastline defences in the UK.

Advanced ***

Facebook

Learning objectives
- **Representing Level 2:** recognise that a real-life situation can be better understood using appropriate mathematics
- **Analysing Level 2:** analyse statistics and patterns, using appropriate mathematical techniques
- **Interpreting Level 2:** interpret results and solutions and make a generalisation about them, sometimes in a social context

APP
Using and applying mathematics Level 8, Calculating Level 8, Algebra Level 8

PLTS
Develops Independent enquirers, Creative thinkers, Effective participators

Every child matters outcome
Enjoy and achieve, Make a positive contribution

Cross-curricular links
Citizenship, ICT, Human geography, English

Underpinning maths
- Standard form
- Percentage increase
- Repeated percentage change
- Quadratic sequences
- Solving a quadratic equation by the quadratic formula

Resources
- *Student book*, pages 142–145
- Calculator
- Stopwatch (optional)

Context
Even students who do not have a Facebook account are likely to understand about social media websites. You could use this activity as an opportunity to emphasise the responsible and safe use of social media; for example, only connecting to people you know, using privacy settings and only communicating in ways you would be happy for everyone to read.

Lesson plan
This activity takes two lessons. Task 6 would make a good homework activity and could be done in pairs or small groups, with students presenting their work to the rest of the class in the next lesson.

Starter
- Tell students that there are now more than 500 million active Facebook users, worldwide.
- Encourage students to discuss with a partner how many zeros there are in the number 500 million. (Answer: zeros)

Advanced ***

- Discuss the difficulty of reading numbers with lots of zeros and how easy it can be to misread them or get them wrong, especially when keying them into a calculator. Ask students to think what happens if they miss just one zero off the number 500 million. Does it make a big or a small difference? (Answer: A big difference of 450 million!)

- Ask students if they know any other ways of representing very large numbers and introduce the idea of standard form. Explain that this means writing numbers in the form of $a \times 10^n$ where $1 \leq a \leq 10$, and n is an integer or whole number. Encourage students to discuss with a partner how they would write 500 million in standard form. (Answer: 5×10^8)

- Discuss advertisements that appear on websites. When someone clicks on one, they are taken directly to the advertiser's website. Explain that some businesses place advertisements on Facebook. Ask students whether they think this is a good idea, and why. (Answer: Students are likely to think it is a good idea because of the number of users, but they may say it depends on the cost and the success rate.)

- Tell students that advertisers use **click-through rates** to assess the success of their advertisements:

$$\text{click-through rate} = \frac{\text{number of times users click on the advertisement}}{\text{number of times the advertisement is shown}} \times 100$$

- Ask students to calculate the click-through rate if 15 000 users click on an advertisement that is shown 50 000 times. (Answer: 0.3 or 30%)

Main activity

- Look at Task 1 with students. Ask three different students to read aloud the facts about Facebook, in question 1. (Students should read numbers as follows: 150 million, 300 thousand, 30 thousand million.) Say that in the US 30 000 000 000 is read as 30 billion, since a thousand million is taken as a billion. Interestingly, in the UK and the rest of Europe, a billion used to be considered to be a million million, but the US definition is now widely adopted.

- Ask the rest of the class to confirm that these students read the numbers correctly.

- **Let students do Task 1**. Encourage them to double-check their answers, as it is easy to make mistakes when dealing with lots of zeros. Make sure that they know that, for example, 70% is the same as the decimal 0.7, 4% is the same as 0.04.

- Ask students to name the website they visit most regularly, and to estimate how long they spend on it on average each month.

- Ask students to look at the diagrams for Task 2. Remind them that, when presented with diagrams, it is important to spend some time looking at exactly what they tell you. Read the title of the diagrams: 'Time spent on Facebook in June 2009 and June 2010 by country (hours spent per person per month)'.

- Ask students what they know about Brazil compared to the other three countries: the US, the UK and Australia. Remind them that Brazil is the only developing country among the four, but it is also one of the BRIC countries (Brazil, Russia, India, China), which are growing very fast and becoming rapidly wealthier.

- Look at Task 2 with students. Discuss the representation of the data in circles. What do they think the circles represent? (Answer: Stopwatches)

- Discuss the representation of the time, and check that students understand that it shows hours, minutes and seconds. You could use a real stopwatch to show the representation of time in this way.

Advanced ***

- Ask students to work with a partner to total the times spent on Facebook in all these countries in June 2009. (Answer: 15:04:33) Discuss how students did their calculations. Students are likely to have taken slightly different approaches, but should talk about converting hours to minutes, and minutes to seconds, and also converting back to an appropriate unit of time when their answer is greater than 60.
- **Let students do Task 2**. Remind them that:

$$\text{percentage increase} = \frac{\text{amount of increase}}{\text{amount before increase}} \times 100$$

- Look at Task 3 (extension) with students who will be doing it. Discuss their approach and the use of repeated percentage increase. **Let these students do Task 3**.
- Look at Task 4 with students. Ask them to look at the diagrams and go through the accompanying description. Ask a student to say, in their own words, what the diagrams represent.
- Read questions 2 and 3 with the students. Discuss how they might set about finding the relationship between n and c. (Answer: Exploring differences between consecutive terms: if the first differences are always constant – in this case if they are always + 4 – then it is a linear sequence; if the second differences are constant then it is a quadratic sequence.)
- Ask students what the answer to question 3 might look like if the relationship is linear, rather than quadratic. (Answer: If it is linear, expect to see n in the equation; if quadratic, expect to see n^2 in the equation.)
- **Let students do Task 4**. When they reach question 4b, encourage them to think about the different ways they know of solving quadratic equations. They may need reminding of the quadratic formula:

$$n = \frac{-b \pm \sqrt{b^2 - 4ac}}{2a} \quad \text{(where } an^2 + bn + c = 0\text{)}$$

- Task 5 (extension) is for A* and A students only. It may take some persistence to find the relationship between n and s. You could offer a hint by suggesting they explore 2^n. **Let the more able students do Task 5**.
- Before they start Task 6, discuss what information students may include in a presentation to persuade a company to adopt Facebook as a marketing tool. Consider the stopwatch circles to represent the data in Task 2. What imaginative ways can they think of to represent data? **Let students do Task 6**.

Plenary
- Ask students if they are surprised by the popularity of Facebook.
- Ask students what other websites are popular. What information would they seek to find out, and from where, to assess the popularity of these other websites?

Outcomes
- Students will have used mathematics to gain insight into a socially relevant phenomenon.
- Students will have used standard form to express large numbers in calculations.
- Students will have explored growth by considering percentages.
- Students will have recognised patterns in sequences, found relationships between terms and used those relationships to solve real problems.

Advanced ***

Answers

Task 1

1 More than 1.5×10^8 active users access their Facebook pages through their mobile phones.

Over 3×10^5 users helped translate Facebook into other languages.

More than 3×10^{10} pieces of content (such as web links, news stories, blog posts, notes, photo albums) are shared on Facebook each month.

2 **a** 7.7×10^5 **b** 1.4×10^7

Task 2

1 12 hours. Students should recognise the US 2010 and UK 2010 diagrams show a little over half a circle shaded and display times of just over 6 hours. Therefore, one can assume a whole circle represents 12 hours.

2 **a** US: 29.7%   **b**   UK: 8.3%
   c Brazil: 134.2% **d**   Australia: 70.3%

Brazil. Because it is a developing country with a fast growing economy, computer sales are increasing rapidly, so users of Facebook are also increasing rapidly.

Task 3 (extension)

2016

Task 4

1

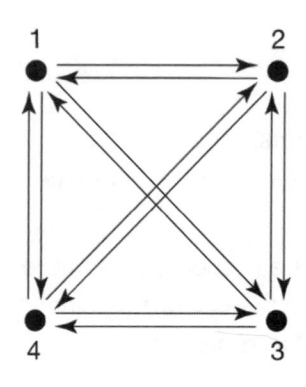

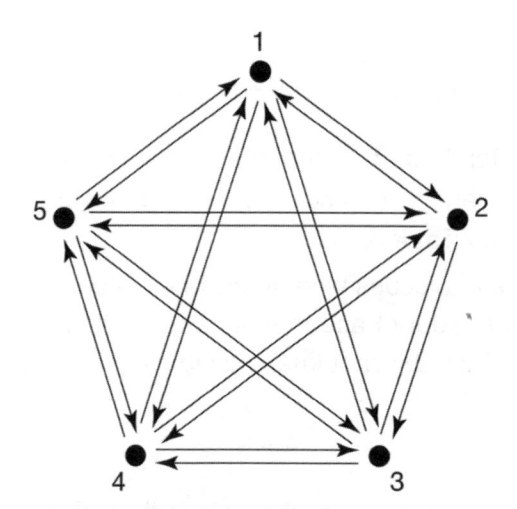

2

n	c
2	2
3	6
4	12
5	20

3 $c = n(n-1)$

4 **a** 870   **b**   33 students

Advanced ***

5 a Australia: 7.6×10^{13}; Brazil: 8.2×10^{14}; UK: 5.9×10^{14}; US: 1.6×10^{16}

b Students should recognise the number of possible connections in Brazil is just ahead of the UK but the percentage increase in numbers of people using Facebook from year to year is far greater in Brazil (134.2%) than in the UK (8.3%). Therefore, the number of possible connections in Brazil in years to come will increase at a much faster rate than the UK.

c People can connect to others outside their country too.

Task 5 (extension)

1

n	s	Sub-group list
2	1	(1, 2)
3	4	(1, 2) (1, 3) (2, 3) (1, 2, 3)
4	11	(1, 2) (1, 3) (1, 4) (2, 3) (2, 4) (3, 4) (1, 2, 3) (1, 2, 4) (2, 3, 4) (1, 3, 4) (1, 2, 3, 4)
5	26	(1, 2) (1, 3) (1, 4) (1, 5) (2, 3) (2, 4) (2, 5) (3, 4) (3, 5) (4, 5) (1, 2, 3) (1, 2, 4) (1, 2, 5) (1, 3, 4) (1, 3, 5) (1, 4, 5) (2, 3, 4) (2, 3, 5) (2, 4, 5) (3, 4, 5) (1, 2, 3, 4) (1, 2, 3, 5) (1, 2, 4, 5) (1, 3, 4, 5) (2, 3, 4, 5) (1, 2, 3, 4, 5)

2 $s = 2^n - n - 1$

3 $s = 1\,073\,741\,793$

4 Students should recognise that there are many more possible connections when considering sub-groups, compared to one-to-one connections. They should also recognise that while groups of friends may comprise more than just paired connections, they are also unlikely to comprise every permutation of sub-group.

Task 6

The types of information students may include in their presentation include:

- statistics for the numbers of active users on Facebook
- the growth of Facebook over time
- the number of possible connections if the company connect with only a few of their customers.

Students should keep their presentation interesting by using different ways of representing their data.

Advanced ***

Population and pensions

Learning objectives
- **Representing Level 2**: find information needed from graphs, diagrams and the internet
- **Analysing Level 2**: calculate variation in population statistics
- **Interpreting Level 2**: interpret results to explain findings and provide mathematical conclusions

APP
Evidence for Using and applying mathematics Level 5, Calculating Level 6, Algebra Level 6, Handling data Level 4

PLTS
Independent enquirers, Creative thinkers, Effective participators

Every child matters outcomes
Enjoy and achieve, Achieve economic well-being

Cross-curricular links
Geography, Business studies, English, ICT

Underpinning maths
- Interpreting graphs
- Extracting information from tables
- Calculating compound interest
- Displaying data graphically
- Working with the mean

Resources
- *Student book*, pages 146–149
- Data sheet: Kamal's bank statement
- Plain paper, coloured pencils
- Scientific calculators
- Internet access

Useful websites
- www.direct.gov.uk/en/Pensionsandretirementplanning/BeginnersGuideToPensions/DG_183705
- www.moneysavingexpert.com/savings/discount-pensions
- http://www.moneymadeclear.org.uk/products/pensions/types_of_pensions.html

Context
All students should be familiar with the terms pension, population and retirement. Students should be familiar with the fact that the population of the UK is increasing and people are living longer. They should have heard on the news that the retirement age is being increased to cover part of the short-fall in money available for pensions. This topic looks at the changing population of the UK and its proportion of workers to retirement-age population.

Advanced ***

Lesson plan
This activity takes two lessons. It could be done in one lesson by focusing on either Tasks 1 and 4 or on Tasks 2 and 3. Task 5 (extension) could be done as homework.

Starter
- Ask students what income they expect to receive when they retire and how much they think the Government will give them, per week, to live on. Say that they would currently get just under £100 a week for food, clothes, heating, rent and any other expenses they have.
- Tell students that the money for pensions comes from the **national insurance** contributions made by the people currently working. These contributions are also used to fund other things such as health care. Suggest that it would a good idea for them to invest in some other form of personal savings, such as a pension, as soon as they start working. The more years you pay into a pension the more money you will get per month when you come to retire.

Main activity
- Ask students why we don't have enough money to pay retired people more in pensions. Remind them that many people of retirement age were in paid employment for most of their working lives, so they have contributed themselves. Discuss how the population is increasing, so more people are taking money in payments such as child benefit and for medical care, also paid out of national insurance contributions.
- Discuss the idea of life expectancy. Explain that this is also increasing. As people are living longer, they are actually taking more money out of the 'pension pot' than they originally put in while they were working.
- Read Task 1 with students. Explain that a census is taken every 10 years, to give the Government an exact picture of the number of people legally in the UK, along with information such as their age, ethnic background and religion.
- **Let students do Task 1.** Help less able students to read the information from the graphs. For question 3, encourage more able students to consider the numbers of people involved as well as percentages. If appropriate, ask them to consider how ratio might be a useful analytic tool.
- Read Task 2 with students. Explain what the **cost of living** is. Discuss the fact that, on average, the cost of items such as fuel, food and other essentials goes up each year. This is called **inflation**. Distribute the data sheet, the example bank statement. Ask if there are any items on the list that students think Kamal would not have to pay once he retired. Explain the idea of **compound interest** and advise students they will have to use this for question 2. However, point out that Kamal withdraws money from his account and they must allow for this. Students could use a spreadsheet for question 2b.
- **Let students do Task 2.** Check that they all have the correct total for the bank statement. When they have done question 1, make sure they all agree what Kamal would not have to pay for when he retires.
- Read Task 3 with students. Ask how they will calculate the amount of tax to be paid on £19 400. (Answer: £19 400 − £6470 gives taxable pay of £12 930, find 20% of that, as £2586.) Tell students that national insurance is worked out on the full or gross salary of £19 400. Explain that pension contributions are set against tax, which means that such payments are not taxed.
- **Let students do Task 3.** Explain to students that they need to find the saving in tax by paying into a private pension. They may also like to consider take-home pay.

Advanced ***

- Read Task 4 with students. Explain that in around 2009, the world went into a **recession**, with Greece probably suffering the worst effects. Ask students what they understand by the term. (Answer: A time of general economic decline; when, for example, a country owes more that it earns, for a sustained period.) Explain that, when the coalition Government came into power in 2010, it had to try to pay off huge debts owed by the UK; for example, the Department for Education had to find a way to cut £5 billion from its budget. Increasing the retirement age brings in more national insurance contributions, at the same time reducing the percentage of people claiming retirement pensions. Discuss whether students think there is a need to raise the retirement age. Encourage objective views, for example: *Yes, otherwise when I come to retire I won't get a pension at all or will have to work until I am over 70 years old.*

- **Let students do Task 4.** Ask students why it might be acceptable to approximate the numbers of males and females aged from 65 to 70. (Answer: The data is only estimated.) Remind students that the census is only carried out every 10 years, with the last one having been taken in 2001. Tell students they can approximate the number of people for each year, from the age of 65 to 70, or find an average over the five years.

- Task 5 (extension) could be done as homework, perhaps in pairs. Make sure students all know the difference between a **final salary** pension and an **average salary** pension, and can describe them in their own words. Explain the term **index-linked**, which means, for example, the pension goes up with the retail price index. They should note whether the pensions they find are index-linked. Make sure students find at least two examples of the interest rate of an investment ISA. Distribute plain paper and make sure students fold it in half, to produce their leaflets. They need to plan carefully what information they will put on the front and back, and what will go inside the leaflet. Alternatively, they could use appropriate software packages to produce their leaflets on computer. Suitable websites for research are listed above.

Plenary

- Ask students their opinions about the increase in the retirement age. Were they surprised at how little – or how much – pension the state provides? Ask if they think they will take out a private pension as soon as they are working.

- Ask students to try to give the percentage population change for their local area, and ask how they think it will affect their chances of getting a job near where they live.

Outcomes

- Students will have used maths to identify a situation and obtained the information needed to find solutions.
- Students will have investigated how to use a range of maths to solve a problem.
- Students will have given opinions, based on mathematical data.
- Students will have interpreted the solutions to their calculations and communicated their conclusions in the form of leaflets and posters.

Answers

Task 1

1   a   There was a steady decline in the rate of population growth from 1962 until 1974 with the exception of a small rise around 1971–1972. Between about 1974 and 1978, and again in 1982, the population was in decline, shown by negative percentage growth. The population increased at a varying rate from 1983 to 2008, when it grew to its second highest growth rate in approximately 50 years.

   b $60\,944\,000 \times 1.007 = 61\,370\,608$

   c $58\,789\,194 \times 1.005^{33} = 69\,307\,071$

Advanced ***

2 a More people are living to 85 and above, there is a greater proportion of people aged from 65 to 84 and a smaller proportion of people of working age (16 to 64). Also shown is a decreasing under-16 population.

b People aged 16–64 = 69 307 071 × 0.6 = 41 584 243
People aged 65+ = 69 307 071 × 0.22 = 15 247 556

3 Students should conclude that as the proportion of people aged 65 and over increases, and as more of these people live past 85, the total pension requirement will increase. At the same time, the proportion of working-age people is decreasing. Proportionally fewer people of working age are required to pay to support proportionally more retired people. The proportion of under 16s is also falling, so there will be proportionally fewer people entering the employment market in future, indicating that the trend shown in the bar chart is likely to continue. Pension contributions from working people will have to rise.

Using the total population figures found for 2009 and 2034 in question 1 confirms that there will be more people of working age in 2034 than in 2009 (61 370 608 × 0.65 = 39 890 895 in 2009 rising to 41 584 243 in 2034). However, the number of people aged 65+ that their NI contributions must support is predicted to increase more quickly (61 370 608 × 0.16 = 9 819 297 in 2009 rising to 15 247 566 in 2034).

In 2009, the ratio of the number of people aged over 65 to the number of people of working age is about 16% : 65% = 1 : 4.06; by 2034 it is predicted to be about 22% : 60% = 1 : 2.73. Effectively, each retired person must be supported by the NI contributions of fewer working-age people.

Task 2

1 a Total outgoings are £1308.13

b Kamal should try to pay off credit cards A and B, his mortgage and his car loan before he retires. After retirement, he will no longer need to make payments for mortgage insurance and protection, union membership or life insurance. Students are likely to decide that Kamal will continue to pay for pet supplies, gas, electricity, his home telephone, television rental, council tax, home insurance, supermarket shopping and a TV licence. They may decide that some of the other items are non-essential or, for example, that Kamal spends less on petrol when he is not working. They should decide on a final figure of £614.32 or less per month. £614.32 × 12 ÷ 52 = £141.77 per week.

2 a Based on the figures given for answers above, £97.65 − £141.77 = −£44.12
Kamal needs to find an extra £44.12 per week.

b £44.12 × 52 = £2294.24 per year.

Year	Balance at start of year (£)	Year's withdrawals ()	Balance at end of year (£)	Interest on balance at end of year (£)
1	50 000.00	2294.24	47 705.76	1144.94
2	48 850.70	2294.24	46 556.46	1117.35
3	47 673.81	2294.24	45 379.57	1089.11
4	46 468.68	2294.24	44 174.44	1060.19
5	45 234.63	2294.24	42 940.39	1030.57
6	43 970.96	2294.24	41 676.72	1000.24
7	42 676.96	2294.24	40 382.72	969.19
8	41 351.91	2294.24	39 057.67	937.38

Advanced ***

9	39 995.05	2294.24	37 700.81	904.82
10	38 605.63	2294.24	36 311.39	871.47
11	37 182.86	2294.24	34 888.62	837.33
12	35 725.95	2294.24	33 431.71	802.36
13	34 234.07	2294.24	31 939.83	766.56
14	32 706.39	2294.24	30 412.15	729.89
15	31 142.04	2294.24	28 847.80	692.35
16	29 540.14	2294.24	27 245.90	653.90
17	27 899.81	2294.24	25 605.57	614.53
18	26 220.10	2294.24	23 925.86	574.22
19	24 500.08	2294.24	22 205.84	532.94
20	22 738.78	2294.24	20 444.54	490.67
21	20 935.21	2294.24	18 640.97	447.38
22	19 088.35	2294.24	16 794.11	403.06
23	17 197.17	2294.24	14 902.93	357.67
24	15 260.60	2294.24	12 966.36	311.19
25	13 277.55	2294.24	10 983.31	263.60
26	11 246.91	2294.24	8952.67	214.86
27	9167.54	2294.24	6873.30	164.96
28	7038.26	2294.24	4744.02	113.86
29	4857.87	2294.24	2563.63	61.53
30	2625.16	2294.24	330.92	7.94
31	338.86	2294.24	−1955.38	

Kamal will run out of money after just over 30 years, well after he reaches 85.

Advanced ***

Task 3

1 a 19 400 × 0.06 = £1164

b 19 400 × 0.08 = £1552 £1552 + £1164 = £2716

2 When not paying into a pension:
tax = (£19 400 − £6470) × 0.2 = £2586; NI = £19 400 × 0.11 = £2134; total tax and NI = £4720

When paying into a pension at 6% of salary:
£19 400 − £1164 = £18 236; tax is (£18 236 − £6470) × 0.2 = £2353.20; NI is £19 400 × 0.11 = £2134 total tax and NI = £4487.20.

When paying into a pension, the tax bill is reduced by £4720 − £4487.20 = £232.80

The amount paid into the pension is £1164. This means that paying into a pension reduces annual take-home pay by £1164 − £232.80 = £931.20.

Task 4

1 Males: aged 65 = approximately 300 000 aged 70 = approximately 250 000.
Average = (300 000 + 250 000) ÷ 2 = 275 000
Estimated total males aged 65–70 = 275 000 × 5 = 1 375 000

Females: aged 65 = approximately 300 000 aged 70 = approximately 250 000
Average = (300 000 + 250 000) ÷ 2 = 275 000
Estimated total females aged 65–70 = 275 000 × 5 = 1 375 000

Total males + females aged 65–70 = 1 375 000 + 1 375 000 = 2 750 000

2 2 750 000 × 28 207 × 0.11 = £8 532 617 500 in NI contributions

3 Not all people will be earning this amount. Higher earners in particular may have paid into a private pension and taken early retirement; others may decide to go part time and/or take a lower-paid job in order to improve their work–life balance. People doing manual labour and other particularly demanding jobs may not be able to continue in the same sort of work as they get older.

Task 5

Students should produce an informative leaflet about retirement, using numerical data to back up their opinions. They should reach some or all of these conclusions:

- Final salary pension is based only on what you earn before retiring; the pension is not as good if pay is frozen just before you retire.
- Calculation of average salary pension is based on the last three years' salary and is linked to the consumer price index.
- Different private pension providers offer different deals, so it is worth shopping around when it comes to buying a pension.
- ISA's are another good way of saving. Interest on savings is not liable for tax, although the capital invested cannot be set against tax (as is the case with pension payments). There are limits on how much can be put into an ISA each year. It is important that an ISA pays more than the inflation rate, otherwise over many years, the money will not be worth as much as it was when it was invested.
- To achieve a reasonable pension on retirement a general rule of thumb is to save a percentage of your salary equal to half your age (for example a 30-year-old should save 15% of their salary).

Advanced ***

London black cabs

Learning objectives
- **Representing Level 2**: recognise that data may be represented in many different ways and can be used for mathematical calculations and problem solving
- **Analysing Level 2**: analyse graphs and data, using appropriate techniques
- **Interpreting Level 2**: interpret results and solutions and make generalisations about them

APP
Evidence for Using and applying mathematics Level 8, Shape, space and measure Level 8

PLTS
Develops Independent enquirers, Creative thinkers

Every child matters outcomes
Make a positive contribution

Cross-curricular links
Science, English

Underpinning maths
- Distance, time, velocity and acceleration
- Drawing and interpreting graphs
- Area under a graph

Resources
- *Student book*, pages 150–153
- Graph paper
- Calculators
- Internet access (optional)

Context
Students may never have travelled in a London black cab but they should have an understanding of taxi services. This activity involves using graphs and tables to obtain useful mathematical information, enabling analysis and comparison of data.

Lesson plan
This activity takes two lessons. You may do it in one lesson by using Tasks 1, questions 1 and 2 only, Task 3, questions 1 and 2 only and Task 4, question 1 only. Other questions or extensions may be used for homework.

Starter
- An article from the internet about the average speed of London traffic could provide an effective introduction to this lesson.
- Discuss with students what they understand by 'average speed' and remind them of the relationships:

$$\text{speed} = \frac{\text{distance}}{\text{time}} \quad \text{or, more specifically,} \quad \text{average speed} = \frac{\text{total distance travelled}}{\text{total time taken}}$$

Advanced ***

- Discuss with students the difference between speed and velocity. (Answer: Velocity includes the direction of travel.)
- Remind students that, on a velocity–time graph, the **gradient** gives the **acceleration**. A negative gradient indicates negative acceleration, which is also called **deceleration**.
- Sketch a velocity–time graph to show acceleration, constant velocity and then deceleration. This will be trapezium-shaped. Ask students what is happening in each of the three parts of the graph.

Main activity

- Based on the discussion of London traffic, ask students to describe a typical short journey in London by car; together, sketch a velocity–time graph of that journey.
- **Let students do Task 1**. The graphs describe very short journeys, so can be assumed to be dealing with velocity, rather than speed. They could do question 4 in pairs or small groups.
- Discuss with students their comparisons between the first cab's journey and the second cab's journey.
- **Let more able students do Task 2 (extension).** Ask students who have done this task how they worked out whether the driver was speeding. Discuss with students the conversions between metres and kilometres, and then kilometres and miles (1.6 km is approximately 1 mile) and how they converted seconds to hours.
- Read Task 3 with students. Refer them back to the velocity–time graph used in Task 1 (from the passenger being dropped off until the zebra crossing). Explain that the area under a velocity–time graph gives the distance travelled. Discuss how to find the area under the graph. Encourage students to identify the shape as a trapezium and remind them how to find its area, using the formula:

    $A = \frac{1}{2}(a + b)h$

- **Let students do Task 3**. Note that, in some cases, finding the area under the graph may involve finding the area of composite shapes; students will have to decide how to split the area into several trapeziums.
- Again, discuss with students their comparisons between the first cab's journey and the second cab's journey.
- Ask students how they think a taxi fare is calculated. What variables do they think are considered? Is a fare that only takes account of distance appropriate? Is a fare that only takes account of time appropriate?
- Read Task 4 with students. Discuss how they may approach it. For example, for question 1, you could suggest they mark on the graph where the first 280 m and the first 60 seconds occur, and then count from there to see if the next 140 m or 30 seconds is reached first.
- **Let students do Task 4**. In groups, they could compare their answers to question 1 before moving on to question 2, so that they have the opportunity to discuss and check their approach.
- **Let students work in small groups to do Task 5 (extension).** Encourage them to create a table with the headings 'Social', 'Environmental' and 'Economic' and list factors for consideration in each column, as they discuss whether to increase or decrease the number of black cabs on London roads. Encourage students to think about the mathematical information they may seek, to help them understand each factor better. For example, under 'Social' they could include 'rush hour congestion', supported by mathematical surveys of the numbers of people who use different forms of public transport at busy times of the day.

Advanced ***

Plenary
- Ask students if they are surprised by how expensive it is to travel by black cab in London, and how slow they can be.
- Ask students what information they might collect in order to compare the speed and cost of taxi travel with other means of transport in London. What mathematical analysis might they do in order to make their comparison?

Outcomes
o Students will have used mathematics to gain insight into a real-life problem.
o Students will have drawn graphs.
o Students will have interpreted graphs to enable them to do calculations, and to make comparisons.

Answers

Task 1

1 a 3 m/s^2 b 0 m/s^2 c -2.25 m/s^2

2

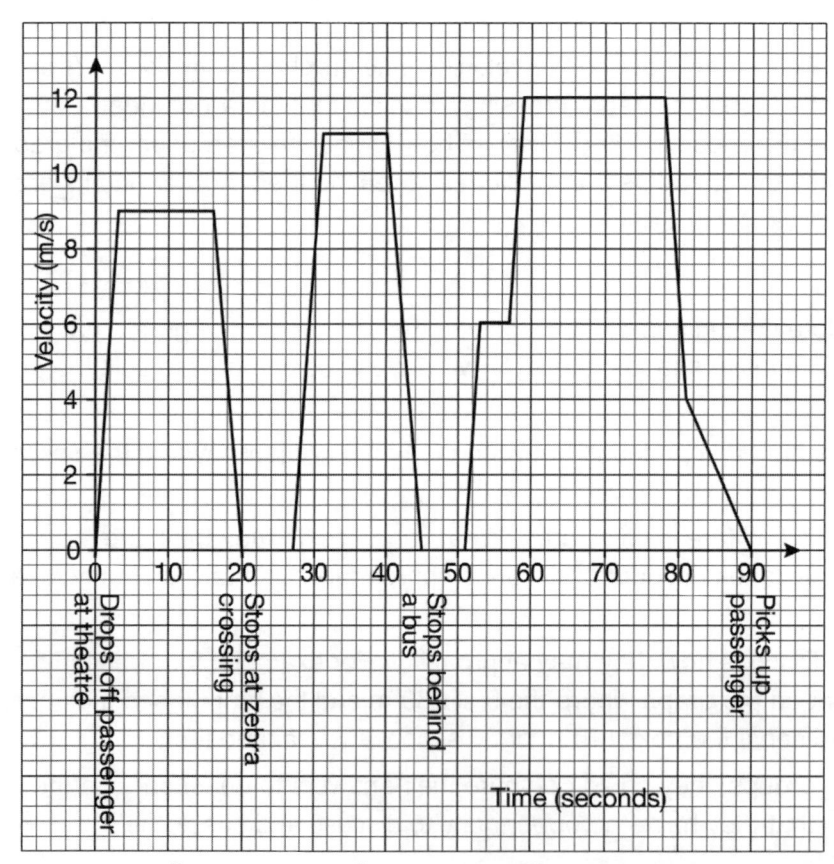

[Velocity-time graph with Velocity (m/s) on y-axis (0 to 12) and Time (seconds) on x-axis (0 to 90). Annotations along x-axis: Drops off passenger at theatre; Stops at zebra crossing; Stops behind a bus; Picks up passenger.]

3 a 2.75 m/s^2 b -2.2 m/s^2 c 3 m/s^2
   d 3 m/s^2 e -2.67 m/s^2 f -0.44 m/s^2

4 a The second taxi driver spends twice the time (3 minutes) as the first taxi driver (1.5 minutes) between dropping off and picking up another passenger.

   b The second taxi driver only stops and starts again once, compared to twice for the first taxi driver, between dropping off and picking up passengers.

   c The second taxi driver achieves a greater maximum velocity when he accelerates, reaching a maximum velocity of 15 m/s, compared to the first taxi driver who reaches a maximum velocity of 12 m/s.

Advanced ***

d The second taxi driver achieves the same kinds of acceleration and deceleration (2.5 m/s^2, 3 m/s^2, –2.6 m/s^2, 3 m/s^2, –2.5 m/s^2) as the first taxi driver.

Task 2 (extension)

For the first part of the journey, the taxi driver reaches a velocity of 13 m/s, which is 0.013 km/s = 46.8 km/h = 29.25 miles per hour; for the second part of the journey, the taxi driver reaches a velocity of 15 m/s, which is 0.015 km/s = 54 km/h = 33.75 miles per hour. For the second part of the journey the taxi driver was speeding.

Task 3

1 148.5 m

2 615 m

3 The distance travelled between passengers by the second cab was 1738 m, that is 1.738 km (almost three times the distance travelled between passengers by the first cab).

Task 4

1 £5.20

2 £5.80

3 £7.60

Task 5 (extension)

The types of mathematical information students may consider collecting:

- a survey of the number of people using black cabs and other means of transport on different days and different times of day
- the carbon emissions of London black cabs
- a typical weekly wage for a London black cab driver
- the cost of travel on alternative means of transport.

Advanced ***

Extreme sports

Learning objectives
- **Representing Level 2**: draw graphs to represent constant speed and acceleration
- **Analysing Level 2**: apply mathematics to find areas, volumes, times and distances
- **Interpreting Level 2**: draw conclusions from complex calculations

APP
Evidence for Using and applying mathematics Level 8, Calculating Level 8, Algebra Level 8, Shape, space and measure Level 7

PLTS
Develops Independent enquirers, Reflective learners, Effective participators

Every child matters outcomes
Enjoy and achieve, Achieve economic well-being

Cross-curricular links
Science, PE

Underpinning maths
- Distance, time, velocity and acceleration
- Drawing and interpreting graphs
- Solving linear equations
- Circumference, surface area and volume of spheres

Resources
- *Student Book* pages 154–156
- Calculators
- Graph paper

Context
Students will have different sporting experiences. Some will take part in more dangerous sports than others. Few will have experienced zorbing or skydiving.

Lesson plan
This activity takes two lessons. The theme for the first lesson is zorbing (Tasks 1–2); for the second it is skydiving (Tasks 3–5).

Starter
- Ask students to discuss, in pairs, which sports they participate in regularly, and which they watch, either live or on television.
- Discuss the most common sports enjoyed by the group (as participants or spectators).
- In pairs, students discuss any extreme sports they are aware of, and whether or not they would like to participate in any of these.

Advanced***

- Collate a class list of extreme sports. Discuss whether they are more likely to be participant sports than spectator sports.
- What is different about extreme sports? (Answer: They often offer a personal challenge rather than competition.)

Main activity

- Read through the notes in the *Student book*, introducing zorbing and skydiving. Ask students which they would enjoy more. Ask them to explain why.
- Look at the information given in Task 1. Ask students to estimate whether there is more air in the inner ball (diameter 2 metres) or in the air cushion between the inner and the outer ball. **Let students do Task 1**.
- Some students might need support in applying the formulae; some might use the diameter instead of the radius.
- Challenge more able students to write simplified formulae for the total surface area of two spheres of radius r and R (Answer: $A = 4\pi(R^2 + r^2)$) and the difference in volumes (Answer: $V = \frac{4}{3}\pi(R^3 - r^3)$).
- The world record speed for zorbing is 51.8 km/h. Discuss what students think typical average speeds over a run of 200 metres might be. (Answer: As it starts from a speed of 0 and gradually increases, the average speed might only be about 10–20 km/h, even though much higher speeds are reached during the run.)
- Discuss the 'thrill' element of zorbing. The speed record might not seem fast (at 32.2 mph) but the excitement factor comes from the spinning of the ball. The participant, who is strapped in, rotates with the ball.
- **Let students start Task 2**. For more able students after question 2, **extend the task** by asking them to calculate how long it takes for the zorb to complete one revolution at different speeds. Discuss the cost of sports. Some students will have participated in sports for which they have to pay. Ask how much they pay, and how long the activity lasts.
- Look at question 3. Discuss whether the students think that £30 is a fair price to pay for a zorb experience. (They might question the cost when, unlike karting or even skydiving, there is no power source to pay for.) For more able students, **extend the task further** by asking: What might be a sensible average cost per second? (Answer: £0.70–1.00 might be a reasonable assumption. Beginners are unlikely to reach high speeds.)
- Ask students whether they think they are more likely to hurt themselves jumping off a roof 20 metres high than one that is 2 metres high. (Answer: Yes, as they would hit the ground at greater speed.) Ask which falls faster, a sheet of stiff paper rolled loosely into a ball, or one that is flat. (Answer: The flat sheet has a greater surface area and so has more air resistance.)
- Discuss these two points in connection with skydiving.
    1 Do skydivers keep falling faster and faster as they freefall? (Answer: No, eventually the air resistance counterbalances the acceleration due to gravity, and they reach terminal velocity.)
    2 Does the skydiver's speed change, according to whether they are in freefall vertically (head above feet) or horizontally (lying down)? (Answer: Yes, vertically they would fall faster as there is less air resistance. Compare to dropping a sheet of stiff paper, as discussed previously.)

Advanced ***

- Read through the introduction to Task 3 with the class, and discuss question 1. Discuss how the graph can be modelled in three different sections. **Let students do Task 3**.

- It might be necessary to support some students by discussing what values of time, t, to take for each part of the graph. Make sure that students realise that for the first 30 seconds the second skydiver's equation will be simply $d = 10\,000$. For more able students, **extend the task** by asking then to derive and solve a pair of simultaneous equations to check their answers.

- Discuss the equations of the first skydiver. Use the equation $d = 10\,000 - 5t^2$ to calculate his height when he reaches terminal velocity after 7 seconds. (Answer: $10\,000 - 245 = 9755$ m) If he free-falls at 75 m/s, what will the gradient of the graph be? (Answer: -75) Ask students to check that the equation of a straight line with gradient -75 passing through (7, 9755) is $d = 10\,280 - 75t$.

- Use this equation to find his height after 60 seconds, when he opens his parachute. (Answer: 5780 m), and use this information, with his speed of 7 m/s, to check the accuracy of the third equation, $d = 6200 - 7t$.

- Remind students that the second skydiver is 30 seconds behind the first. Ask what effect this has on the graphs. (Answer: The first part of the second skydiver's graphs should be a translation of $\begin{pmatrix} 30 \\ 0 \end{pmatrix}$ of the first skydiver's; they join up when she opens her parachute.) Ask how students would amend the equation to produce this transformation. (Answer: Replace t with $t - 30$.) Students can derive the equations of the second skydiver from those of the first, using this method.

- **Let students do Task 4**. They will need to work out the time taken for each section of the fall, and then find a cost per second. To support those who need help, give hints. Ask:

    1. What is your altitude after 7 seconds? (Answer: 3755 metres)
    2. How much longer will it take to reach 1650 m? (Answer: 28 seconds)

- Discuss which activity, zorbing or skydiving, is cheaper per second. (Answer: Skydiving, but only just.)

- Discuss Task 5 (extension) with students. They are required to research any world records that relate to skydiving, and then suggest ways in which these records compare to the figures they used in Task 4. Then students should research any other zorbing world records, such as the longest zorbing run. **Let students do Task 5**.

Plenary

- Ask students if the fact that skydiving is cheaper per second is what they would have expected. (Answer: You might expect skydiving to be more expensive because of fuel costs and the one-to-one staffing costs.)

- Ask students if they think it is sensible to compare costs in this way. (Answer: Probably not, but it does make zorbing appear to be very expensive.)

Outcomes

- Students will have calculated with perimeters, circumference and volume, time, distance and speed, and with unit costs (cost per second).
- Students will have drawn graphs that combine quadratic and linear elements and solved problems graphically.
- Students will have solved simultaneous equations algebraically.

Advanced***

Answers

Task 1

1 40.8 m² (to 1 dp)
2 4.2 m³ (to 1 dp)
3 9.9 m³ (to 1 dp)   (The air cushion has over twice the air of the inner ball.)

Task 2

1 9.4 m (to 1 dp)
2 **a** 21.2 (to 1 dp) **b** 31.8 (to 1 dp)

Extension

Speed (km/h)	10	20	30	40	50
Time (seconds)	3.4	1.7	1.1	0.8	0.7

3

	10 km/h	20 km/h	30 km/h	40 km/h	50 km/h
200 m	72 sec	36 sec	24 sec	18 sec	14.4 sec
300 m	108 sec	54 sec	36 sec	27 sec	21.6 sec

4

	10 km/h	20 km/h	30 km/h	40 km/h	50 km/h
200 m	£0.42	£0.83	£1.25	£1.67	£2.08
300 m	£0.28	£0.56	£0.83	£1.11	£1.39

Task 3

1

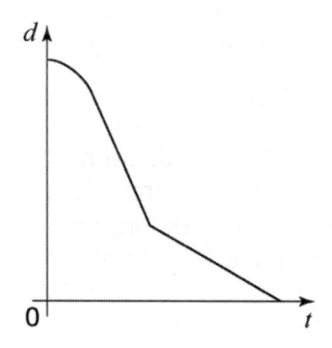

Advanced ***

2, 3 The first skydiver is shown as a solid line, the second as a dashed line.

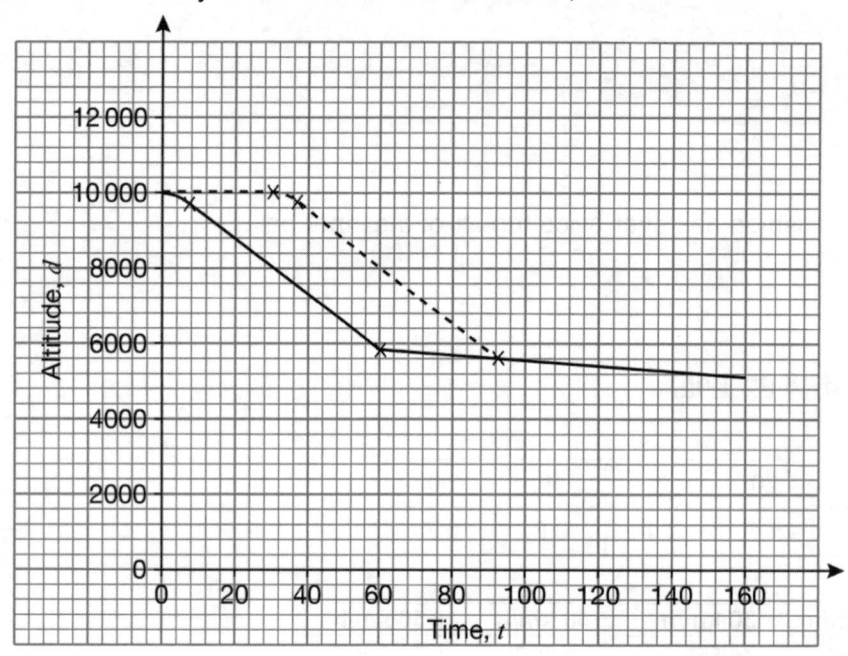

The skydivers are at the same altitude after 93 seconds at a height of 5500 m.

Extension

The equations are: $d = 6200 - 7t$ and $d = 12\,530 - 75t$, the solution is $t = 93.1$ seconds, $d = 5548$ metres.

Task 4

1 After 7 seconds, height $= 4000 - 5 \times 7^2 = 3755$ m

To fall from 3755 m to 1650 m at 75 m/s will take $(3755 - 1650) \div 75 = 28$ seconds

The last 1650 m at 7 m/s takes 236 seconds.

Total time = 271 seconds.

Cost per second = £155 ÷ 271 = £0.57

2 There is little to choose, but skydiving is probably a little cheaper per second.

Task 5 (extension)

Skydiving: The greatest freefall delay made in one jump was carried out by Captain Joseph Kittinger. He jumped from an altitude of 84 700 feet (25 820 m) from a balloon in Tularosa, New Mexico, USA on 16 August 1960. His freefall lasted for 4 minutes and 37 seconds before his canopy automatically opened. Throughout his skydive he achieved freefall speeds of up to 614 miles per hour (1000 km/h).

This is 2.5 times higher than the height used in Task 4, and his maximum speed was about four times the 75 m/s used as a terminal velocity.

Zorbing: Steve Camp holds the record for the greatest zorbing distance when he travelled 570 metres in a single roll in Paengaroa. This is about double the length of a usual zorb run.

Advanced ***

Maths – music to your ears?

Learning objectives
- **Representing Level 2**: identify information to solve a non-routine problem in an unfamiliar context
- **Analysing Level 2**: apply a range of mathematics to solve a problem
- **Interpreting Level 2**: interpret and communicate a solution to the problem, using graphical methods to draw conclusions

APP
Evidence for Using and applying mathematics Level 7, Numbers and the number system Level 6, Calculating Level 6, Algebra Level 6

PLTS
Develops Independent enquirers, Creative thinkers, Reflective learners

Every child matters outcomes
Make a positive contribution, Enjoy and achieve

Cross-curricular links
Music, Science, Design and technology

Underpinning maths
- Extracting information from tables
- Calculating ratios and fractions
- Constructing line graphs
- Rearranging formulae
- Finding reciprocals

Resources
- *Student book*, pages 157–159
- Data sheet 1: Background information
- Data sheet 2: Fretting a ukulele
- Answer sheet: Task 5 questions 3 & 4
- Graph paper
- Slinky spring
- Calculators
- Access to keyboards

Useful websites
- www.bgfl.org/bgfl/custom/resources_ftp/client_ftp/ks2/music/piano/ (virtual keyboard)

Context
This activity encourages students to look at the maths that is implicit in music, to identify patterns and explore how these relate to other aspects of our lives. Many students may be familiar with reading music and the names and values of the different notes. Students should be familiar with the terms period and frequency but will not need to use them to perform calculations in the activity.

© HarperCollins*Publishers* 2010

Advanced ***

Lesson plan
This activity takes one or two lessons. Task 5 (extension) could be set as homework.

Starter
- Ask students whether any of them play musical instruments. Ask what they play, and how long they have been playing. Encourage them to discuss their music and to say why they like doing it.
- Explain that a musical note, like any other sound, is produced by oscillations or **waves** in air molecules and travels at the speed of sound. The peaks of the waves for the note are evenly spaced and the time between successive high points is the **period**. The shorter the period, the higher the **pitch** or **frequency** of the note. The frequency, which is the number of times the wave oscillates per second, is measured in **hertz**, which is equivalent to cycles per second.
- Mention that historically, there is a strong relationship between music and maths. Emphasise that Pythagoras was able to determine that there were mathematical relationships between different musical notes, based on ratios, long before it was realised that sound was produced by waves.

Main activity
- Ask students if they know what an **octave** is and how many notes it comprises. (Answer: An octave is a set of thirteen notes, each one a semitone higher than the one before it. Two semitones equal one tone.)
- A scale is a selection of eight notes from the octave, in a particular sequence. Taking as an example the scale of C major, the notes are: C, D, E, F, G, A, B then back to C. The sequence is produced by starting at C, then moving one tone to the note D, then a tone further on to E, one semitone to F, and so on so that the whole sequence is:

  key note, tone, tone, semitone, tone, tone, tone, semitone

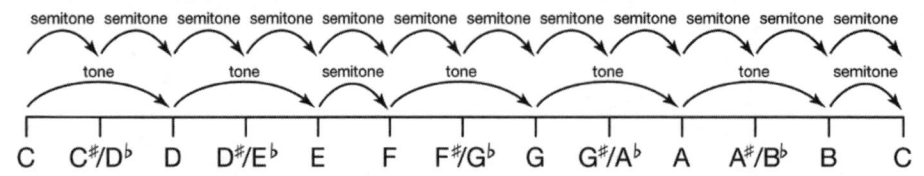

  semitone semitone semitone semitone semitone semitone semitone semitone semitone semitone semitone semitone
  tone   tone   semitone   tone   tone   tone   semitone
  C   C$^\#$/D$^\flat$ D   D$^\#$/E$^\flat$ E   F   F$^\#$/G$^\flat$ G   G$^\#$/A$^\flat$ A   A$^\#$/B$^\flat$ B   C

- Use the picture of the piano keyboard to show the students that they can start a scale on any note (including sharp or flat notes) provided that the same sequence of tones and semitones is followed. Some students may know that the piano is set up to make C major an easy key to play. Explain that music that is written using notes that are in the same scale tends to sound pleasing.
- **Let students do Task 1**. The students should draw up a table that has the header row as follows, in order to fit in with common musical nomenclature: 1st, 2nd, 3rd, 4th, 5th, 6th, 7th, 8th.
- You could offer students the chance to play out these scales on a virtual keyboard (see the website listed above). They should work out that the intervals between the notes sound the same in every key, following the same sequence as above.
- Before students start Task 2, distribute data sheet 1 and read though it with the class. Explain that notes can be played in more than one octave. The human ear can hear a range of about 10 octaves, starting with the lowest note C0, and going up to A9. In this activity they will use notes near to C4, commonly called **middle C**. Notes in higher octaves have a higher pitch or frequency, meaning that the peaks of the sound wave reach our ears closer together than lower notes.

Advanced ***

- Stress that octaves form a repeating pattern. Use the virtual keyboard or the table in the *Student book*, to demonstrate that, after they go up from C4 to C5, they could start again and go from C5 to C6.

- **Let students do Task 2**. Question 1 is a simple exercise in ratios. For question 2, encourage students to draw up a table of the required frequencies before they start drawing their graphs. The graph should have frequency as the vertical axis (*y*-axis) and the position of the note in scale as the horizontal (*x*-axis), i.e. 1st, 2nd, 3rd, 4th, 5th, 6th, 7th, 8th. The students should notice that they cannot draw a straight line through all the points that make up a scale, but should join each point to the next, using short straight lines. Students should realise that the spacing between the notes increases on the right-hand side of the graph.

- Before moving on to Task 3, discuss **frequency** and **period**. Ask if any students can explain the terms. Show students the equation:

$$\text{frequency} = \frac{1}{\text{period}}$$

- Ensure that the students can rearrange the formula to find the period from the frequency of each note. Students may need to be shown that they have a reciprocal button $\boxed{\tfrac{1}{x}}$ on their calculators.

- You could use a slinky spring to demonstrate how longitudinal waves occur. Explain that once the sound of the note arrives at the listener's ear, the next peak will arrive at the time given by the period, and that the second will arrive the same amount of time after that, and so on. When working out the timing of peaks, the students need to complete a series of repeated additions. Encourage them to use their calculator's constant function key $\boxed{K}$ or press the $\boxed{+}$ key twice to make their task easier.

- **Let students do Task 3**. When they are plotting the peaks for each frequency, show students how to produce the appropriate type of graph. The horizontal axis should be time (in seconds) and the peaks for each frequency should be plotted in a horizontal line and labelled correctly.

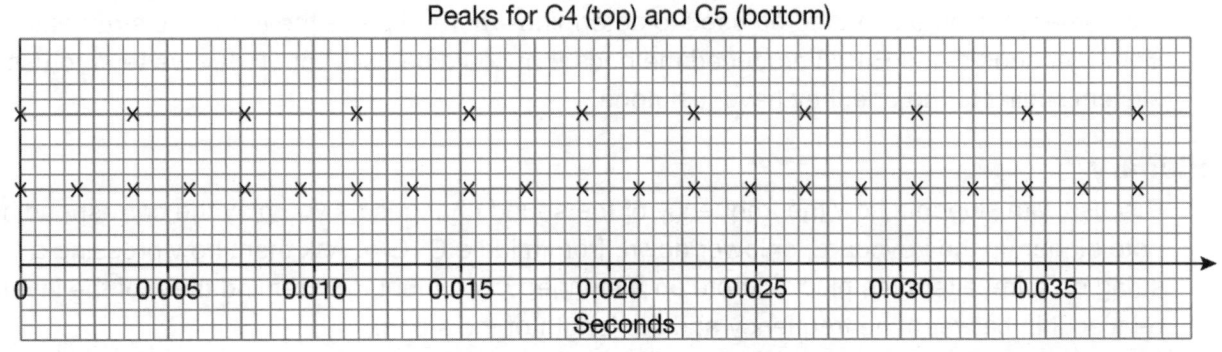

Peaks for C4 (top) and C5 (bottom)

When students are interpreting the graphs it should be obvious to them where the peaks line up. However, the given frequencies have been rounded and so may not line up perfectly on every student's chart.

- In Task 4 students should take care to compare the peaks of the notes that the question requires, which is C to its 3rd and C to its 5th, not the 3rd to the 5th.

- **Let students do Task 4**. The ratios are of the form $a : b$ and $a : c$. In question 5, students need to find a ratio of the form $a : b : c$. if they multiply the ratio for the 5th by 2 they get a ratio of fundamental : 3rd : 5th as 4 : 5 : 6. Students may need help to realise that they can treat ratios in a similar way as they would fractions.

Advanced ***

- Tell students that they have just worked out the chord of C major, which consists of C, E and G. Explain that the major chord for any key can be played using the notes they highlighted in their table from Task 1. The ratios identified above will be true for the notes that comprise all the major chords. If possible, give students the opportunity to try out different chords on a keyboard (real or virtual). More able students may work out the major chords of flat or sharp notes, though these are not covered in this activity. **Extend the task** by asking students to plot a graph of the peaks of the notes C4 and F#4. Ask how often the peaks line up. Ask what they can predict about the sound of this chord. Students should realise that the peaks do not line up in a repeating pattern, which suggests that the notes will not give a chord that sounds harmonious.

- Look at Task 5 (extension) with students. Distribute data sheet 2, which gives a diagram of a ukulele. The aim of the task is for students to work out where the 12 frets need to be positioned along the neck of the ukulele in order to produce the 13 notes of an octave. The students can calculate all the measurements they need by knowing the length of the string and using the ratios of frequencies to the frequency of the fundamental note, C4, from the table they used on data sheet 1.

- The distance from the bridge to the fret is calculated from the formula:

$$\text{distance from bridge} = 32 \text{ cm} \times \frac{\text{frequency of fundamental note}}{\text{frequency of desired note}}$$

- The students have previously calculated the correct ratio to determine where to place the fret for the notes E and G (Task 4 **Q3** and **4**). Ensure that the students don't get confused by the terms 3rd and 5th, which refer to the position of the note in the scale of C major. In the full octave E will be five semitones above C and G will be eight semitones above C.

- **Let students do Task 5 (extension)**. They should be able to complete the table on their own, perhaps as homework, using the formula on the worksheet, and then draw the frets in position. They should note that the frets get closer together as they go down the neck of the ukulele.

- Explain to students that before people were able to measure the frequency of a note, other mathematical methods had to be used to determine where to place the frets on instruments. Both Pythagoras and Euclid produced methods that could be used, but today we tend to use a system similar to the one they have just done.

Plenary

- Discuss with students how the frequency of the sound changes as you play the corresponding note higher up the keyboard, or lower down, from middle C (C4). Ask them how pressing a string on a fret alters the plucked note on a stringed instrument, and remind them of the inverse relationship between the frequency and the length of the string.

- Ask the students how many notes are in a scale, and how many in an octave.

- Ask them what a chord is. Why do some chords sound pleasant when played together? (Answer: The ratios of their frequencies is a simple fraction). Mention that any combination of a key note, its 3rd and 5th will produce a pleasant chord, and ask them for some examples (they can read them from their answers to Task 1).

Outcomes

o Students will have used maths to identify a situation and identified the method needed to find solutions.

o Students will have used appropriate checking procedures.

o Students will have interpreted the solutions to their calculations and shown their results graphically.

Advanced ***

Answers

Task 1

a 2, 2, 1, 2, 2, 2, 1 or tone, tone, semitone, tone, tone, tone, semitone

b D, E, F$^\#$(G^b), G, A, B, C$^\#$(D^b), D

c

Note	1st	2nd	3rd	4th	5th	6th	7th	8th
C major	C	D	E	F	G	A	B	C
D major	D	E	F$^\#$(G^b)	G	A	B	C$^\#$(D^b)	D
E major	E	F$^\#$(G^b)	G$^\#$(A^b)	A	B	C$^\#$(D^b)	D$^\#$(E^b)	E
F major	F	G	A	B^b(A$^\#$)	C	D	E	F
G major	G	A	B	C	D	E	F$^\#$(G^b)	G
A major	A	B	C$^\#$(D^b)	D	E	F$^\#$(G^b)	G$^\#$(A^b)	A
B major	B	C$^\#$(D^b)	D$^\#$(E^b)	E	F$^\#$(G^b)	G$^\#$(A^b)	A$^\#$(B^b)	B

Task 2

1 A2 = 110 Hz, A5 = 880 Hz

2 Students should note that the graphs have a similar shape, but that the notes get further apart towards the right-hand end of the graph, both in terms of the separation between scales, and the difference in frequency from the preceding note.

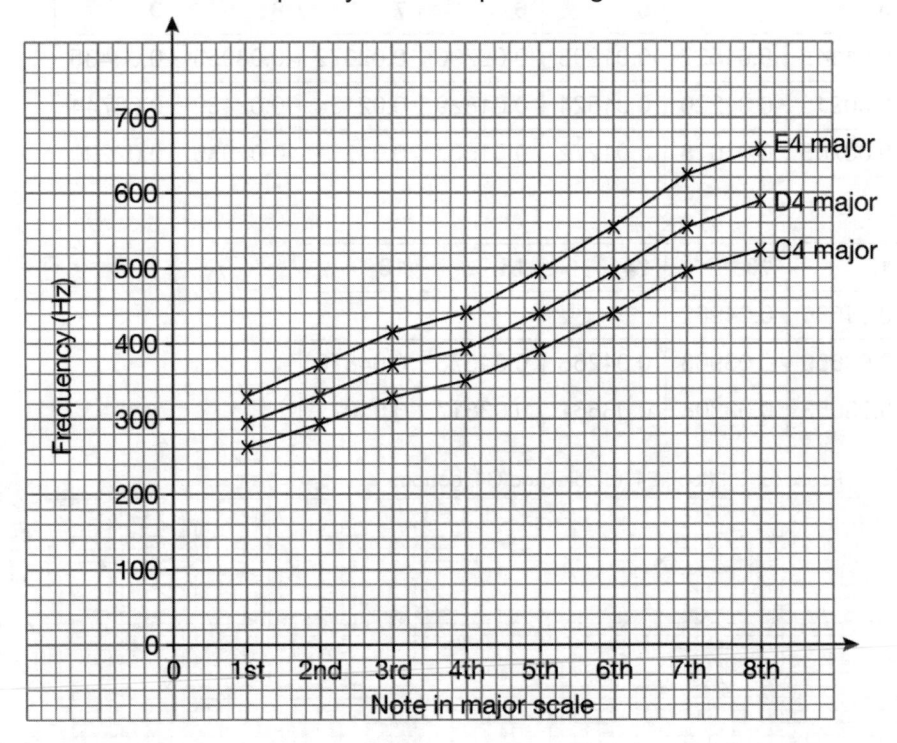

Advanced ***

Task 3

1

Peak	1	2	3	4	5	6	7	8	9	10
C4	0.00382	0.00763	0.01145	0.01527	0.01908	0.02290	0.02672	0.03053	0.03435	0.03817
C5	0.00191	0.00382	0.00573	0.00763	0.0095	0.01145	0.01335	0.01527	0.01718	0.01908

Peaks for C4 (top) and C5 (bottom)

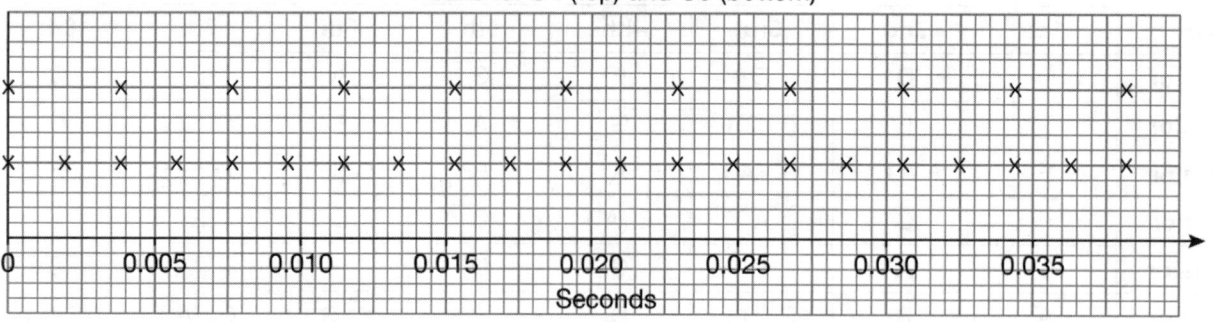

The frequency of C5 is twice that of C4, so every other peak will line up.

2 20 peaks, ratio 2 : 1

Task 4

1 In the scale of C major the 3rd note is E, the 5th note is G

2

Peak	1	2	3	4	5	6	7	8	9
C4	0.00382	0.00763	0.01145	0.01527	0.01908	0.02290	0.02672	0.03053	0.03435
E4	0.00305	0.00610	0.00915	0.01220	0.01524	0.01829	0.02134	0.02439	0.02744
G4	0.00254	0.00509	0.00763	0.01018	0.01272	0.01527	0.01781	0.02036	0.02290

Peak	10	11	12	13	14	15	16
C4	0.03817	0.04198	0.04580	0.04962			
E4	0.03049	0.03354	0.03659	0.03963	0.04268	0.04573	0.04878
G4	0.02545	0.02799	0.03053	0.03308	0.03562	0.03817	0.04071

Peaks for C4 (top), E4 (middle) and G4 (bottom)

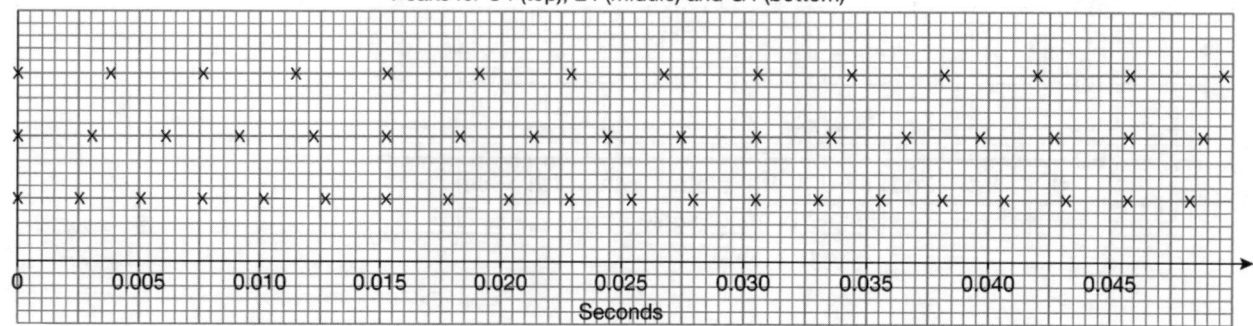

3 The 3rd note E has five peaks in the time the key note C has four. Ratio 5 : 4

4 The 5th note G has three peaks in the time the key note C has two. Ratio 3 : 2

5 They all line up every four peaks of C4, five peaks of E and peaks six of G. Ratio 4 : 5 : 6

The notes of the C major chord will sound pleasant when played together because the peaks line up at regular intervals and have a simple ratio between their frequencies.

Advanced ***

Extension

Peak	1	2	3	4	5	6	7	8	9
C4	0.00382	0.00763	0.01145	0.01527	0.01908	0.02290	0.02672	0.03053	0.03435
F#4	0.00270	0.00541	0.00811	0.01081	0.01351	0.01622	0.01892	0.02162	0.02432

Peak	10	11	12	13	14	15	16	17	18
C4	0.03817	0.04198	0.04580	0.04962					
F#4	0.02703	0.02973	0.03243	0.03514	0.03784	0.04054	0.04324	0.04595	0.04865

Peaks for C4 (top) and F#4 (bottom)

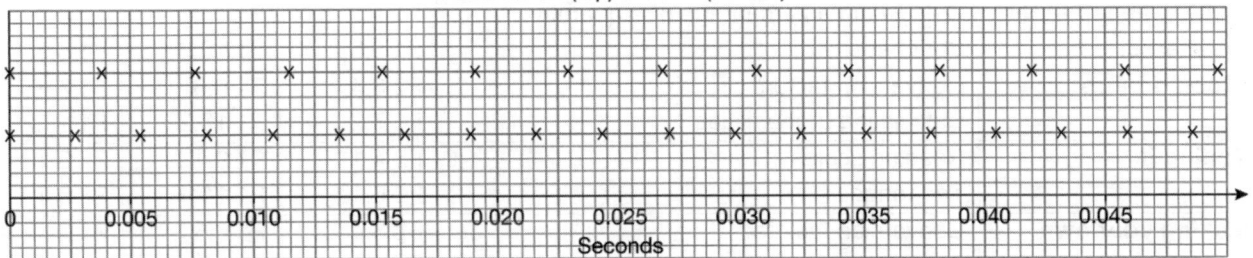

The chord of C4 and F#4 will sound discordant because there is no repeating pattern of peaks lining up.

Task 5 (extension)

1. 16 cm from the bridge

2. Fret for 3rd note 25.6 cm from the bridge, $\frac{4}{5} \times 32$ cm

   Fret for 5th note 21.3 cm from bridge, $\frac{2}{3} \times 32$ cm

3, 4. Answers can be found on the CD-Rom.

New GCSE Maths Functional Skills matching chart for Foundation 1 and 2

Each functional skills topic in the table below has been matched to relevant lessons of the Collins New GCSE Maths Foundation Student Books 1 and 2. These are indicated under the AQA Modular, Edexcel Modular and Edexcel Linear headings.

Think about the ability of your students and their stage of development. A good approach could be to use the activities a topic or two later to recall, revise and consolidate learning.

Beginner Topics*	Lesson	AQA Modular	Edexcel Modular	Edexcel Linear
Birds	Which average to use	F1 6.5	F1 11.5	F2 5.5
	Surveys	F1 8.3	F1 12.3	F1 15.3
Getting ahead in the job market	Calculating a percentage of a quantity	F1 4.2	F1 4.2	F2 3.2
	Bar charts	F1 5.3	F1 10.3	F1 5.5
Blood donors	Conversion factors	F2 3.4	F1 6.6	F1 7.4
	Calculating probabilities	F1 7.2	F1 13.2	F1 11.2
Tuning in	Reading scales	F2 4.1	F1 6.1	F2 6.1
	The range	F1 6.4	F1 11.4	F2 5.4
Making your own fuel	Conversion factors	F2 3.4	F1 6.6	F1 7.4
	Statistical diagrams	F1 5.2	F1 10.2	F1 5.2
Thumbelina	Scale drawings	F2 4.3	F2 3.1	F1 6.3
	Solving problems using Pythagoras' theorem	F2 14.3	F2 17.3	F2 16.3
Off your trolley	Best buys	F2 5.3	F1 4.4	F2 7.4
	Conversion factors	F2 3.4	F1 6.6	F1 7.4
The honey bee	Scale drawings	F2 4.3	F2 3.1	F1 6.3
	Tessellations	F2 10.2	F2 15.2	F1 12.2
Money – making the world go round?	Approximation of calculations	F1 11.5	F1 5.5	F1 14.6
	Conversion graphs	F1 13.1	F1 9.1	F1 9.1
Flags	Lines of symmetry	F2 7.1	F2 9.1	F1 8.1
	Rotational symmetry	F2 7.2	F2 9.2	F1 8.2
Commuting	Calculating a percentage of a quantity	F1 4.2	F1 4.2	F2 3.2
	Pie charts	F1 8.1	F1 12.1	F1 15.1
Website design	The language of algebra	F1 10.1	F1 8.1	F2 4.1
	Flow diagrams and graphs	F1 13.3	F1 9.3	F1 9.3

Improver Topics **	Lesson	AQA Modular	Edexcel Modular	Edexcel Linear
Eat well, live longer	Equivalent percentages, fractions and decimals	F1 4.1	F1 4.1	F2 3.1
	Approximation of calculations	F1 11.5	F1 5.5	F1 14.6
Coastguard search	Area of an irregular shape	F2 6.2	F2 4.2	F2 6.2
	Pythagoras' theorem	F2 14.1	F2 17.1	F2 16.1
Photography: Past, present and future	Ratio	F1 4.5	F1 4.3	F2 7.1
	Conversion factors	F2 3.4	F1 6.6	F1 7.4
Teabag design and production	Nets	F2 4.4	F2 3.2	F1 6.4
	Perimeter	F2 6.1	F2 4.1	F2 6.1
Small-scale farming	The mean	F1 6.3	F1 11.3	F2 5.3
	Powers	F1 9.6	F2 8.6	F1 4.6
Coastguard rescue	Scale drawings	F2 4.3	F2 3.1	F1 6.3
	Bearings	F2 8.8	F2 13.3	F1 10.8
Tomorrow's world	Best buys	F2 5.3	F1 4.4	F2 7.4
	Sensible estimates	F2 4.2	F1 6.2	F1 6.2
Time Management	Statistical diagrams	F1 5.2	F1 10.2	F1 5.2
	Rearranging formula	F1 12.4	F2 6.3	F2 8.6
GM foods	Frequency diagrams	F1 5.1	F1 10.1	F1 5.1
	Increasing or decreasing quantities by a percentage	F1 4.3	F2 11.2	F2 3.3
Flying the world	Everyday use of negative numbers	F1 3.2	F1 3.2	F1 3.2
	Speed, time and distance	F2 5.1	F1 4.5	F2 7.2
Your plaice or mine?	Statistical Diagrams	F1 5.2	F1 10.2	F1 5.2
	The mean	F1 6.3	F1 11.3	F2 5.3
Sleep	Scatter diagrams	F1 8.2	F1 12.2	F1 15.2
	Surveys	F1 8.3	F1 12.3	F1 15.3
Selling online	Best buys	F2 5.3	F1 4.4	F2 7.4
	Calculating probabilities	F1 7.2	F1 13.2	F1 11.2
Jewellery design	Measuring and drawing angles	F2 8.1	F1 7.1	F1 10.1
	The circumference of a circle	F2 9.2	F2 14.2	F2 13.2
Buying your first car	Conversion graphs	F1 13.1	F1 9.1	F1 9.1
	Which average to use	F1 6.5	F1 11.5	F2 5.5
Fish and chips	Powers	F1 9.6	F2 8.6	F1 4.6
	Increasing or decreasing quantities by a percentage	F1 4.3	F2 11.2	F2 3.3

New GCSE Maths Functional Skills matching chart for Higher 1 and 2

Each functional skills topic in the table below has been matched to relevant lessons of the Collins New GCSE Maths Higher Student Books 1 and 2. These are indicated under the AQA Modular, Edexcel Modular and Edexcel Linear headings.

Think about the ability of your students and their stage of development. A good approach could be to use the activities a topic or two later to recall, revise and consolidate learning.

Improver Topics**	Lesson	AQA Modular	Edexcel Modular	Edexcel Linear
Eat well, live longer	Expressing one quantity as a percentage of another	H1 2.4	H1 2.3	H1 2.6
	Grouped data	H1 3.3	H1 4.3	H1 9.3
Coastguard search	Pythagoras' theorem	H2 5.1	H2 5.1	H1 6.1
	Area and volume of similar shapes	H2 9.2	H2 9.2	H2 7.2
Teabag design and production	Surveys	H1 3.6	H1 4.6	H1 9.5
	Circumference and area of a circle	H2 4.1	H2 4.1	H1 4.1
Small-scale farming	Increasing and decreasing quantities by a percentage	H1 2.3	H1 2.2	H1 2.5
	Basic algebra	H1 8.1 & H2 2.1	H1 11.1	H1 5.1
Coastguard rescue	Speed, time and distance	H2 3.1	H2 3.2	H1 3.2
	Solving real-life problems	H1 1.1	H1 1.1	H1 1.1
GM foods	Box plots	H1 4.5	H1 5.5	H2 10.2
	Surveys	H1 3.6	H1 4.6	H1 9.5
Flying the world	Negative numbers	H1 7.3	H1 1.3	H1 1.6
	Speed, time and distance	H2 3.1	H2 3.2	H1 3.2
Sleep	Surveys	H1 3.6	H1 4.6	H1 9.5
	Scatter diagrams	H1 4.3	H1 5.3	H1 11.3
Selling online	Expressing one quantity as a percentage of another	H1 2.4	H1 2.3	H1 2.6
	Two-way tables	H1 5.4	H1 6.4	H1 12.4
Jewellery design	Circle theorems	H2 6.3	H1 13.1	H2 4.1
	Circumference and area of a circle	H2 4.1	H2 4.1	H1 4.1
Buying your first car	Averages	H1 3.1	H1 4.1	H1 9.1
	Compound interest and repeated percentage change	H1 2.5	H2 2.2	H1 2.7
Fish and chips	Standard form	H1 9.2	H1 9.2	H2 5.2
	Limits of accuracy	H1 6.1	H2 3.1	H2 14.1

Advanced Topics ***	Lesson	AQA Modular	Edexcel Modular	Edexcel Linear
The Milky Way	Density	H2 3.4	H2 3.4	H1 3.5
	Spheres	H2 4.8	H2 4.5	H2 2.3
On your bike	Solving linear equations	H1 8.3 & H2 2.2	H2 7.2	H1 5.3
	Find the equation of a line from its graph	H1 12.3	H2 12.2	H1 14.3
Water usage	Cumulative frequency diagrams	H1 9.2	H1 5.4	H2 5.2
	Box plots	H1 4.5	H1 5.5	H2 10.2
	Cylinders	H2 4.5	H2 4.2	H1 4.5
Crash investigation	Speed, time and distance	H2 3.1	H2 3.2	H1 3.2
	Changing the subject of a formula	H1 13.5	H2 7.1	H2 12.2
Glastonbury Festival	Limits of accuracy	H1 6.1	H2 3.1	H2 14.1
	Solving problems using trigonometry 1	H2 5.10	H2 5.10	H2 3.6
Leaving smaller footprints	Averages	H1 3.1	H1 4.1	H1 9.1
	Basic algebra	H1 8.1	H1 11.1	H1 5.1
Can we hold back the sea?	Scatter diagrams	H1 4.3	H1 5.3	H1 11.3
	Area of a trapezium	H2 4.2	H1 8.1	H1 4.2
Facebook	Compound interest and repeated percentage change	H1 2.5	H1 2.4 & H2 2.2	H1 2.7
	Solving a quadratic equation by the quadratic formula	H2 2.8	H2 11.4	H2 6.4
Population and pensions	Grouped data	H1 3.3	H1 4.3	H1 9.3
	Line graphs	H1 4.1	H1 5.1	H1 11.1
London black cabs	Area of a trapezium	H2 4.2	H1 8.1	H1 4.2
	Speed, time and distance	H2 3.1	H2 3.2	H1 3.2
Extreme sports	Spheres	H2 4.8	H2 4.5	H2 2.3
	Solving linear equations	H1 8.3 & H2 2.2	H2 7.2	H1 5.3
Maths – music to your ears?	Rational numbers and reciprocals	H1 9.3	H1 9.3 & H2 2.5	H2 5.3
	Which ratio to use?	H2 5.9	H2 5.9	H2 3.5